P9-DWY-071

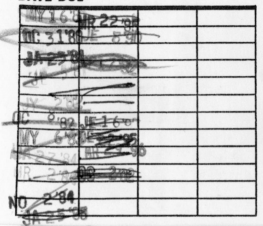

THE BEST SHORT PLAYS *1978*

Chilton Book Company
RADNOR, PENNSYLVANIA

THE BEST SHORT PLAYS *1978*

edited and with an introduction by

STANLEY RICHARDS

Best Short Plays Series

for H. K. Baskette

BOOKS AND PLAYS BY STANLEY RICHARDS

ANTHOLOGIES:

The Best Short Plays Series, issued annually 1968–1977
Great Musicals of the American Theatre: Volume One
Great Musicals of the American Theatre: Volume Two
America on Stage: Ten Great Plays of American History
The Tony Winners
Best Plays of the Sixties
Twenty One-Act Plays
Best Mystery and Suspense Plays of the Modern Theatre
10 Classic Mystery and Suspense Plays of the Modern Theatre
Great Rock Musicals
Modern Short Comedies from Broadway and London
Best Short Plays of the World Theatre: 1968–1973
Best Short Plays of the World Theatre: 1958–1967
Canada on Stage

PLAYS:

Through a Glass, Darkly
August Heat
Sun Deck
Tunnel of Love
Journey to Bahia
O Distant Land
Mood Piece
Mr. Bell's Creation
The Proud Age
Once to Every Boy
Half-Hour, Please
Know Your Neighbor
Gin and Bitterness
The Hills of Bataan
District of Columbia

CONTENTS

INTRODUCTION

Shortly before this volume went to press, I was asked by a well-intentioned acquaintance whether an editor found it somewhat arduous or tedious to compile an annual collection of plays. My reply was both rapid and emphatic: No! To the contrary, as editor of *The Best Short Plays* series, now in its eleventh year, I find each volume challenging, stimulating and, often, inspiring.

To me, each volume represents a new and fresh endeavor, not a continuous clothesline of sorts. Each year brings a new stimulus and, just as there are changes of seasons, there are constant new trends and developments in the theatre, in both the writing and production aspects. And one must keep abreast of these developments, for it is only by doing so that there is a stream of vitality and immediacy flowing through one's work.

Another, and major, factor in retaining an editor's enthusiasm is the discovery of new writers. In this present collection there are at least eight authors who fall into this category. True, some of them may have attained regional prominence, but to me they are significant and outstanding "discoveries." Joanna M. Glass, for example, is widely known in her homeland, Canada, but until I saw and read *Canadian Gothic,* I was unfamiliar with her work and there was a sincere pleasure of discovery when I did finally come across this vastly talented writer. The same is true of Lanie Robertson, whose *The Insanity of Mary Girard* ignited a Philadelphia stage last year, or the gifted English writer-performers John Harding and John Burrows, who are being introduced to American readers (and, hopefully, audiences) with the ingenious *For Sylvia* which appears in this collection.

As faithful readers know, it has been the policy, from the

beginning, to juxtapose new and established writers in each edition of *The Best Short Plays*. This year, quite true, less familiar dramatists outnumber the second category and this is a happy portent, for it is the emerging author who in time will become the "established" contributor to the theatre.

Within a period of less than three years, this has been forcefully demonstrated by David Mamet and Albert Innaurato. Mr. Mamet was represented in *The Best Short Plays of 1977* with *The Duck Variations*. At the time the play was selected for inclusion, he was widely regarded as a "promising new playwright." Today, Mr. Mamet has gained the status of "important American playwright" and currently is represented on Broadway with *The Water Engine* and Off-Broadway by the very successful *A Life in the Theatre*. (It may be added that his *American Buffalo* won the New York Drama Critics' Circle Award for best American play of the 1976–77 season.)

Similarly, Albert Innaurato (contributor to these pages of *The Transfiguration of Benno Blimpie*) has more than fulfilled his "promise" with *Gemini*, now in its second Broadway year, and other works.

Nor is an editor's pleasure of discovery limited to new writers. Dozens of bright new plays by some of the best-known names writing for the theatre have been introduced here and have gone on to considerable success on stages throughout the country, while at least two dozen plays that first appeared in *The Best Short Plays* have been presented on network television.

Preparing this volume, as well as its predecessors, then, has been a rewarding experience. Now the final gratification will come in sharing these plays and playwrights with my readers, for the theatre is and always will be a communal experience.

STANLEY RICHARDS
New York, N. Y.

Joanna M. Glass

CANADIAN GOTHIC

Joanna M. Glass

A moving and imaginatively conceived study of love and loss by one of Canada's most highly regarded young playwrights, Joanna M. Glass, *Canadian Gothic* (and its companion piece, *American Modern*) was produced twice in New York City within a period of three years. Presented in 1976 by the noted Phoenix Theatre, it garnered much praise from the critics and led Clive Barnes to declare in *The New York Times* that ". . . interest in Joanna Glass is understandable. She has an original voice and a quizzical way of looking at the world."

A native of Saskatoon, Saskatchewan, Ms. Glass gained early experience as a writer for Canadian radio and television, while studying acting in a theatre workshop. While appearing in a production that developed from that workshop, she was awarded a Canadian Arts Council scholarship to further her studies at the Pasadena Playhouse in California.

Her first play, *Santacqua,* was produced at the HB Playwrights Foundation, New York, in 1969. Next came the author's double bill, *Canadian Gothic* and *American Modern,* which was first staged by the Manhattan Theatre Club in 1973 and, subsequently, in many areas of Canada. The reporter for the *Daily Colonist* in Victoria, B. C., described *Canadian Gothic* as ". . . a beautiful play about a young woman's recollection of growing up with a no-nonsense father, a somewhat free-spirited mother who dies at age thirty, and later the girl's first and only love affair with a native Indian. The play touches on love, death and even birth, yet ultimately latches onto the defiance of spirit in the face of rationality. . . . It combines the poetry of both a prairie sunset and dust storm." The Canadian press reception probably was best summarized by the reviewer for the Montreal *Gazette,* who hailed Ms. Glass as ". . . one of the finest and tightest users of the English language Canada has produced for the stage."

The author's next venture in the theatre was the full-length drama, *Artichoke,* which had its world premiere in 1975 at the Long Wharf Theatre in New Haven, Connecticut, with Colleen Dewhurst in the starring role. Like its predecessors, it later was widely performed in various parts of Canada. Following this, Ms. Glass was commissioned by the Canadian Arts

Council to write a play for the twentieth anniversary of the Manitoba Theatre Centre in Winnipeg. The play, *The Last Chalice,* held its premiere there in November, 1977.

Joanna M. Glass also has written a successful novel, *Reflections on a Mountain Summer,* many short stories, and a screenplay, *Surfacing.*

Characters:

FATHER
MOTHER
JEAN
BEN REDLEAF

Scene:

A small town on the Saskatchewan prairie in the 1950s.

There are three wooden chairs onstage, approximately three yards apart. The middle chair is not on a parallel with the other two, but is slightly to the back of them. The Father is seated in the chair down right. He is blind, and wears dark glasses. He is dressed in a business suit. He is in his early sixties. The Mother is seated in the chair down left. She is thirty years old. The Daughter is not present at the opening. When she enters, she sits in the middle chair. She, also, is thirty. There may be, suspended at the rear, a large window with a plain, slightly warped wooden frame.

FATHER: After all's said and done, the town of Cardigan's been good to me. I was born here, in the year 1910. My father was a shoemaker who'd emigrated from the Highlands. I never had any complaints against this town. Pioneers of hardy stock built it in the middle of the prairie. Built the schools and hospitals, the stores and libraries, and finally, the university. Civilized institutions for civilized people. I received my degree in dentistry from the university in 1932.

MOTHER: Rare he was, in 1932, having a degree in dentistry. The university was mostly an agriculture school at the time, being, as we were, in the heart of the wheat country. A little prim he was, and I knew he'd never known a woman. I knew he'd never visited that famous clapboard house on the outskirts of town. I knew he didn't get drunk in the beer parlour, and his conduct was never disorderly at hockey games. After our wedding I knew, and it nearly killed me at the time. I knew the routine we'd set that first week of marriage was the one we'd follow for the rest of our lives.

FATHER: In choosing a wife I looked for a woman with spirit. When I met Natalie, I walked her down by the river—that shady spot there by Grant Island. I put my hands on her breasts. She said, "Tut, tut, Jack, don't you know? God made those for babies!" And off she ran, laughing, a fine filly of a lass.

MOTHER: *(Sighing deeply)* So many things I never understood. What was most attractive became a bone of contention. The spirit he admired before we wed became a thorn in his side by the first anniversary. And I knew the thorn would fester there for the rest of our lives. Both of us helpless, in our natures, to either remove it, or ignore it.

FATHER: She never did the things that other women did! The house was put to rights by noon. She could hoe and weed the garden quick as you could say Jack Robinson. Spring cleaning in every other house took a full week. In ours, one frantic day. All the curtains, all the rugs—shazaam!—down before breakfast, up again by dinnertime. "Busy work," she'd say, and bring down the wrath of the neighborhood with those two words.

MOTHER: "Too much idle time," he'd say. I liked to do charcoal drawings. I went to the river almost every afternoon, summer and winter, ninety above and thirty below. It gave me great pleasure to sketch and draw there, and try to master the arcs of our two bridges, spanning the river. The arcs were so hard to get right! I worked like a demon on them, but never did master the exact geometry of those two bridges. *(The Father opens his mouth to speak, the Mother interrupts and continues)* I'd get the one in the foreground *just right*, but the one up-river, behind the first, escaped me.

FATHER: Her little fingers, at dinnertime, were blue at first, and then beet red. Thirty below she'd go down to the river-bank with her pieces of charcoal and pad of paper. She never learned to sketch with gloves on, although you'd think that would have been the first order of business. I remember frost-bite on at least three occasions. All because she couldn't get that second bridge right. My God, what a lot of effort, day after day! The truth was, I was ready to go down there and dynamite that damned second bridge. But amazingly, one day she said:

MOTHER: All right, Jack. I guess the time has come to settle for the one.

FATHER: And damned if she didn't sell that first picture right off, for thirty dollars. Back in those days I used to work a whole week for thirty dollars.

MOTHER: The Mayor bought my first completed picture. I said, "Mr. Mayor, don't you notice the absence of something in that picture?" "No," he said. "There's great technique in that one bridge—at least thirty dollars worth, I don't mind telling you." I said, "But Mr. Mayor, from that spot on the bank you can see the Fulton Bridge." "Yes, I know," he said, "and thanks for leaving it out. I expect you'd make me pay sixty for two of 'em."

FATHER: *(Shifting in his chair)* They say in every person's life there comes a time when we're faced with a fork in the road. We stop, we consider the two choices, we make our decision. In the third year of our marriage it happened to us. Nothing monumental caused it. We had a simple conversation. And after that she went one way, and I went the other.

MOTHER: There was a polio epidemic in Cardigan. It was a terrible time. There was fear, and panic, and endless prayer. For nearly a year, everyone's conversation was the same:

Didja hear? Didja hear? The Ferguson boy's in a brace for life!

Didja hear? Didja hear? It's hit poor Mr. Jamison. He's in a brace for the rest of his life.

I had no stomach at all for sick or crippled people. I went to pieces whenever I had to be around them. Every morning during the epidemic I'd cry into my coffee and tell Jack the news from the day before. *(They turn, slightly, toward each other)*

FATHER: Really, Natalie! Must I face this waterfall every morning at breakfast?

MOTHER: Yes, you must. *(Quietly)* Unless you choose to eat somewhere else.

FATHER: *(Resigned)* Well, who is it now?

MOTHER: The Ferguson boy.

FATHER: *Which* Ferguson boy? The town's full of Fergusons.

MOTHER: You wouldn't want to waste sympathy on one you didn't know. *(Pause)* Dougie Ferguson. He's in a brace for the rest of his life.

FATHER: Dougie Ferguson . . .

MOTHER: He's a *patient* of yours, Jack! And he's—he *was*—goalie on the Pee-Wee team! We've watched him many times.

FATHER: Oh, yes, little Dougie. Yes. Too bad.

MOTHER: Jack, *listen* to me! I'm losing my mind! How can I *face* Mrs. Ferguson? What can I *say* to Mrs. Ferguson?

FATHER: The less said, the better. Things are easier dealt with when they're not put into words.

MOTHER: He reached for the marmalade and spread it on his toast. *(Pause)* I began to get a fixed image of Jack in my mind. I thought of him as a man in a brace—a mechanical man. There was no way to penetrate this thing that he wore. I asked him. I said, "Jack, tell me. What is it that makes you harness yourself against life like this?"

FATHER: I wanted to answer as best I could, because I never, ever, wanted it asked again. *(Pause)* An awareness, I guess, of the softness at the middle.

MOTHER: I don't understand that, Jack.

FATHER: Natalie, a man needs a crust. This bread has a crust. The earth has a crust. That maple there, out the window—its bark is its crust. It's all protection for the softness at the middle. *(He turns away, in his chair)* Natalie, we're unequal partners. Accept it, and leave me be.

MOTHER: We never talked of it again. I let him be. *(She frowns)* As far as a woman's able.

(The Daughter, Jean, enters youthfully. She sits in the middle chair)

FATHER: I was very happy when our daughter, Jean, was

born. I remember thinking this new child would fill her afternoons for twenty years to come. That just goes to show you how much I knew. I said, "Natalie, this'll take up the slack of all those afternoons." And she said:

MOTHER: There's no slack! There's no slack anywhere. Every hour is taut and I mean to keep it that way.

FATHER: So, the house, and the garden, and the *baby* were put to rights by noon. *(Pause)* God in Heaven, why did I let it gall me so? I wasted myself on petty victories—speck of dust on the sideboard, dandelion among the iris, a wet diaper, the beginnings of a rash. "Neglect," I'd say. "Too much idle time." "Busy work," she'd say, and thereby lost her last remaining female friend in Cardigan. *(Pause)* As time went on, she befriended Jean.

JEAN: Every day, before I started school, my mother took me past the city limits, to the fields around Cardigan. In the spring we collected wild prairie crocus. I wore dirndl skirts then. I'd lift the whole front of my skirt and fill it with stubby mauve crocus. When the skirt was full, and I couldn't bend down any more without the flowers spilling out, I stopped. She always hummed one song: *I Dream of Jeannie With the Light Brown Hair*. When I couldn't hear it, I knew I'd strayed too far. We did the same thing with tiger lilies in the summer, bringing them home and stuffing them into old honey cans and pickle jars. I never believed when they closed at night they'd open again in the morning. *(Pause)* Why do they do that, Mama?

MOTHER: It's magic. Nature's magic.

JEAN: Daddy says there's no magic. He says all magic is tricks.

MOTHER: Then maybe you'd better ask your Daddy.

JEAN: I already did.

MOTHER: And what did he say?

JEAN: I forget.

MOTHER: Well, until you remember, let's just call it nature's magic. *(Pause, the Mother shifts back to the audience)* In the fall we went into the fields to watch the mallards. The fields were one big sanctuary then, before the bricks and lumber got that far. "Isn't it a miracle," I'd say, "the way they inform each other when it's time to take wing and fly south. I wonder how they know?"

JEAN: Daddy says it's the most spectacular phenomenon in the world. He says there's vertical migration, when they move down the mountains to the valleys, and there's long migration, when they move from here to South America. They move on the Atlantic flyway and the Mississippi flyway, and they mostly move nocturnally. We know about their routes because of bird banding.

MOTHER: Oh? My, my, my.

JEAN: Yes. Scientists put numbered aluminum bands around their legs and make records of the flights.

MOTHER: But I wonder how so many millions of them can agree on the *exact time* to go?

JEAN: Personally, I think it's nature's magic.

FATHER: They went in the spring and the summer and the fall, frittering away whole seasons. And damned if they didn't go out there and skate on the frozen sloughs in January! A block away from our house there was a spanking new rink my taxes helped to build. You could open the front door of a winter's evening and hear "The Skater's Waltz" wafting up our street. Do you think they'd go to that rink? No, sir! Oh, it was picturesque on the sloughs, all right, but it wasn't safe. Fell in, both of 'em, ass over teakettle, several times. I remember them coming home drenched, with purple lips, and joints so stiff they wouldn't move. *(Pause)* I remember the stink of wet wool as it dried on the radiator. *(The Mother rises, touches Jean, and exits. The Father and Jean slouch over, heads hanging down. There is a brief pause)* Well, they didn't have much in the way of medications back in those days. Hell, one way or another it didn't matter. I'd bawled her out for falling in, and she wouldn't have the doctor after that. I told her if she ever went again I'd break her bloody neck. She said, "Let's wait till *then* for the doctor, Jack. They're best at mending broken bones." We got to the hospital on the heels of her last breath. She died the minute they put her under the oxygen tent. *(Pause)* I remember thinking that tent was like the old snuffers we used to use to put out candles.

(Jean rises, moves down left, and sits in the Mother's chair. Her voice is harder, more mature, in the following segments)

JEAN: Fortunately, there's gold in dentistry. My father wouldn't have live-in help under foot in the evenings so we hired a woman to do the washing, and we hired a woman to do the cooking. In accordance with his nature, we took care of these things first, and then we mourned.

FATHER: And we hired a woman to come in and do the spring cleaning. What took Natalie one frantic day, and the neighbor ladies one full week, took that hired woman two full weeks. At a dollar an hour, I remember. I mourned, publicly, for half a year. I will mourn, privately, for the rest of my life. But even in that mourning there's bitterness and rancor. For she had handed down that temperament intact. No, not intact. Threefold. And if I couldn't cope with it in the adult, God knows: spirit in a child is a terrible thing!

JEAN: There was no time when I could look across a room and say, "He's lonely now. He misses her." He went about his business, his grief was private. And I resented that. It seemed to me that he was free at last, free from a voice that once asked for his time, his ear, his company, his heart.

The wonder of my mother's voice was this: it asked, it was refused, it never asked again. It found some other place to sing its song. It didn't seek its answers in other men, clubs, church, civic activities. It never aired its tale of woe over any neighbor's back fence. Once refused, it was forever silent.

She was just thirty when she died. I knew that in the fields around Cardigan there was still stubby crocus. There were lilies and mallards. Only her song was gone.

FATHER: Well, that's her side of the story. What she didn't know, and what her mother knew too well, was that in her silence she could mock me, accuse me, deny me, defy me. But Jean was artless. It took her years to learn those skills. *(Short pause)* And so she asked, and asked, and asked again. No soul on earth petitions like a child.

JEAN: I defied him every inch of the way. When he sent me to my room, I made him haul me there, kicking and screaming until we both were bruised. In school I was called an imaginative child. I loved to read horror stories. *(She smiles)*

Late one night, when I was nine, I attached two cardboard fangs to my eye teeth, and went into his room. I woke him up and grinned a fangy grin. *(She does so)*

FATHER: For *Christsake!* What do you *want?*

JEAN: *I vant to bite your neck!!*

FATHER: Ketchup sandwiches! I always thought a sandwich was two pieces of bread with a slice of meat in between. No, sir! Ketchup sandwiches. She had a two hundred dollar solid mahogany dresser in her bedroom. Wouldn't use it. Ugly as sin, she said. She went to the store and got some orange crates and built herself a thing with a big organdy skirt around it. *"Vanity,"* she said. "You're damned *right,"* I said. "In no small measure!" At fourteen she was five feet eight inches tall. She took the heels off every pair of shoes I bought her. I took them to the shoemaker and had the heels put back. She refused to leave the house until those heels came off again. She missed three whole days of school one week, on account of that. *(Pause)* At fifteen, on the eighth anniversary of her mother's death, she started going out to the fields again.

(A young man enters. He is darkskinned; a full-blooded Cree Indian. He wears a pale blue shirt, open at the neck, and jeans. He sits in the middle chair)

JEAN: One day in late June, I saw him at the edge of a slough, crouching down, fiddling with something. His hair was jet black—blue in the sunlight. Hair like that on the prairie could only belong to an Indian.

BEN: They called us all half-breeds, whether we were or not. I was not. I was full-blooded Cree. On the farms they said one thing: they said we stole their chickens. In the cities they said another: they said we could be found, lurking, in the back seats of white women's cars. *(He shrugs, and smiles)* I paid no attention. That day I was setting a trap. She was very young. She had light brown hair. I thought she'd go away when she saw me.

JEAN: Are you setting a trap?

BEN: That's right.

JEAN: What for?

BEN: Oh, I dunno. Jackrabbit, I guess.

JEAN: What for?

BEN: Oh, I dunno. It's what I do in June.

JEAN: I mean—for fun, for food, for recreation?

BEN: Geez, I dunno. Something to do.

JEAN: Well, I guess I have to say I don't like you much for that.

BEN: Well, paleface, I guess I have to say I don't give a damn one way or the other.

JEAN: Sassy Indian!

BEN: Yessiree!! Getting sassier every day. G'wan home and tell your Maw you met a sassy Indian.

JEAN: I told him my mother died when I was seven. He said he was sorry. He said his name was Ben Redleaf. I told him mine was Jean MacPherson. "Well, there you are," he said. He smiled, and said . . .

BEN: I'll bet they call you bonnie Jean. *(Pause)* I told her about the time my brother set a trap for jackrabbit, and when he got there to check it one day, he couldn't believe his eyes. There was a bloody rabbit's foot in the trap, but the animal was gone. That rabbit chewed off his foot and part of his leg in order to get away. I made it as bloody as I could—and I watched that white girl. I told her the blue veins were hanging off the foot—*dangling*—*glistening* in the sun. Crazy white girl. When I finished, her eyes filled with tears and she said, "Oh, Ben, that's a beautiful story!"

JEAN: I met him in the fields every day all that summer, sunshine or rain. I knew he came into the city sometimes, and one day I persuaded him to have a Coke with me at the Sunset Cafe. I don't know what was in my head, thinking he and I could sit and have a Coke in the Sunset Cafe, plain as day. When we were finished, and out on the sidewalk, he turned to me and said, "Well, Jeannie, I guess we'll never do that again." "No," I said, "I guess we won't."

BEN: Just for the hell of it, I walked down Third Street one day and stopped in front of her Dad's practice. I wanted to get a look at the old buzzard. I was hanging around there, waiting for a glimpse of him, when I could see the nurse at the desk getting all upset. Suddenly, there he was, right beside me in front of the window.

FATHER: Can I do something for you, boy?

BEN: No, thanks. Nothing.

FATHER: Got a toothache, have you?

BEN: No, sir. Just wanted to see how the other half lives.

FATHER: Well, I'll tell you. You g'wan down to Eighth Street there and see Dr. Lutz. He's the one they all go to when they've got a toothache.

BEN: *(To audience)* I didn't have a toothache. As a matter of fact, I'd *never* had a toothache. My mother used to say we had strong teeth from chewing buffalo hide. I used to say, "Yeah, that accounts for the women. They did all the chewing. What about the men?" To that she'd say, "God takes care of Indians in small ways." Then my father would chime in. "Yeah," he'd say, "in ways so small nobody's ever noticed."

All the kids in town went to dances every Saturday night, and guzzled beer in some back room. The Indian kids did the same at a place out on Willow Road. I couldn't take her; she couldn't take me. One day I got a bottle of wine and met her in the fields. *(He takes Jean's hand)* Guess what we're going to do today?

JEAN: How many guesses do I get?

BEN: Two.

JEAN: We're going to make love.

BEN: Right, that's one. What's the other?

JEAN: We're going to make love again.

BEN: That's a possible *third*. What's the second?

JEAN: Geez, I dunno. I give up.

BEN: We're going to dance.

JEAN: *Dance?*

BEN: Yeah.

JEAN: *(After a moment) Rain* dance?

BEN: How'dja like a fat lip? We're gonna drink some wine and we're gonna dance.

JEAN: To the music of whom?

BEN: I brought the wine. I guess you'll have to sing.

JEAN: O.K. What'll I sing?

BEN: I dunno. It's up to you.

JEAN: How about *Rose Marie?*

BEN: Nah.

JEAN: How about *Ramona?*

BEN: Don't think so.

JEAN: How about: *(She sings)* "One little, two little, three little—"

BEN: *(Holding up his fist)* How about a *big, fat, lip?*

JEAN: O.K. How about *Stardust?*

BEN: Yeah! How about that?

(There is a pause. Jean turns away from Ben and faces front)

JEAN: There is, among friends, a catalogue of virgin crossings. They like to relate, with grins and hindsight, first gropings, adolescent clumsiness. *(Pause)* Doris Meyers lost her virginity at noon one day in her uncle's hayloft, and broke out in hives immediately afterward. Sheila Fraser lost hers in a canoe at Waskesui. Evelyn Davidson lost hers in the boiler room of the Biology Lab. They say, "Come on, Jean, tell us yours!" I am, after all's said and done, my father's daughter. Things are easier dealt with when they're not put into words.

We would lie in the fields for hours and look at the sky till it nearly hypnotized us.

(They lean back in their chairs and stretch out their legs. They fold their arms over their eyes, as if to provide protection from a blinding sun)

BEN: Tell me about your Dad.

JEAN: What's to tell? A dad's a dad.

BEN: Has he got a girlfriend?

JEAN: Are you kidding?

BEN: He's not that old. I'll bet he's hiding a lady friend somewhere.

JEAN: He wouldn't know what to *do* with a lady friend.

BEN: He knew what to do with your mother.

JEAN: I doubt it.

BEN: Aw, come on. You're the proof of it.

JEAN: I look at him, and I look at her picture, and I just can't imagine them doing it. You know? Maybe it's always that way with parents.

BEN: I can sure as hell imagine *my* Dad doing it.

JEAN: Has he got a lady friend?

BEN: Always. Always has, always will. He's a real horny old

bugger. And he's always promising to turn over a new leaf. And he never does. *(Pause)* I made up a limerick about him once.

JEAN: Tell me.

BEN: Nah. It's dirty.

JEAN: How dirty?

BEN: Real dirty.

JEAN: That's the way I like 'em.

BEN: Jeannie, you're a raunchy little girl.

JEAN: I know I am. But it's normal.

BEN: Who says?

JEAN: I've got a book about teenage behavior. My Dad bought it for me. He's like that, you know. Whenever there's something he'd rather not talk about, he writes to Toronto for a book. Anyway, this book says fifteen's a raunchy age. Come on, tell me your limerick.

BEN: Oh, O.K.

There was an Old Injun from Cardigan
Who promised to make a clean start again
He said that he would
We hoped that he could
But each squaw that he saw made it hard again

(They both laugh. Jean faces front, Ben sits upright in his chair)

JEAN: I spent each afternoon alone with Ben, and I spent each evening alone in my room. I could hear my father downstairs, fixing tea, listening to the radio, taking the newspaper out to the porch. I sat up there, and it struck me that we were more than a flight of stairs apart. In our minds, he was my old man, downstairs; I was his little girl, upstairs. I remembered the events of the afternoon and I thought how innocent he was, really, sitting in the kitchen, waiting for the kettle to whistle. Sometimes I wondered if Ben Redleaf fit into the picture at all.

BEN: I was not alone in my room all that often. I shared a room with my older brother, and my younger brother. Our house was one of those concrete block things—my brother called them "urban igloos." Anyway, when I was alone in my room those summer evenings, strange things began to happen in my mind. I started thinking about my future. I'd been drifting along, thinking the future was something you worried about when you were thirty. I began to think I'd better look into some kind of government aid, and get myself into a trade school. I could take apart a V8 engine and put it back together again blindfolded. So I thought maybe I'd make a good mechanic. But as the summer went on, I really went off the deep end. I began to have all kinds of pipe dreams. I imagined myself as a lab technician. I wore a white coat and I carried around trays of test tubes. And I always had a book of litmus paper in my pocket. I imagined all this because I'd convinced myself that this girl was in my league. That just goes to show you what a really screwy summer it was. Sky and sun and tiger lilies, and white people's pipe dreams. *(Pause, and transition)* On Friday, October 14th, she came to the fields and told me. On Saturday, October 15th, at breakfast, she told her father. On Sunday, October 16th, she boarded the train for Winnipeg.

JEAN: Dad, I'm going to have a baby. *(There is no reaction)* I thought he'd fly off in a fit and call me names. I thought he'd leap up, wail, berate me. I thought he'd at least turn ashen gray. No, sir! He reached for the marmalade.

FATHER: I think you're overstating the case. I think you misunderstand.

JEAN: No, Dad! *You* misunderstand. I'm going to have a baby.

FATHER: Jean, you're fifteen years old. You are not going to *have* a baby. If you are carrying a child you'll go to Winnipeg and leave it there in a doctor's pail.

JEAN: I watched him spread the marmalade on his toast. I marvelled at his steady hand. He didn't look at me, but then, he never did. I should have let it go at that. I thought of my mother. I thought of all the times she'd watched his steady hand. I had a trump card. I decided to play it.

Whose do you think it is?

FATHER: I bit my tongue. I tried to count to ten. I didn't make it. "The better question *is*," I said, "whose do *you* think it is?" She didn't answer. She tapped her finger, nonchalantly, on the chair. "How far along?", I said.

JEAN: About two months.

FATHER: Well, they're not really *babies* at that stage.

JEAN: Oh, Jack! I've got a punchline! This one isn't a *baby*, this one's a *papoose!* (*Pause*) It was not his nature to fly off in a fit. He didn't wail, he didn't berate me. He did turn ashen gray. In retrospect, it was a petty victory.

BEN: We'd decided, the day before, that I was to come by around eleven. I don't know what was in our heads even to consider such a meeting. Oh, I guess I know. She was fifteen, I was twenty. We were going to stand together, heads erect, a united front. We were going to deliver our message and let the chips fall where they may. That worn out, threadbare message. We were going to tell him that we loved each other. (*Pause. Tension*) Did you tell him?

JEAN: I told him.

BEN: What'd he say?

JEAN: He already made a phone call. Long distance. I'm to go to some doctor in Winnipeg and leave it there. (*Pause*) Imagine him even knowing where to call!

BEN: Over my dead body!

JEAN: I don't know, Ben. It's a closed subject.

BEN: Where is he?

JEAN: In the basement. Doing something at his work-bench. He made the call and went right down.

BEN: She nodded toward the door that led to the basement. I went down the stairs, having to grope, because he hadn't turned the light on. He wasn't doing anything, just standing there, hunched over his workbench. He squinted at me for a minute. Then he began to mumble.

FATHER: You—bastard! You—fucking Indian!

BEN: (*Incredulous*) *Fucking Indian?* What could I do? I laughed.

FATHER: That red-skinned bastard laughed at me! Jean was standing at the top of the stairs. It was like an echo, reverberating through the basement. "Fucking Indian?" she said, and threw her head back and laughed. Their laughter was—arrogant. It was the most arrogant laughter I'd ever heard. I picked up the nearest thing to me, a hammer. I threw it at him. It missed him by an inch and hit the water meter. I remember the crash and the broken glass from the water meter falling on the floor. I picked up a wrench—

BEN: I picked up the nearest thing to me and threw it at him. It was metal and round. It hit him in the face. It was a can of lye.

(All three slouch over in their chairs, elbows on knees, heads hanging down)

JEAN: An ambulance, sirens, howling neighbors, two police cars, and for some reason, the Fire Chief came, too. My father was put into the back of the ambulance. Ben was handcuffed and put into the police car. Fifteen years have passed since then, and a thousand nightmares. The nightmare is always the same. There is a miniature police car and a miniature ambulance. There are infinite miniature doors hanging open on each. They hang there, gaping. They beckon to me. A stranger pushes my shoulder and says, "Go, child, go!" I wear metal shoes and there are magnets under the sidewalk. I'm held there, straining but powerless, until dawn. In actual fact I was pushed, and I went. In the back of the ambulance I was grateful that they'd covered my father's face. *(Ben rises, and exits)* That evening in the hospital, I sat on his bed and held his hand.

FATHER: Is it still Saturday?

JEAN: Yes. Eight o'clock.

FATHER: Are you crying?

JEAN: Yes.

FATHER: I wonder—for whom?

JEAN: All of us. *(Pause)* Why did we have lye in the basement?

FATHER: You have an appointment in Winnipeg.

JEAN: Dad, he grabbed the nearest thing! What were we doing with lye in the basement?

FATHER: The sight is gone, Jeannie, but the child is growing. First things first. Get rid of that papoose.

(There is a pause. Jean leans forward and cups her hands over her mouth)

JEAN:

Didja hear? Didja hear? She's up and going

to Winnipeg and leaving her blind father!
Doctor ordered it, they say. Terrible state
of shock she's in. And Lord knows, wouldn't
it be? Finding an Indian in your basement?
Who was he, anyway?
Paper says some half-breed from Willow Road.
It's a blessing her mother's gone.
Did you know her mother? Strange woman.
Artistic. Never did a lick of work, I knew of.

FATHER: Ben Redleaf was accused of assault with intent to kill. He was sentenced to four years in the Provincial Penitentiary.

JEAN:
Didja hear? Didja hear? Four bloody years
is all that savage got!
He'll come out again and do the same. It's
the courts, y'know, the judges. They're a
bunch of bleeding hearts where the Indians
are concerned.

My father sold his practice. It seemed he had to sign a hundred papers to complete that transaction. The lawyers were amazing. They'd hand him a sheet and say, "Sign right there, please." "Oh, yes," he'd say, and scribble his name across the middle. Finally, he let me guide his hand.

FATHER: The sight was gone, the child was gone, the pride remained a problem.

JEAN: He put salt in his tea for the first few days. He put lard on his bread. His meat ended up in his lap until he let me cut it for him. The part in his hair was never straight. His socks were never the same color. Our first caller was the paper boy.

Collecting, sir. Three dollars, please.

FATHER: Oh, yes. Yes. Right here. Just a minute now. Yes. There you are.

JEAN: That's a five and two ones, sir. Do you have three ones?

FATHER: Oh, yes, just a minute. I'm sure I—yes, I think I can—

JEAN: No, sir, you haven't got it. *(She leans forward)* Here, I'll take this five and change it—

FATHER: *(Bellowing)* Get your damned hands off my money!! *(He calls)* Jean? Jean?? Jeannie, will you come help me?

JEAN: We tried going for walks together during the day, but he wouldn't let me guide him.

FATHER: *(With a small smile)* She had a running commentary that drove me crazy. This is Mrs. Bradley's house—remember, they have nasturtiums up their walk. It's a very pungent smell. You'll always know the Bradleys' by that smell. There's a crack in the walk, there, where it's buckled. If you veer too far to the right you'll hit the fire hydrant. Watch it! Some kid's left a tricycle here! Hold it! Oh, *damn.* You've stepped in a big wet dog mess. *(Pause)* After that we walked at night, and I held her arm.

JEAN: He'd feathered his nest very nicely over the years. We hired whatever help we needed. We took the train to Banff every summer. We never, ever, spoke of Ben Redleaf. I have four Christmas cards in a box upstairs. None is signed. They say, "Merry Christmas, bonnie Jean, four to go. Merry Christmas, bonnie Jean, three to go. Merry Christmas, bonnie Jean, two to go. Merry Christmas, bonnie Jean, one to go." *(Pause)* He came to see me when he got out of jail. We talked for about five minutes. It was around ten o'clock at night. It was twelve years ago. *(She suddenly claps her hands, twice, sharply and quickly)*

FATHER: *(Calling)* What's that noise on the porch, Jean?

JEAN: *(Calling)* Just the screen door, Dad. It bangs in the wind.

FATHER: Oh, yes. Have to get somebody in to fix that.

JEAN: Yes. One of these days. *(She turns, and whispers)* Ben? Ben Redleaf, is that you? *(Ben enters, as described in the following, but for hat and blade of grass. He stands behind the middle chair)* His face, in the half-light, had changed. He'd matured. He looked like a real Indian now—pronounced cheek bones, a black felt cowboy hat, a blade of grass sticking out of his mouth. His eyes were sly, his expression cocky. He leaned against our porch rail and spat, over the edge, on our honeysuckle bush.

BEN: Hiya, Jeannie.

JEAN: Hello, Ben.

(Pause. Ben nods to the right)

BEN: Is he in there?

JEAN: Yes.

BEN: How's he doing?

JEAN: Pretty well. He's learned braille. He still has pains in his forehead.

BEN: Watcha been doing with yourself?

JEAN: I'm in my second year at the university. How about you?

BEN: *(Broad smile)* Just can't make up my mind, got so many offers. Royal Bank of Canada, Richardson and Sons— they all want me real bad.

JEAN: Ben, what did you do there all those years?

BEN: Swung a pick-ax every day. Kept my back against the wall at night.

JEAN: Oh?

BEN: Yeah.

JEAN: He turned and spat on the honeysuckle bush a second time. He was lean and hard. Oh, my God, he was lean and hard. I didn't dare touch him.

FATHER: Jean? I'm just damned sure I hear something out on that porch!

JEAN: No, Dad. Just me. Nothing to fret about. *(Turning to Ben)* What are you going to do, Ben?

BEN: Got to get off this prairie, that's for sure. Lot of talk around the pen about some white man in northern British Columbia. He owns a big lumber camp. Seems he only hires Indian ex-cons. Doesn't pay anything at all, but I hear the food is good. And the quarters, fair. Guess I'll get my ass up there for awhile.

JEAN: And then my father came out to the porch.

(The Father moves down left. He stands between Jean and Ben)

FATHER: Jean? Sure you're all right out here alone?

JEAN: Just fine, Dad, really. There's a chill tonight. You'd better stay inside.

FATHER: Oh, you're such an old granny! There's no chill. It's a very pleasant night. *(He sniffs at the air, and sighs)* Come what may that honeysuckle bush just keeps on blooming. Full bloom now?

JEAN: Not quite yet. Another day or two. *(Pause)* Ben stood so still—I never saw a man stand so still. Then, suddenly *(She claps her hands again)* the screen door banged in the wind. It startled my father and he jumped slightly.

FATHER: That's a hell of a nuisance! Have to get somebody in here to fix that one of these days.

JEAN: Ben Redleaf tipped his hat, and crept away. *(There is a tableau for a moment)* It's habit now to look for him wherever they gather in groups. Saturday afternoons we often drive to Grant Island. I see them crouched along the road, selling beads, moccasins, toy wig-wams. I see them on the bus late at night, drunk and mumbling to themselves. I've looked up alleys along Eighth Street and seen them huddled there with cheap wine, vanilla extract, canned heat. Sunday mornings I've seen them vomiting in the park.

FATHER: She's moody and depressed when she sees these things. Nothing I could say would comfort her. I know, and I knew, that her contribution to that scene was better left in Winnipeg.

JEAN: I've looked for him riding at fairs and rodeos. I've looked for him climbing oil rigs in Alberta. I've looked for him picking sugar beets, near Lethbridge; cherries in the Okanogan. I've looked for him posing for pictures, in borrowed regalia, at Lake Louise. The slant of a forehead, the nape of a neck can make my palms grow wet, can make me ache. There are a thousand dead ringers for Ben Redleaf, but he's gone. *(She rises, and moves behind her chair, in reverie)* It's a shame, in a way, that I have so little tangible evidence of him. There are the four Christmas cards, but there are none of the ordinary mementos. No snapshots, no dried orchid from any high school prom. There is one piece of paper. The receipt from the doctor in Winnipeg. My father keeps it in his strongbox, upstairs. For some reason, he used my mother's maiden name when he made the call. So the receipt is made out to Miss Natalie Duncan. And it is stamped in purple ink—*Paid in Full.* I have very little evidence of my mother, either. Her spirit, her vitality, have become dimmed by time. My memory of her is like a rumor I once heard, and can't quite remember, and can't quite forget. Once a year I go down to City Hall to pay our taxes. I always pause at the Mayor's office. The Mayors have changed several times, but the receptionist is always the same, and she expects me. Mother's picture still hangs there. The riverbank, the water, the one perfect bridge.

(Jean and the Father sigh, exhale, touch their foreheads. The Father loosens his tie. He moves the middle chair down, closer to Jean's. Gradually, they settle into the chairs)

FATHER: That damned thing they call spring comes and goes before you notice it. Then it's heat, heat, heat.

JEAN: Yes, with no let-up in sight. Not much better out here than in the house.

FATHER: Not much. Don't hear a single leaf moving *(Pause)* I've been thinking about this summer. We've gone to Banff for fourteen years now. Seems to me we're in a helluva rut.

JEAN: I'd just as soon stay here, if you would.

FATHER: Oh, I don't know. The mountains, the Maritimes—it's all the same to me. Just a different smell, s'all, hotel to hotel. It's you I think about.

JEAN: It's all the same to me, too, Dad.

FATHER: I used to think you'd find a beau on one of those holidays.

JEAN: If you look for a beau, I guess you can find one.

FATHER: Yep, I guess so. *(Pause)* I used to think about moving, too.

JEAN: So did I. I think the time has come, Dad, to settle for Cardigan.

FATHER: Yep. After all's said and done, Cardigan's been good to us. Everything's changing, though. I heard on the radio families move an average of once every four years nowadays.

JEAN: Mobile Society.

FATHER: I wonder if it stacks up any different in the long run.

JEAN: How so?

FATHER: Well, it might be easier, making your mistakes and leaving them behind. In the old days we just piled 'em up in one place and scratched a living off the top.

JEAN: Don't you think you do that whether you move or not?

FATHER: I guess so. *(He groans, and puts his palm to his head)*

JEAN: Got some pain tonight?

FATHER: Just a tad. Guess I'll take a couple of those new pills and go to bed.

JEAN: Get the right bottle now. Here, I'd better—*(She begins to rise)*

FATHER: Never mind, never mind! I know which ones. It's all *aspirin*, anyway.

JEAN: No, Dad. These new ones are pink.

FATHER: *Pink, yellow, red, green.* The pharmacist's artistry. It's wasted on me.

JEAN: Dad, I taped a safety pin on the lid.

FATHER: All right, I'll feel for it. *(Muttering, as he exits)* They play their little games. My gullet knows it's all aspirin. Will you lock up?

JEAN: Yes.

FATHER: And you'd better check the windows. You never know, it might—

JEAN: I don't think so—

FATHER: I don't think so, either. But you never know. Better to be safe than—

JEAN: Right. I'll close them. Good night, Dad.

FATHER: Good night, Jeannie.

Blackout

Israel Horovitz

THE 75TH

Israel Horovitz

Israel Horovitz makes his fifth appearance in *The Best Short Plays* series with *The 75th,* the third work to be published here from the author's *The Quannapowitt Quartet,* a bill of four related short plays. The complementary plays are *Stage Directions (The Best Short Plays 1977), Spared (The Best Short Plays 1975),* and *Hopscotch.*

Mr. Horovitz won his first acclaim in 1968 with *The Indian Wants the Bronx,* a powerful and terrifying study of violence on a New York street. A striking Off-Broadway success with Al Pacino in the pivotal role, it also scored heavily in other major American cities, at the 1968 Spoleto (Italy) Festival, the World Theatre Festival in England (1969), as well as in numerous other foreign countries. The play (which was published in *The Best Short Plays 1969*) won a 1968 Drama Desk–Vernon Rice Award and three "Obies," as well as a commendation from *Newsweek* magazine citing the author as one of the three most original dramatists of the year.

Israel Horovitz was born on March 31, 1939, in Wakefield, Massachusetts. After completing his domestic studies, he journeyed to London to continue his education at the Royal Academy of Dramatic Art and in 1965 became the first American to be chosen as playwright-in-residence with Britain's celebrated Royal Shakespeare Company.

His first play, *The Comeback,* was written when he was seventeen; it was produced in Boston in 1960. In the decade that followed, Mr. Horovitz' plays tenanted many stages of the world. Among them: *It's Called the Sugar Plum* (paired with *The Indian Wants the Bronx* on the New York stage); *The Death of Bernard the Believer; Rats; Morning* (originally titled *Chiaroscuro,* it was initially performed at the Spoleto Festival and later on a triple bill, *Morning, Noon and Night,* Henry Miller's Theatre, New York, 1968); *Trees; Acrobats* (introduced in *The Best Short Plays 1970); Line* (included in this editor's anthology, *Best Short Plays of the World Theatre: 1968–1973); Leader;* and *The Honest-to-God Schnozzola* (for which he won a 1969 Off-Broadway "Obie" Award).

His other works for the stage include: *Shooting Gallery; Dr. Hero* (presented at Amherst and various other colleges, as well

as Off-Broadway by The Shade Company, 1973); *Turnstile;*
The Primary English Class (a 1976 Off-Broadway success with
Diane Keaton as star); *The Reason We Eat* (which held its world
premiere at the Hartman Theatre, Stamford, Connecticut, in
November, 1976, with Academy Award-winning actress Es-
telle Parsons in one of the principal roles); and an adaptation
of Eugene Ionesco's French drama, *Man With Bags*.

Mr. Horovitz' most ambitious project to date is his full-
length trilogy, *The Wakefield Plays*. Set in Wakefield, Massachusetts, where he grew up, the three plays are *Alfred the*
Great, Our Father's Failing and *Alfred Dies,* and they are sched-
uled for a major Broadway production in the near future.

A collection of his plays, *First Season,* was published in 1968.
His first novel, *Cappella,* was issued in 1973, followed by a
novella, *Nobody Loves Me,* in 1975.

Twice the recipient of a Rockefeller Foundation Playwriting
Fellowship, he also won a similar fellowship from the Creative
Artists Program Service, funded by the New York State
Council on the Arts. In 1972, he received an Award in Litera-
ture from the American Academy of Arts and Letters, and in
1973 he was honored with a National Endowment for the Arts
Award.

The author, who divides his time between New York and
Massachusetts, with frequent sojourns in France, also has
written several major screenplays, notably *The Strawberry*
Statement, which won the *Prix de Jury,* Cannes Film Festival,
1970.

The People of the Play:

AMY CHAMBERLAIN, *thin, well-groomed, attractive, ninety-three*
ARTHUR "COOKIE" SILVERSTEIN, *tall, thin, well-groomed, handsome, ninety-three*

The Place of the Play:

Small private dining room in a restaurant overlooking Lake Quannapowitt, Wakefield, Massachusetts.

The Time of the Play:

September; evening.

A Note on the Music:

John Hall's song, "Still the One," should be used to start, interrupt, and conclude the play. The music source should be the onstage jukebox. N.B. "Still the One" is recorded by Hall's group, Orleans.

Darkness in auditorium.
Up-tempo popular music is heard at substantial volume.
Garish lights of coin-operated jukebox switch on, revealing jukebox on stage.
A human figure, back to audience, leans over front of machine, thumping same with her hands.
It should appear that figure is beating time to rhythm of music.
Lights to soft glow, revealing section of small-town, small restaurant.
The figure is Amy Chamberlain. She is extremely old, thin. She wears a long overcoat. Her back is still to auditorium, but it has become evident that she is trying to stop the jukebox from playing. She is now kicking the machine, as well as beating same with her hands.
There are two round tables on stage: four small chairs surround each. The stage is otherwise clear.

AMY: *(Yells) How d'ya' stop this goddam racket???* *(She kicks machine again; music ends; record has completed its play)* That's better. *(She moves to table, chooses chair, removes coat, folds same over back of chair; sits. She looks about for a waiter. There is none. Another record begins to play on jukebox. This one is even louder and more raucous than the first. She is amazed) Anybody here???* *(No response)* Hello!

(She stands and moves to jukebox, kicks and whacks same several times. She exits, leaving her coat on chair. The stage is empty awhile, but for furniture, jukebox and coat. The music continues. Arthur "Cookie" Silverstein enters. He is, like Amy, nearly ancient. He, too, wears a long overcoat. He carries brown bag. He looks about the room and, seeing no one, moves to jukebox and tries to stop same from playing loud music. Unable to stop same, he kicks machine and soon begins to whack it with hands and brown bag. Music continues. Silverstein goes to second table and removes coat, sets down brown paper bag, folds coat over back of chair and sits in chair next to coat. He searches through brown bag and removes rolled banner. He stands, goes to jukebox, carrying rolled banner. He kicks jukebox several times. He yells)

COOKIE: *Anybody here???* *(No response; He continues to kick jukebox) Anybody know how to shut this goddam thing off???* *(He screams now) THIS IS OFFENSIVE!!!* . . . *(Music ends abruptly, as song is completed. Cookie's scream is now in the clear) I SAID THAT THIS IS OFFENSIVE!!!* . . . *(Realizes his screams have not been covered by music)* . . . Thank you very much. Thank you.

(He looks about room. Sees he is still alone. He fastens banner to wall, after unrolling same. Lettering on banner reads:

WELCOME 75TH

He stands back and looks at banner. Amy's coat catches his eye. He walks to same and touches it, then lifts it to look at it. Amy pokes her head on to stage again. Watches a moment)

AMY: Alan Roberto?

(Cookie turns and faces her)

COOKIE: Eleanor Fritz!

AMY: No.

COOKIE: Me, neither . . .

AMY: Frank Lazzaro?

COOKIE: I'm not Italian . . .

AMY: Oh, my God! Jimmy Kiley!

COOKIE: Nope! *(Pauses)* Annie MacGlennon!

AMY: Not at all . . . Edgar Lancing?

COOKIE: Nope.

AMY: Philly Drinkwater?

COOKIE: Nope.

AMY: Angel-face Beech?

COOKIE: He's dead.

AMY: I thought not. *(Pauses)* Are you Wakefield High?

COOKIE: Yup.

AMY: Don't tell me. Let me guess. *(Smiles)* You wouldn't be Hannah's cousin Adrian?

COOKIE: Right. I wouldn't be.

AMY: Everybody else is . . . well . . . accounted for, in terms of men.

COOKIE: Silverstein.

AMY: A what?

COOKIE: Silverstein. Arthur Silverstein.

AMY: I'm sorry . . .

COOKIE: *Cookie* Silverstein . . .

AMY: Oh, of course, *Cookie* Silverstein! That's you!

COOKIE: *(Smiling)* Yup.

AMY: Cookie!

COOKIE: And you're . . . ?

AMY: Amy.

COOKIE: Amy?

AMY: Chamberlain . . .

COOKIE: Amy *Chamb*erlain!!!

(There is a pause in which they both smile at one another)

AMY: I don't think I remember you at all.

COOKIE: Nor I you.

AMY: Where did you live?

COOKIE: In high school? Elm Street.

AMY: Elm Street? West Side?

COOKIE: Elm Street. Runs up from the tracks on North Avenue all the way to Reading . . .

AMY: Well, I know that. It's just that . . . well . . . I know everybody on Elm Street and . . . Silverstein?

COOKIE: Cookie!

AMY: I beg your pardon?

COOKIE: Me. Cookie. That's my name.

AMY: Well, listen, at my age, why do I doubt *anything*? *(Pauses)* Silverstein, you say?

COOKIE: Silverstein. My father was Samuel Silverstein . . . the mover . . . He had his shop in Medford and another one later in Stoneham. Silverstein the Mover. You remember?

AMY: Well, listen. At my age. *(After a pause)* How have you been?

COOKIE: Oh, very well, very well.

AMY: Cookie?

COOKIE: Cookie.

AMY: What an odd name for a boy!

COOKIE: You were up Lynnfield way, right?

AMY: When?

COOKIE: High school.

AMY: No. We were in the park. West Side. Parker Road, in fact . . .

COOKIE: Parker Road?

AMY: Number twenty-seven . . .

COOKIE: White house with green trim.

AMY: Yellow. Bright yellow.

COOKIE: There's no yellow house I can remember on Parker . . .

AMY: There was a Taffy.

COOKIE: A Toffy*house?*

AMY: Taffy *Turner*. But never a Cookie . . . *(Pause)* Tuffy, I mean. Tuffy Pottle! You remember?

COOKIE: Do I remember Tuffy Pottle? Do I remember Tuffy Pottle? Didn't we play together every day on the West Ward hill?

AMY: You did?

COOKIE: Every day.

AMY: Tuffy.

COOKIE: Tuffy.

AMY: Wonderfully good-natured boy . . .

COOKIE: Salt of the Earth . . .

AMY: Never wanted much . . .

COOKIE: Never got much . . .

AMY: What became of Tuffy?

COOKIE: Tuffy? *(Pauses)* Dunno' . . . *(Pauses)* Probably quite successful.

AMY: No doubt. *(She pauses; sits. Leans back)* Just us?

COOKIE: I suspect so.

AMY: How many were we?

COOKIE: Then? *(Pauses)* Eighty-one.

AMY: Eighty-one?

COOKIE: *If* we count the Reilly girl . . .

AMY: Carol?

COOKIE: Her sister: Helen.

AMY: Why wouldn't we count Helen?

COOKIE: She never actually graduated with us—with our class. She had . . . trouble.

AMY: Ah, yes. *(Pauses)* What sort of trouble?

COOKIE: Family.

AMY: With her family?

COOKIE: Excuse me?

AMY: She had trouble with her family?

COOKIE: Who?

AMY: Helen Reilly?

COOKIE: Family *way:* she was in it.

AMY: Ah, yes. Did we know the father?

COOKIE: There was none.

AMY: There *had* to be one. There always is . . .

COOKIE: Not from us: from our graduating class. *(Pauses)* She always turned her affection away from our year. Either above us or beneath us. *(Pauses)* She was fond of my brother.

AMY: Was she?

COOKIE: Very fond. You might even say she was *keen* on him.

AMY: Was she?

COOKIE: *He* said so . . . *(Pauses)* I suppose she was. *(Pauses)* He was a full head taller than me.

AMY: Was he?

COOKIE: I can vouch for that myself. A full head. Two years younger, too. One of those flukes of genetics . . .

AMY: I'm sure.

COOKIE: My entire family was flukish, genetically speaking.

AMY: Were they?

COOKIE: Not my mother and father. They were normal. I mean, who *knows* if they were? It's just that the genetic fluke I'm speaking of was found out in their children: me and my brothers and sister.

AMY: Bald?

COOKIE: Short.

AMY: Really?

COOKIE: I was nearly a foot shorter than my younger brother . . .

AMY: Helen Reilly's friend?

COOKIE: Right. Him. And he was nearly a head taller than me, but a foot shorter than my father . . .

AMY: That would make you a head and a foot shorter than your father . . .

COOKIE: At the minimum.

AMY: That *is* strange!

COOKIE: Oh, yes. A fluke. My sister, poor thing, she was incredibly short.

AMY: Was she?

COOKIE: Nearly a legal midget.

AMY: *Was* she?

COOKIE: Becky! Poor Becky . . . , incredibly short, really . . .

AMY: Little Becky Roberto?

COOKIE: Excuse me?

AMY: Was that the way we knew your sister?

COOKIE: Little Becky Silverstein.

AMY: I don't think so.

COOKIE: I *know* so!

AMY: I don't think I remember her . . .

COOKIE: Couldn'ta' forgot her, once you saw her. Tiny little thing, but very well formed, for her size and all. Very attractive to the multitude of men here in town . . .

AMY: Was she?

COOKIE: Oh, very much so. The Lazzaro boys couldn't keep their hands off her . . . *(Pauses, embarrassed)* . . . I hope you pardon my bein' so blunt.

AMY: Oh, well. Times have changed, haven't they?

COOKIE: And for the better, too, I'd have to say!

AMY: I knew the Lazzaro family quite well. Funny, you should mention them in relation to your poor stunted sister.

COOKIE: They lived closeby. On Eustis Avenue . . .

AMY: They did indeed. And I on Parker. Number twenty-seven . . .

COOKIE: And we were thirty-three Elm. *(Smiles)* You place us now, do you?

AMY: I suppose.

COOKIE: It was an enormous gray house with a Dutch-shaped roof. My uncle built it for my grandfather . . . *(Smiles)* Very wealthy.

AMY: Your grandfather?

COOKIE: My uncle.

AMY: Your *grandfather* lived in Wakefield?

COOKIE: Born here. Same house as me.

AMY: Native Wakefieldians?

COOKIE: Yankees . . . *Puritans*, almost.

AMY: Goldstein?

COOKIE: Silverstein.

AMY: And your sister married a Lazzaro?

COOKIE: Excuse me?

AMY: Your sister married a Lazzaro. You said that. Am I getting it bolixed up? I do that . . .

COOKIE: Oh, not bolixed badly. You're very close to what I said. *(Smiles)* I said, my sister Becky was tremendously bothered by the Lazzaro brothers' sexual advances to her body . . .

AMY: Was she?

COOKIE: Something terrible!

AMY: I am simply amazed! Simply amazed! *Sexual?*

COOKIE: With their hands.

AMY: I don't completely understand . . .

COOKIE: While walking . . . on the street . . . their hands!

AMY: In an acrobatic fashion, you mean?

COOKIE: No, you've made a major bolix of it now. Now you have. *(Pauses)* My sister, the stunted one, was tremendously bothered by the Lazzaro boys fondling her breasts when she took walks . . .

AMY: *Are you serious???*

COOKIE: Deadly so.

AMY: I am simply amazed!

COOKIE: Italians.

AMY: I am simply amazed.

COOKIE: So was she, the first dozen or so gropes . . .

AMY: I can well imagine!

COOKIE: It made her a bit frightened to take walks . . .

AMY: Which brother in particular?

COOKIE: All of them.

AMY: There were five or six . . .

COOKIE: Six. And we suspected the father as well . . .

AMY: You *can't* be serious???

COOKIE: Is the Pope Catholic?

AMY: He certainly is!

COOKIE: Then there you are.

AMY: I would have to say shocked and amazed. I am simply shocked and amazed . . .

COOKIE: Sorry to have brought it up . . .

AMY: Not at all. These things are good to know . . . *(Pauses)* Which brother, in particular. Did she say?

COOKIE: It was always difficult for her to be sure . . . She bein' so short . . .

AMY: . . . and they bein' so tall!

COOKIE: Exactly.

AMY: Poor little thing.

COOKIE: It was horrible . . . for her . . . first dozen or so times . . . until she learned.

AMY: To stop them?

COOKIE: Opposite. To just let them do it. *(Pauses; tight-lipped)* It was the only way. *(Pauses)* Get it over with, quickly.

AMY: I am simply beside myself.

COOKIE: As were we all.

AMY: Why, do you suppose, am I hearing this for the first time?

COOKIE: Oh, well, you can understand *that* . . .

AMY: I suppose I can . . .

COOKIE: You knew the Lazzaro family well then, did you?

AMY: Well, my God! Not *that* well!

COOKIE: I wasn't insinuating.

AMY: Of course not. I'm just a bit shaken from the news.

COOKIE: Oh, Christ, it was more than sixty years ago . . .

AMY: I suppose, but the sting's still there . . . *(Pauses; smiles)* I had quite a crush on a Lazzaro. You might even say I was . . . you know . . .

COOKIE: Keen?

AMY: Oh, that, too . . .

COOKIE: Which one of them?

AMY: Alan.

COOKIE: Alan?

AMY: He pitched a no-hitter against Reading . . .

COOKIE: Of course, Alan . . . *(Pauses)* I remember him well . . . *(Pauses)* Oh, I don't think he hardly groped her at all . . . Maybe once or twice, just to keep up the family image, but that's all.

AMY: I shouldn't think so. He wasn't very happy in that family.

COOKIE: You don't say?

AMY: Couldn't wait to leave town.

COOKIE: Did he?

AMY: For the War.

COOKIE: Of course.

AMY: Came back very well decorated, too.

COOKIE: I think I'd heard that . . .

AMY: But never really happy again . . .

COOKIE: Did you see him?

AMY: Excuse me?

COOKIE: *Date* him, I suppose you'd say?

AMY: Oh, no. *(Pauses)* An occasional dance. A walk . . . *(There is a pause)* He was quite tall. A six-footer, I think.

COOKIE: Oh, I don't think so. Not Alan Lazzaro. Maybe, Angelo . . .

AMY: Really, Mr. Silverstein, I should know . . .

COOKIE: Cookie.

AMY: Oh, no, thank you . . . Stuffed.

COOKIE: My name. My name is Cookie.

AMY: Your given name?

COOKIE: Nick.

AMY: This is very confusing.

COOKIE: My given name is Arthur. My nickname is Cookie. *(Smiles)* I prefer Cookie. I don't know why. It suits me . . .

AMY: I wish I could say I remember you. I don't.

COOKIE: May I be truthful?

AMY: I wish you would.

COOKIE: I don't remember you, either.

AMY: But that's just ridiculous!

COOKIE: But it's the truth!

AMY: I was a cheerleader, for God's sake!

COOKIE: You were?

AMY: K.

COOKIE: You were K?

AMY: Senior year. I was L, junior year . . .

COOKIE: *(Trying to remember)* L, junior year . . . K, senior year . . . *(Squinting now)* K, K, K . . .

AMY: Judy Beebe was W . . .

COOKIE: Carol what's her name was A . . .

AMY: And I was K!

COOKIE: I can do no more than draw a blank on K . . . *(Pauses)* Christ! *(Squints. He visualizes and points to each imagined cheerleader in line, on the air between him and Amy)* W . . . A . . . a blank . . . E . . . F . . . I . . . E . . . L . . . *(Remembers)* Let's just wait a minute! L! Junior year! *(Sings to melody of "My Old Kentucky Home")* "Oh, the moon shines bright . . ."

(He points to Amy, who completes the song by singing the final line)

AMY: "O'er my Quannapowitt home . . ." *(She laughs)* You remember!

COOKIE: *(Laughing as well)* Ah, yes. You were L . . .

AMY: Between E and D . . .

(They both laugh)

COOKIE: Elaine Hawkins was E, and Maud what's-her-name was D . . .

AMY: *(Stops laughing)* Not at all . . .

COOKIE: Huh?

AMY: Not at all! It was Maud Anderson and she was a majorette, not a cheerleader. Elaine Hawkins was neither a cheerleader, nor a majorette. She was quite hefty, if I recall correctly.

COOKIE: *(Stunned)* Christ! She was more than hefty! She was a battleship . . .

AMY: Could you please not use that expletive?

COOKIE: What?

AMY: I've never taken to people just saying "Christ!" like Christ was just a word. I'm sorry.

COOKIE: Oh, God! I'm really sorry.

AMY: No, *I'm* sorry. I don't mean to embarrass you . . .

COOKIE: I'm embarrassed . . .

AMY: There, you see? *(Pauses)* I'm sorry. I apologize. *(Looks about the room)* Where are the others?

COOKIE: The others?

AMY: There are supposed to be twelve of us. Alice and Rosemary Simon . . .

COOKIE: Oh, no . . .

AMY: What?

COOKIE: There's just us, I think . . .

AMY: No, there are twelve of us. *(Looks for her coat and pocketbook)* There's a letter with the ticket . . .

COOKIE: It's from me.

AMY: There's a list in with the ticket: those lost, those . . . well . . . gone . . . and those found. There are twelve of us.

COOKIE: I sent the letter.

AMY: Rosemary . . . *(Hears)* You what? You sent the letter?

COOKIE: I did.

AMY: Oh. *(Pauses)* Did you? *(Finds letter by now and looks at it)* Arthur "Cookie" . . . *(Looks at Cookie)* You?

COOKIE: Me.

AMY: Then you should know. About the others . . .

COOKIE: I do.

AMY: All of them?

COOKIE: Our class had a bad year.

(There is a silence)

COOKIE: One of the worst.

AMY: Rosemary?

COOKIE: Car wreck. Horrible.

AMY: A car wreck? At her age?

COOKIE: Ironical.

AMY: I should say. Rosemary?

COOKIE: Route One-twenty-eight, down near Manchester. *(Smiles)* Read it in the *Globe*. A very nice sized notice.

AMY: Large?

COOKIE: Oh, very large. Excellently thought out, too. At least *I* thought so.

AMY: Well, then. I can just stop waiting for the others, can't I?

COOKIE: I was quite relieved to find you here. I didn't get your form back.

AMY: I don't understand.

COOKIE: There was a personal history form. I didn't get yours back.

AMY: Were you a class officer?

COOKIE: Me? *(Laughs)* No.

AMY: I should think not. *(Pauses)* Oh. Not to cast any insinuendoes, but I do remember our officers . . .

COOKIE: John and Janette . . .

AMY: Lovely couple . . .

COOKIE: Did they date?

AMY: John and Janette? Oh, more than that. They married.

COOKIE: Did they?

AMY: They reunited at our own reunion. It was a beautiful thing to see.

COOKIE: I can imagine . . .

AMY: Dancing, cheek to cheek and all . . . It was our thirty-fifth . . .

COOKIE: I missed that one.

AMY: His first marriage, her fourth, I believe . . .

COOKIE: They must have been fifty . . .

AMY: Fifty-three.

COOKIE: Must have been.

AMY: Precisely.

COOKIE: I was off fighting . . .

AMY: For whom?

COOKIE: For us! For whom? Whom did you think? There was no time for me to be dancing cheek to cheek, I'll tell you that!

AMY: That old and fighting still?

COOKIE: I re-enlisted after the Second War . . .

AMY: Did you?

COOKIE: I was piss and vinegar . . . *Excuse* me!

AMY: Not at all. Don't you worry . . .

COOKIE: I wouldn't now.

AMY: I shouldn't think so . . .

COOKIE: I missed our thirty-fifth . . . Couldn't get the weekend. I remember it well . . .

AMY: You would have won "Traveled Longest Distance" . . .

COOKIE: Oh, no. I was just up at Devens . . .

AMY: England?

COOKIE: Fitchburg. Just up here. Fort Devens.

AMY: Oh, were you? Fitchburg?

COOKIE: Not much of a town.

AMY: Never was.

COOKIE: I tried for the weekend, but I couldn't get it. Paid for my tickets, too . . .

AMY: Tickets, were they? In the plural?

COOKIE: Married, no children. Married late for children. She was sixty . . .

AMY: Local girl?

COOKIE: No. Fitchburg. A spinster, but very nice. Taught English in the junior high . . .

AMY: *I* taught English . . .

COOKIE: Oh, I didn't mean . . . *(Pauses; embarrassed)* Nothing wrong with not marrying. I think not-marrying is a fine institution! *(He laughs; pleased by his small joke. No response at all from Amy)* That was a play on words.

AMY: I married twice.

COOKIE: Did you?

AMY: Once to a Frenchman and once to a Californian.

COOKIE: You seen the world, then, haven't you?

AMY: I have some memories.

COOKIE: Sounds like it. Sounds like it. *(Smiles)* In France then, with the Frenchman?

AMY: Providence.

COOKIE: Ah, yes. Rhode Island French. Quite a few of them in Providence, aren't there?

AMY: Oh, thousands. Even still . . .

COOKIE: Children?

AMY: No.

COOKIE: Neither time?

AMY: No.

COOKIE: *There's* something in common then . . . between us, I mean.

AMY: Yes.

(There is a silence)

COOKIE: Do you remember Evelyn whoosis?

AMY: Who could forget?

COOKIE: She won the award for "The Most" every time . . .

AMY: Catholics.

COOKIE: Insanely so, I'd say . . .

AMY: She stayed in town, didn't she?

COOKIE: Married a MacShane . . .

AMY: Never moved from town, did they?

COOKIE: They couldn't, could they? Fourteen screaming children all around them all the time . . .

AMY: Shocking way to waste your time!

COOKIE: I agree.

AMY: Cleaning noses . . .

COOKIE: Wiping up spilled milk . . .

AMY: Packing lunches . . .

COOKIE: Sunday meals . . .

AMY: Telephone bills from long distances . . .

COOKIE: Tragedy befalling . . .

AMY: *(After a pause)* Yes. That would've been the worst.
(There is a silence)

AMY: Who wins the award for "Distance Traveled" then?
You or me?

COOKIE: I'm down from Burlington . . .

AMY: Vermont?

COOKIE: No, Burlington . . .

AMY: Just up here? *(He nods)* Burlington's only four miles
from here.

COOKIE: As the crow . . . you know . . .

AMY: . . . flies?

COOKIE: Flies. *(Looks down; embarrassed)* I did live once, for
a month, in D.C. . . . *(Pauses)* But that was a hotel. Hotels
don't really count. *(Pauses)* Very little traveling done. I
guess I never wanted to, because, I . . . well . . . I didn't.
(Looks up) You?

AMY: What?

COOKIE: In from the Coast?

AMY: Oh, no. He passed on almost immediately after we
married. *(Pauses)* Very soon after. *(Pauses)* Within the week, in
fact.

COOKIE: Did he?

AMY: Very sudden.

COOKIE: Tragic business. Heart?

AMY: Lungs. They both collapsed . . .

COOKIE: Simultaneously?

AMY: Spontaneously, as well.

COOKIE: Tragic business. No warning?

AMY: He coughed.

COOKIE: Not much warning in a cough . . .

AMY: One never knows.

COOKIE: That's the truth.

AMY: I had a great deal of trouble locating his family.
(Pauses) I'd not yet actually met them. *(Pauses)* Californians.

COOKIE: You mentioned that.

AMY: We were living up Stoneham way . . .

COOKIE: Were you?

AMY: Do you know Gould Street?

COOKIE: Near the junk shop?

AMY: Scrap yard.

COOKIE: Oh, yes, I do. I'm very interested in that . . .

AMY: In junk?

COOKIE: In the phenomenon . . .

AMY: I don't completely understand . . .

COOKIE: Those of us who move away . . . far away . . . from birthplaces . . . and those of us who . . . you know . . . don't.

AMY: Ah, yes, I see. *(Smiles)* I've always quite liked it here . . .

COOKIE: As do I.

AMY: Never saw the need to move about . . .

COOKIE: Nor I . . .

AMY: I've had my work . . .

COOKIE: Teaching English?

AMY: Precisely.

COOKIE: In Stoneham?

AMY: Not for a while. Not since my retirement.

COOKIE: *(Smiles)* Well, it looks as though I win. I must say, this is a surprising victory . . .

AMY: I would call it a tie myself . . .

COOKIE: Nonsense. In order to reach Burlington, you have to pass through Stoneham *and* Woburn . . . *(Smiles; shrugs)* No question who wins "Longest Distance Traveled" . . .

AMY: *Longer* distance traveled.

COOKIE: I see. Yes.

AMY: If there were three of us, it could be longest . . .

COOKIE: I remember that, now that you bring it up. *(Smiles)* Do you remember Miss Caswell?

AMY: Remember her? She started me out!

COOKIE: All of us! Wonderful teacher, wonderful woman as well . . .

AMY: On my career, I mean! I actually taught English!

COOKIE: Oh, yes. I see what you mean.

AMY: I remember the day she took me aside. (*Smiles. Imitates still older woman*) "Amy Chamberlain, you have a talent." (*Pauses*) "For what?" I asked. I was young. (*Pauses; smiles. Changes vocal pitch to older woman's timbre*) "For teaching the language, its rules and uses." And she was right . . .

COOKIE: Nearly always.

AMY: I do have a talent . . .

COOKIE: A way with words . . .

AMY: Do you think so?

COOKIE: Very certainly so.

AMY: Thank you . . . Cookie.

COOKIE: It's something I notice in an English-speaking person . . .

AMY: You're very kind.

COOKIE: Would you have any interest in dancing?

AMY: The ballet?

COOKIE: With me.

AMY: Oh, I see. (*Smiles*) It's been a while. (*Pauses*) I would. Yes. I think we should. It's an occasion, after all . . .

COOKIE: We're the seventh-fifth . . .

AMY: Together again . . .

COOKIE: We're the lucky ones . . .

AMY: I should say!

COOKIE: (*Fishing in his pockets*) Do you have a favorite?
(*She stares at him blankly. He nods to jukebox*)

COOKIE: Song?

AMY: I doubt if it's there.

COOKIE: You might be surprised.

AMY: "Don't Fence Me In."

COOKIE: Is it?

AMY: It is. Never known why. (*She hums a melody, smiling happily*)

COOKIE: Let me have a look . . . "Don't Fence Me In," huh?
(*He stands and moves to jukebox.
She continues to hum, smiling*)

AMY: (*Her smile fades; suddenly*) I can't seem to remember the words to the song.

COOKIE: It's been years since I've played one of these

things . . . *(Jiggling coins; reading price)* My Christ! It's certainly risen from two-for-a-nickel, I'll tell you that!

AMY: *(Hums again, this time worried)* Do you remember what comes in between *commences* and *fences?*

(Cookie drops coin in slot and lights on machine flash signal for him to choose a song)

COOKIE: Let's just have a peek here . . . *(Puts on his eyeglasses)* Right!

AMY: I've lost it completely . . . right between *commences* and *fences* . . . a perfect rhyme . . . *(Pauses, hums)* Like a sieve! *(She hums again a while; stops)* Well, that's gone now. All gone.

COOKIE: I don't see the song here. I'm afraid it's not on the machine . . .

AMY: It doesn't matter . . .

COOKIE: It was so popular, too . . .

AMY: Play anything you like . . . Play one of *your* favorites . . .

COOKIE: Mine? Oh, well, I never knew too much about music . . . *(Looks over selection list)* I always admired "Those Wedding Bells Are Breaking Up That Old Gang Of Mine."

AMY: Oh, good, then. Play that.

COOKIE: I don't see it.

AMY: *(Hums again a while, this time clearly panicked)* It fits perfectly between *commences* and *fences.* I don't know *how* I could have forgotten! I sang that song a hundred times a day! *(She hums again)* Gone!

COOKIE: I don't think it's here!

AMY: Surprise us, then!

COOKIE: You mean just pick any number that comes to mind?

AMY: Certainly.

COOKIE: Oh, well, then . . . *(Smiles)* Fifty cents.

AMY: For a song?

COOKIE: That's what it costs now.

AMY: It's all relative, isn't it?

COOKIE: Relative to what you've got, you mean . . .

AMY: *(Smiles)* That's very good, yes. *(Pauses)* I've got my pension. I foxed them on that one, didn't I? Worked thirty years, pensioned for thirty-five! . . .

COOKIE: So far . . .

AMY: Right! So far! They'll change the retirement dates one day, when they smarten up, won't they?

COOKIE: I've been pensioned nearly forty-seven years now.

AMY: You're not serious?

COOKIE: Imagine if I'd' a quit at forty, like they wanted?

AMY: You went straight in after high school, did you?

COOKIE: Many of us did. Things were different then.

AMY: Never any thought of college?

COOKIE: College of Life and Hard Knocks. That's me. *(He smiles; She doesn't)*

COOKIE: College of Life and Hard Knocks.

AMY: I suppose.

COOKIE: And you? Radcliffe, I suppose.

AMY: Smith.

COOKIE: *(Amazed)* Did you? I was making a joke there. I really thought you'd come back with "Salem Normal." I never dreamed you'd be comin' back with "Smith." *(Pauses)* You've been beautifully educated, haven't you?

AMY: Miss Caswell's the wonder behind all that.

COOKIE: I'm sure she is. Wonderful woman. Wonderful teacher and a wonderful human being to boot. *(Pauses; suddenly upset)* Oh, God!

AMY: What's the matter?

COOKIE: You remember old Mrs. Nicker . . . Warren School?

AMY: Fourth grade?

COOKIE: That's her.

AMY: Died when we were in fifth . . .

COOKIE: *You* were Warren School, too?

AMY: Parker Road . . .

COOKIE: God! What *is* it with my brain???

AMY: *You* were Warren School?

COOKIE: Elm Street.

AMY: God bless us. My brain is a bowl of Quaker Oats . . .

COOKIE: Do you remember old Nicker then?

AMY: Certainly.

COOKIE: She had a problem with flatulency, so to speak . . .

(Amy looks down)

COOKIE: Sorry. Anyway, you remember her?

AMY: Yes, of course. She died when I . . . we . . . were in the fifth . . .

COOKIE: My fault.

AMY: What?

COOKIE: My fault. In fourth grade, I kicked her. Her leg never healed and she died from it. My fault. It was my fault.

AMY: You're not serious?

COOKIE: She took us out for recess. We were playing kickball, when the bell rang. I was up. I'd been waiting for my up about ten minutes, about half the recess. The pitcher pitched . . . I kicked . . . Miss Nicker stepped in to stop me from kicking and end the game . . .

AMY: And you kicked her?

COOKIE: Kicked her? Damn near sent her into the trees!

AMY: You can't be serious?

COOKIE: Deadly so. She was in her grave within the year. Her leg never healed. I think they took it off before she finally went, nothing could've saved her . . .

AMY: You've got it all wrong!

COOKIE: Would that I did!

AMY: But you do! She lived right next to us . . .

COOKIE: Parker Road . . .

AMY: Right next to us. Twenty-nine!

COOKIE: That's a fact!

AMY: It was her stomach that killed her. Some sort of tumor . . . They were Christian Scientists. I heard the screams for weeks. Terrible thing. I'll never forget.

COOKIE: Emily Nicker, fourth grade, H. M. Warren School?

AMY: Twenty-nine Parker Road. Flatulency problem . . . so to speak . . .

COOKIE: My God!

AMY: I remember it like yesterday . . .

COOKIE: All these years . . .

AMY: Poor old thing . . .

COOKIE: What a relief!

AMY: I can imagine! . . .

COOKIE: You can't. You really can't . . . *(Pauses)* I . . . am . . . so . . . relieved!

AMY: I'm very happy for you . . .

COOKIE: I'd like very much to dance. Would you?

AMY: I wouldn't mind.

COOKIE: I say number 6. How's that sound?

AMY: Fine.

COOKIE: *(Inspecting machine)* That doesn't seem to be the way this works. Would you choose 6-A, 6-B, 6-C, 6-D, E, or F?

AMY: F.

COOKIE: Really?

AMY: F.

COOKIE: *(Pushes buttons)* Here goes.

(Machine clicks into action.

He goes to her.

She rises.

They assume ballroom dance position in each other's arms.

Up-tempo music.

They stare awhile at one another.

They attempt a few steps of a waltz.

Amy sits.

Cookie goes to machine and pushes all buttons then kicks and whacks same. Amy stands, goes to machine, removes plug. Music and lights on machine fade out together)

COOKIE: I thought I would lose my senses! *(Cookie is exhausted from whacking machine. He leans against chair)*

AMY: *(Suddenly screams)* That's it!

COOKIE: *(Amazed; he sits at other table)* What's it?

AMY: *Lose my senses! (Laughs)* Isn't that ironical? Lose my senses?

COOKIE: I've missed the context, I think . . .

AMY: It fits . . . between *commences* and *fences* . . .

COOKIE: It does?

AMY: It rhymes. With *commences* and *fences*. *Commences, fences, lose my senses*.

COOKIE: There's rhyme there. That's true enough.

AMY: I . . . am . . . so . . . relieved.

COOKIE: Glad to have helped out . . .

AMY: It's the biggest fear I have.

COOKIE: Fences?

AMY: *(Laughs; whoops)* You are so *clever*, Cookie! You really are! *(Laughs)* I haven't had a laugh like this in Christ knows how long! *(Laughs again; stops. Dries eyes)* That was a good one.

COOKIE: *(Begins to laugh)* I see. *(A deep laugh here)* Whewwwww!

(She joins his laugh with her own)

AMY: My sides!

COOKIE: Our sides!

(They both whoop again with laughter, looking across the space from table to table at one another. The laughter ends. They dry their eyes. There is a silence. They are lost in a memory)

AMY: *(Breaking the long frozen silence)* How were your grades?

COOKIE: *(Quickly)* Not much.

AMY: Weren't they?

COOKIE: I didn't click into real concentration until . . . later on . . . Later on in life.

AMY: Yes.

COOKIE: Your grades were excellent?

AMY: Quite good, yes.

COOKIE: B-pluses and A-minuses? That sort of thing?

AMY: Oh, yes. And then some.

COOKIE: Higher?

AMY: A bit.

COOKIE: A-minuses and As?

AMY: As and A-pluses, mostly.

COOKIE: Were you the . . . ?

AMY: No . . .

COOKIE: I didn't think so . . .

AMY: . . . Bruce B. Webber . . .

COOKIE: . . . I remember that . . .

AMY: . . . Every A I got, he got an A-plus. Every A-plus I got, he matched . . .

COOKIE: Always higher . . .

AMY: On the average . . .

COOKIE: Must've bothered you . . .

AMY: Not at all.

COOKIE: Must have.

AMY: Not any more . . .

COOKIE: 'course not . . .

AMY: Sixty years now . . .

COOKIE: Seventy-five!

AMY: Ah, yes . . .

COOKIE: That's why we're here . . .

AMY: Seventy-five . . .

(A pause)

AMY: I remember being two.

COOKIE: Two years old?

AMY: I do. I have a memory.

COOKIE: Extraordinary mind you have.

AMY: Do you think so?

COOKIE: Oh, I do.

AMY: So much fed in.

COOKIE: Must be a burden . . .

AMY: Our age is supposed to dull it all . . .

COOKIE: Blend it together . . .

AMY: Not I.

COOKIE: Me, neither . . . *(Pauses)* Hell of a burden. *(Smiles)* Whatever became of him?

AMY: Bruce B. Webber?

COOKIE: I'd heard Tech . . .

AMY: Tech?

COOKIE: M.I.T. . . .

AMY: Oh, no! He quit there . . .

COOKIE: Really?

AMY: Quit during his first year. They say he was failing . . .

COOKIE: His *health?*

AMY: His grades!

COOKIE: You're joking!

AMY: Small fish, big pond . . . That sort of thing.

COOKIE: Bruce B. Webber? Failing? Doesn't seem possible, does it?

AMY: Smith girls often spent a weekend in Cambridge, Harvard or M.I.T. Clara Ellison, from Great Neck, Long Island, New York, dated Bruce B. Webber's cousin, Alfred, also an M.I.T. man . . .

COOKIE: Poor Alfred.

AMY: Oh, yes. Poor Alfred, indeed . . . You may remember . . .

COOKIE: Which of us could forget? Poor Alfred.

AMY: Clara brought the news of poor Alfred's cousin, our own Bruce B. Webber . . .

COOKIE: And he was in fact failing?

AMY: And despairing, too!

COOKIE: Not drinking as well?

AMY: I don't think so . . . *(Pauses)* Clara didn't mention any drinking . . . *(Pauses)* Perhaps . . .

COOKIE: Who would have guessed?

AMY: Small fish.

COOKIE: But you certainly did well at Smith . . .

AMY: Quite well.

COOKIE: Same pond for both of you . . .

AMY: That's true enough. *(Smiles)* Lake Quannapowitt.

COOKIE: Terrible, the pollution formed in that lake in seventy-five years!

AMY: Do you take walks?

COOKIE: I do. I do.

AMY: I do, as well . . .

COOKIE: Now, of course, with Route One-twenty-eight cutting right into my property, it's . . . well . . . it's not as nice, not as relaxing.

AMY: Noise can bury you!

COOKIE: You needn't say *that* above a whisper, I can tell you that! *(Leans in)* I've foxed them.

AMY: Mmm?

COOKIE: The Route One-twenty-eight Commission. I've foxed them. *(Looks around room before he speaks)* I requested, procured and installed an absolutely official, state-provided sign for the road at my property-edge: "BLIND CHILD." *(Smiles)* Isn't that terrific?

AMY: *(Smiles)* Blind child?

COOKIE: *(Chortles a while)* Cut the noise to half . . .

AMY: Really?

COOKIE: You can see the cars and trucks visibly lose speed the moment they see the sign . . . Feet loosen right off their accelerators! *(He chortles again)* I'm very proud of *that* idea!

AMY: Do you own a great deal of property?

COOKIE: A modest amount.

AMY: How lucky for you.

COOKIE: I planned.

AMY: Good for you!

COOKIE: I bought the original parcel back about forty years now. At the time I first bought, I insisted on taking options on five adjoining parcels . . . *(Pauses)* Or would I say "adjacent"?

AMY: You might. You might even say "contiguous" . . .

COOKIE: Ah, yes, contiguous parcels. That has a nice ring!

AMY: How clever of you! And you've managed to buy them all?

COOKIE: And then some.

AMY: Have you?

COOKIE: Twelve parcels in all.

AMY: My God!

COOKIE: It's an eyeful.

AMY: All near the highway, is it?

COOKIE: Oh, no. Just the tip of two. The bottom edges, you might say . . .

AMY: I see.

COOKIE: I've got a pond . . .

AMY: On your property?

COOKIE: It's very nice.

AMY: I love a small pond.

COOKIE: I wouldn't exactly call it a *small* pond. It's quite large . . .

AMY: Really?

COOKIE: Half-a-mile across in width; three-quarters-of-a-mile, in length . . .

AMY: Sounds enormous!

COOKIE: Very pleasant, I should say.

AMY: I should think so!

COOKIE: Stocked with pickerel . . .

AMY: Pickerel?

COOKIE: Pickerel are young pike. They like the deep, cool, fresh water . . . *(Smiles)* They're quite a large, long fish.

AMY: How marvelous for you!

COOKIE: *(He returns to her table; sits. He talks quickly, confidentially)* A bit saved every year and, by the time you hit *my* age . . .

AMY: Not I.

COOKIE: I'm sorry . . .

AMY: Never had a business head . . .

COOKIE: But you've got your pension . . .

AMY: Yes, that. But I never used it well . . .

COOKIE: Do you own or rent?

AMY: Rent.

COOKIE: Oh, I see. *(Pauses)* Renting can be nice.

AMY: Not the same as owning.

COOKIE: I know many a happy renter . . .

AMY: I know a few . . .

COOKIE: I know many an unhappy owner . . .

AMY: Yes, I suppose . . . *(Smiles)* You have a very pleasant way.

COOKIE: Do you think so?

AMY: I do.

COOKIE: Well, aren't you nice to say it . . .

(There is a pause. Cookie reaches across the table and touches Amy's hand. She smiles. Tableau. Cookie withdraws his hand. He smiles)

COOKIE: Bruce B. Webber never impressed *me* much, I can tell you *that!*

AMY: Oh, I wouldn't sell him short . . .

COOKIE: I don't. I don't. But he did have an arrogant streak!

AMY: You have to in this life. If you want to get ahead . . .

COOKIE: I don't agree!

AMY: I'm afraid it's true . . .

COOKIE: And where did it get Mr. Bruce B. Webber? . . .

AMY: I suppose . . .

COOKIE: All that drinking and despairing! . . .

AMY: I suppose . . .

COOKIE: As if that family didn't have enough trouble and grief, with poor Alfred's untimely end . . .

AMY: That was pretty much of a freak accident, wouldn't you say?

COOKIE: I wouldn't. I wouldn't say murder ever really happens in an accidental fashion. As far as I'm concerned, it's always premeditated and hangin's never good enough, even for the best of them . . .

AMY: Still and all, Alfred's death was bizarre . . .

COOKIE: Familicide.

AMY: Familicide's not the word you want . . . That's not even a *word!* (*Shakes her head*) There's no word invented for what that family did to Alfred L. Webber. . . . Not in Greek, not in Italian, probably not even in the Irish tongue . . .

COOKIE: Were you friendly with Alfred?

AMY: . . . L. Webber? Yes, I suppose I should say yes . . . (*Pauses*) Which of us was, really. He was so . . . well . . .

COOKIE: Odd?

AMY: Odd's too harsh . . .

COOKIE: Despairing?

AMY: Yes, that's it. And, of course, his problem . . .

COOKIE: The drinking . . .

AMY: Like a fish . . .

COOKIE: Awful to see . . .

AMY: Tried to stop him . . .

COOKIE: I'm sure you did . . .

AMY: Never could . . . .

COOKIE: (*After a pause*) You were *that* close, were you?

AMY: We took walks. In the afternoons. Not many, but they had quality . . . *(Smiles)* He knew the lake like a friend . . . the wildflowers . . . by name . . . butterflies . . . by name, as well . . . the trees . . . *(Pauses)* He was the first to make me see the beauty of the old headstones . . .

COOKIE: *(Amazed)* In the cemetery?

AMY: Can you imagine? I was terrified at first . . .

COOKIE: *(Increasingly amazed)* The headstones in the cemetery?

AMY: We made rubbings.

COOKIE: *(Shocked)* Of the headstones in the cemetery?

AMY: Some of them were quite beautiful . . . Seventeenth Century . . . Very early Wakefield families . . .

COOKIE: This is a little difficult for me to follow . . . *(He is clearly amazed)* You and Alfred . . . together . . . took walks in the cemetery? . . . and made rubbings of tombstones?

AMY: Yes, we did.

COOKIE: Christ!

AMY: I know it sounds a bit odd . . .

COOKIE: Odd? Weird, you mean.

AMY: Well, I . . .

COOKIE: *(Interrupting her)* My entire family's buried there . . .

AMY: Not *that* cemetery.

COOKIE: Huh?

AMY: We did our rubbings in the other cemetery.

COOKIE: Oh, yes.

AMY: Near the Congo church . . .

COOKIE: Back of the Hartshorne House . . .

AMY: Precisely.

COOKIE: Alfred was as weird as they come.

AMY: *(Sudden anger, after a pause)* I think we've carried this subject to a conclusion, Mr. Silverman. *(Pauses)* I think this conversation of ours is . . . exhausted.

COOKIE: I didn't realize . . .

AMY: That we were close? *(Smiles)* Yes, we were.

COOKIE: I'm really sorry.

AMY: I'm sure you are. *(Smiles)* Alfred L. Webber was the

gentlest man I have known in my entire ninety-three years of knowing men . . . and I have known many, Mr. Silverman, many. *(Pauses)* I think we have touched, as they say, a ticklish spot.

COOKIE: I'm really sorry, Miss Chamberlain. I hope you can forgive me . . .

AMY: I do. I do . . . *(Pauses)* I'm a bit overprotective with my memories . . .

COOKIE: I understand . . .

AMY: So much of it has been so difficult . . .

COOKIE: Tragedy befalling you, over and over again . . .

AMY: *(Looks about room)* Well . . . *(Smiles)* I'm feeling a bit tired . . . *(Pauses)* No one else expected. Just us, I suppose . . . *(Smiles)* We didn't get an awful lot for our money, did we?

COOKIE: Oh! I have your money! *(Reaches in his pocket; finds check)* Here!

AMY: Oh, not at all!

COOKIE: No, it's your check. I never cashed it. *(Pauses)* Please.

(She takes check)

COOKIE: When you failed to return the form, I assumed . . . *(Pauses)* I only came myself on an outside chance that someone . . . *(Smiles)* I'm very pleased I did . . .

AMY: *(Pocketing check)* Yes. As am I.

COOKIE: I didn't order a meal, because . . .

AMY: I understand . . .

COOKIE: I canceled the caterer . . .

AMY: There was a caterer?

COOKIE: Oh, yes. I thought there might be as many as ten of us . . .

AMY: Really?

COOKIE: Tragic year for our class . . .

AMY: Perhaps next time . . .

COOKIE: What's that?

AMY: We'll keep the caterer.

COOKIE: And a proper dancing band!

AMY: Dance band. I'm sure that's what you mean: dance band.

COOKIE: Precisely!

AMY: Perhaps next time.

COOKIE: Should we wait the five years?

AMY: It's the tradition?

COOKIE: We might bend the tradition a bit . . .

AMY: In which way?

COOKIE: Why not wait just *one* year?

AMY: And have a seventy-sixth? I suppose. We could call it "The Spirit of Seventy-Six."

COOKIE: It certainly has a ring . . .

AMY: I wouldn't mind at all, really. Not at all . . . *(She stands)* You have my address, don't you?

COOKIE: Twenty-seven Parker Road . . .

AMY: No, Thirty Gould . . .

COOKIE: Oh, yes!

AMY: Will you remember?

COOKIE: Etched on my brain already!

AMY: *(He helps her into her coat)* Next year then? *(She smiles; extends her arm for a handshake)*

COOKIE: *(Takes her hand; holds it a while)* Could we do it next week?

AMY: Next week?

COOKIE: Next week. I would like that very much, Miss Chamberlain.

AMY: I suppose so. What would we call it?

COOKIE: Seventy-Five-*A*.

AMY: Yes. Do you have a telephone?

COOKIE: I do. I do. I'll write out my address and number for you. *(He fishes for and finds a wallet with pad and gold pen, in his jacket's inside pocket)* Here. I'll write it down.

(She is looking through her pocketbook)

AMY: I'm afraid I haven't a pencil . . . *(Sees his)* Isn't that elegant?

COOKIE: *(Hands paper to her)* That's my address and telephone there . . . May I ask yours?

AMY: I'll write it for you . . . *(She takes pen and paper and writes her address and telephone number upon paper)* Wonderful pen . . .

COOKIE: Thank you . . .

(She hands pen and paper to him)

COOKIE: Ah, yes. Gould Street, Stoneham. I know it . . .

AMY: Just past where the scrap yard used to be . . .

COOKIE: You have lovely handwriting . . .

AMY: Do you think so?

COOKIE: Perfect Palmer Perfect. . . . Wonderful to see.

AMY: Not quite so perfect as it was . . .

COOKIE: Lovely . . . *(Pockets her address, his wallet, etc.)* I'll call you . . . when? . . . day after tomorrow? What's a good time of day for you?

AMY: Late afternoon. I enjoy a call in the late afternoon.

COOKIE: Four-thirty, day after tomorrow. You'll hear my ring.

AMY: I look forward to it.

COOKIE: Do you have a ride now? . . . I could have my driver take you . . .

AMY: You have a driver, do you?

COOKIE: Been with me for years now. Excellent driver. Highly skilled.

AMY: Do you have a limousine?

COOKIE: I do.

AMY: My goodness! *(She giggles)* What a small world . . .

COOKIE: Could I arrange then for you to be driven . . . *(Smiles)* I could ride along, if you'd like.

AMY: Thank you, but my ride is arranged. *(Looks at her watch)* Well done by now, I should think. I'm nearly twenty minutes late. *(Smiles)* Good company.

COOKIE: You're very kind to say that . . .

AMY: I can't promise you we'll meet next week, but we can discuss it . . . the possibility of our meeting . . . when you call.

COOKIE: I understand.

AMY: *(Extends hand again)* Well, then . . .

COOKIE: I'll walk you to your car . . .

AMY: Please, don't! *(Smiles)* I'm perfectly capable . . .

COOKIE: I know that. I just thought it would be nice . . .

AMY: I'd rather you didn't!

COOKIE: Fine. We'll say "Good-night" here then . . .
(They shake hands)
COOKIE: I'm very pleased to have met you . . . to have seen you again, I mean.
AMY: As am I . . . Pleased to have met you again . . . Mr. Silverman.
COOKIE: . . . *Stein*. Cookie.
AMY: Good-night.
(She exits.
There is a silence.
Cookie walks to the jukebox and replugs electrical join to the wall outlet.
The jukebox lights relight.
The music fades in again, winding up to full sound and speed, at the precise spot on the recording at which the plug was pulled earlier in the play.
Cookie crosses to the chair, collects his coat, puts it on, stops a moment.
He begins to exit, thinks better of it, returns to chair, sits.
The music continues.
Cookie sits at table, staring straight out, listening to music, lost in a fantasy.
He taps his fingers on the table-top, to the rhythm of the music.
The lights fade out)

Curtain

Lanie Robertson

THE INSANITY
OF MARY GIRARD

Lanie Robertson

When *The Insanity of Mary Girard* was presented in Philadelphia in 1976, it was hailed in the *Inquirer* as ". . . a spellbinding and finely crafted play that deals boldly with the questions of insanity and women's rights. Set in the basement ward for the insane in Pennsylvania Hospital in 1790, it explores the psychic landscapes of Mary Girard, wife of the financial wizard, Stephen Girard, who committed her to an asylum (which was a husband's legal right at the time) but committed her knowing that she was pregnant. Out of historical fact, Robertson has created a sinister and intelligent encounter and a compelling piece of experimental theatre."

The reviewer for the Philadelphia *Daily News* was equally impressed: "Bravos go to the Theatre Center of Philadelphia for coming on strong with a finely sculptured, frighteningly provocative piece of total environment, 'theatre of cruelty' drama."

In response to a request for biographical data, Mr. Robertson wrote to this editor: "I was born in Knoxville, Iowa, in 1940 and raised in southern and southwestern states, spending much of my youth traveling cross-country with my parents as my father's work was pipeline construction. I attended fourteen schools in twelve states before graduating from high school. Later, I attended the University of Kansas, the University of London, and received a Ph.D. in English from Temple University in 1974.

"Although I have lived longest in Philadelphia, where I currently reside, I feel that Texas is my ancestral home as my grandparents either lived there or came from there, as did my parents. My spiritual home is the theatre: I am an actor and I have written approximately eighteen plays."

The author's most recent drama, *Back County Crimes,* was presented at the Williamstown (Massachusetts) Theatre Festival during the summer of 1977 and later, in the autumn, at Playwrights Horizons in New York City.

The Insanity of Mary Girard appears in print for the first time in *The Best Short Plays 1978*.

Characters:

MARY GIRARD, *a very attractive woman of twenty-nine years*
THE FURIES, *three women, two men of any age*
THE WARDER, *a man of middle age*
MRS. LUM, *Mary's mother*
STEPHEN GIRARD, *Mary's husband, ten years her senior*
MR. PHILLIPS, *a steward of Pennsylvania Hospital and a man in his forties*
POLLY KENTON, *a young woman*
MRS. HATCHER, *a woman approximately Mary's own age*

CHORUS: *The* FURIES *should be presented in the following way:*
FURY #1 *should play the role of* THE WARDER
FURY #2 *should play the role of* MRS. LUM
FURY #3 *should play the role of* POLLY KENTON
FURY #4 *should play the role of* MR. PHILIPS
FURY #5 *should play the role of* MRS. HATCHER
FURY #1 *should think of himself as a "regressed child"*
FURY #2 *should have "delusions of grandeur"*
FURY #3 *should be an "obsessive/compulsive"*
FURY #4 *should be "active/passive," usually in a catatonic state*
FURY #5 *should be an "hysteric"*

The segments of lines should be almost equally divided among FURIES *1, 2, 3, and 5.* FURY #4 *should say much less but always the "Dr. Rush" references.* FURY #5 *should deliver most of the "God" and "Jesus" words, etc.*

Time:

A Saturday night in the Fall of 1790.

Place:

A lunatic cell in the basement of the Pennsylvania Hospital in Philadelphia.

NOTE: Although the events presented in this play are based on fact, there has been no attempt to accurately portray the personalities of those responsible for the incarceration of Mrs. Stephen Girard.

At rise the stage is bare except for Mary Girard who is seated, bound in the Tranquilizing Chair. This was a device used for "excitable patients" who were insane or believed to be. There are leather straps to bind down the wrists, the arms, the chest and thighs, iron rings to go about the ankles, and a square box that swings down over the head. As the lights gradually come up, several figures enter from different directions. These are the Furies. They circle about the chair. One of them lifts the box and we see Mary's face for the first time.

Mary Girard is a very attractive woman, twenty-nine years old. Her eyes and hair are dark. She seems at first asleep or in a coma. Then she becomes very agitated and strains against her bonds.

FURIES: *(Tauntingly)* Mary. Mary Girard. Polly. Polly-Mary. Girard.

MARY: *(Screams)* Who are you? Stay away from me! No! Let me out of here. Do you hear me? Set me free at once!

FURIES: Oh, she wants. To be set. Free. At once. Oh, no. We mustn't. Do that.

MARY: Set me free, I tell you! Who are you? How dare you laugh at me! How dare you!

FURIES: Oh. She's so. Indig. Nant. Quite the fine lady. Isn't she? No one would think. Her husband was. Well-to-do. Would they, Mary?

MARY: What do you want of me? Did you come here to torment me?

FURIES: We want nothing, Mary. Only to comfort you. To aid you. Be with you in time of travail. Do whatever we can. Or may. Or might.

MARY: Then for God's sake set me free! If I stay in this chair any longer I shall go mad.

FURIES: Oh, say that and. We'll never let you out. Dr. Rush's chair is always successful. Such a good doctor! Dr. Rush!

MARY: Please set me free. Please!

FURIES: Does she promise? To behave? Would she try? To run? Away?

MARY: No. I promise I won't run away. I won't.

FURIES: Besides. She has no place. To run. Except into the wall. Which we can do, but not her. Not you, Mary. Not you.

MARY: Who are you? What are you? Tell me.

FURIES: We're no one. Nothing. Inmates of the asylum. Like you, Mary. Figments of your imagination. Air. Less than. Smoke. A puff. A poof. Of nothing. Nothing, nothing. Nothing.

(The Furies set Mary free)

MARY: If you are nothing, then I must be mad. I can see you, hear you.

(Mary grabs at them but they elude her)

FURIES: No, you mustn't touch us. For then we would have to. Tear you apart. We don't exist. We are ghosts. Your friends. Selves of yourself. Friends and angels. We know nothing. Except everything. You know. Or want. To know.

MARY: You know everything I want to know?

FURIES: Certainly. Assuredly. Definitely.

MARY: Then tell me. Tell me everything I want to know.

FURIES: What do you? Want to know, Mary?

MARY: Tell me where I am? And how long I've been here.

FURIES: *(Disappointed)* That's too simple. It's no fun. You know that already. The Penn. Sylvania. Hospital. The same. As it was. This morning.

MARY: This morning? How long have I been here?

FURIES: It's the same day. As it was before.

MARY: I can't have been here only a matter of hours. It's not possible! Oh, being in that chair is horrible. Horrible!

FURIES: Of course, it's horrible. It's supposed. To be. That's what you. Get for. Being crazy. Crazy Mary Girard.

MARY: But I'm not crazy. You know I'm not.

FURIES: You must be! Mr. Girard had you admitted. As a lunatic, paying patient. The doctors have agreed. To keep you here. As long as Mr. Girard. Continues to pay. Your bills. And quite a lucrative account. You'll prove to be. For a lunatic, Mary.

MARY: *(Furies laugh at her frustration through this)* It's all a misunderstanding. When I see the doctors, when I speak to Mr. Girard, it will all be corrected. It's a mistake, I tell you. And that chair. I thought I'd go mad.

FURIES: She will. In time. She sounds positively. Stark raving. Mad. That chair is one of the. Prized possessions. And inventions of. Dr. Rush. He positively. Loves it. And. So do we.

MARY: I couldn't move. I couldn't see anything. No sooner was I strapped into it than I began to itch.

FURIES: Only nerves. Or madness.

MARY: I couldn't even scratch my arm. And then my eyes began to tear and I couldn't wipe them. And there was such a roaring in my ears. I thought I would go . . . that it would drive me . . .

FURIES: Yes? Go. on. Don't stop. We want. To hear. Everything.

MARY: All sounds were strange, distant, as though I were under water, drowned without being dead, and it seemed so terribly hard to breathe. Later I fell asleep and had such dreams that I woke up screaming. Then I thought I was being smothered, coldly, carefully smothered with an enormous pillow that kept getting larger and larger. First it seemed the size of that box, but then it was as large as the room. Then it grew to the size of the entire hospital. And I knew that it would continue growing. Smothering not only me but everyone. The size of the city. And then the state. And then the size of the entire United States. And I awoke screaming.

FURIES: And you see. No one was. Smothering you at all. You were only here. Experiencing the effects. Of the Tranquilizing Chair.

MARY: And the echo in the box of my own screams. . . . It was horrible! Oh, why would they put me in such a thing? Surely they know I'm not mad.

FURIES: But it's the. Proper treatment. For your type. Of madness. Everybody knows. There are two kinds of. Madness.

The Torpid. And those subject to. Excitation. Dr. Rush. Has invented. Two appliances. To be used for. The treatment of. The mad. The gyrator. Or revolving machine. That shakes them up. The other is. The Tranquilizing Chair. For types like you. Ones subject to. Excitation. Or claims of. Sanity.

MARY: I feel weak, faint.

FURIES: It's only natural. After the. Bloodletting.

MARY: Bloodletting?

FURIES: It's quite regular. Quite customary. Mary. Quite natural. It lessens greatly. Your protestations. Of sanity. From you they took. Thirty ounces. Of blood.

MARY: Was that the itching of my arm?

FURIES: Yes, you see. You didn't feel. A thing. You see how well. The chair works. Now, Mary?

MARY: Ah! I must get out of here. I must. I can't have been here for only one day. It isn't possible.

FURIES: Less. It's only now. Near midnight. Soon it will be Sunday. You'll be able to hear. The bells. From all the churches. Stephen Girard will be in his usual pew. Mary. Praying for your soul. No doubt.

MARY: I must see him, talk with him. I'll ask him to forgive me or to let me pass away to some other place, pass out of his life as though we'd never met.

FURIES: The idea! Did you ever? Hear of such a thing? Horrid. Shocking. Disgraceful. A dreadful idea. For a married woman. To have. Leave her husband? She must be. Mad.

MARY: If you know anything about me you know that my marriage was the worst thing that ever happened to me. Until this.

FURIES: The hussy! I must say. I'm shocked. And this from. A woman legally bound. To a husband for thirteen years. She sounds like. A woman of. The streets. A common whore. A bawdy house tart. A ten-penny slut.

MARY: (Furious) How dare you speak to me like that. I'm Mrs. Stephen Girard! I don't have to tolerate your taunts and jeers. Get out. Get away from me and get out!

FURIES: (Afraid of being sent out) Oh, no, don't, Mary. Don't send us off. Or shut us out. We're only trying. To help you.

Mary. To put mildly. What you're bound to hear. Tomorrow. Only then it will be. So very much. Worse.

MARY: No one would dare talk to me in such a manner!

FURIES: They will, Mary. And worse. Much worse, Mary. The ones on the streets. The ones at those windows. The ones who come daily. To stare and point. And laugh at the lunatics. To mock them. Try to frighten them into fits. Or convulsions. Or seizures. Of the most horrid kinds. And it works beautifully, Mary. You'll be surprised how often. And how violently the seizures come.

MARY: I don't believe you. I don't believe there are people like that, people who do things like that. It's . . . cruel! People aren't like that. I'm sure they're not.

FURIES: (*Laughing*) She has so much. To learn. You mustn't undervalue the power of an accusing finger. The amusement people derive from the suffering of others. The superiority they feel when they see those less fortunate. They relish it. Revel in it. Rejoice for it.

MARY: It mustn't be allowed. I'll speak to someone about it!

FURIES: (*In glee*) Speak to someone! Mustn't be allowed! Glorious! Wonderful. Mary, can't you see how large? The windows were made? So the people wouldn't have to stoop? To see in?

MARY: They'll not look at me. Not here. I couldn't stand it. I'll be gone before they come. And if I'm not I'll hide from them. Under the covers of the bed or under the bed if necessary. I won't have them laughing at me. I couldn't stand it, I tell you.

FURIES: No! Poor Mary. If you hide. It'll make matters. So much worse. The attendants will pull you out. Chain you there where the manacles are. Facing the windows. No, Mary. It's much better. If you don't hide.

MARY: You said you know all I want to know. Then tell me how to get out of here. Please. Please!

FURIES: We can only. Show you. Yes, show you. You have to start. At the beginning. By seeing. The Warder of. The cells.

MARY: But I saw him this morning. He won't help me.

FURIES: You have to. See him for. He's the beginning. And if you are to. Know the end. You have to begin at the. Start.

(Furies place a short cape on Mary's shoulders, a muff on her hands, and a hat on her head. Warder enters. He is a young man about Mary's age)

WARDER: Here ye go. This way. In here, Mary. That's yer name, ain't it?

MARY: My name is Mrs. Stephen Girard. You will call me by that name if you address me again.

WARDER: Oh, no, I don't. I calls ye Mary. I have it on strictest orders not to call ye any such false name as that.

MARY: I am *Mrs. Girard.* There is nothing false about that.

WARDER: Oh, well, ye'll be right at home. We got the Queen of France an' the King of Poland in here, too. Call yerself whatever ye will. It'll cut no ice with me. I calls ye Mary because I was told by Mr. Girard hisself I was to so call ye.

MARY: But you know who I am. You came to my home in your carriage to bring me to see the doctor. You know I'm Mrs. Girard.

WARDER: I went to Mr. Girard's home. Not yers. All I know is yer Mary. More than that I don't want to know.

MARY: But I'm his wife, Mary Girard.

WARDER: I'm tellin' ye true. It's Mary ye be and Mary ye'll remain as far as I'm concerned. Unless ye take to bein' the Queen of Sheba or somebody else. Then I'll be callin' ye that.

MARY: *(Handing him some money)* Look, I have some money . . .

WARDER: *(Taking it)* Oh, ye'll be glad ye give this to me. I'll see ye get some real food some of the time. Somethin' to keep up yer strength instead of this gruel all the time. Maybe a pint 'a something' warmin' on occasion, huh?

MARY: You don't understand. I came to see the doctor, and you're to take me back to my home at once.

WARDER: Home? This room's yer home now, Mary. It's cheery, too, in daylight. That is, if ye'll be able to see much daylight fer all the admirers ye'll be entertainin' in them winders up there.

MARY: What admirers?

WARDER: Tomorrow's Sabbath. Lots of folks'll be out an' in a holiday mood. You'll see fer yerself then, I figure.

MARY: I won't be here tomorrow. I came to see the doctor about a . . . a personal condition. Where is he, sir?

WARDER: Me name's Frankie. Ye be good to Frankie, an' Frankie'll be good to ye, too, Mary.

(Pause)

MARY: I demand that you take me to the doctor at once!

WARDER: Snooty, ain't ye? Wants to see the doctor at once, do she? Well, doctors don't come round at once. They're due sometime week after next. I guess ye'll wait till then, all right. I'll just take yer hat an' cap an' muff so's ye can get to feelin' right at home, Mary.

MARY: Stay away from me!

WARDER: If that's the way ye want it. *(Calls)* Aides here!

(Furies enter and snatch Mary's cape, muff and hat from her)

MARY: No, stop! Please! You mustn't do this.

(Furies exit)

WARDER: Oh, things will be worse by a yard if ye act like that too frequent.

MARY: Do you have any idea who my husband is?

WARDER: Yep. I know who ye claims he be.

MARY: He's the wealthiest man in the City of Philadelphia.

WARDER: Wouldn't serprize me a notch.

MARY: Possibly the wealthiest in all the Republic.

WARDER: Yep. That, too.

(Pause)

MARY: *(Speaking rapidly)* If you keep me here against my will, you will be making a terrible mistake. He might sue this hospital, its board of directors, you and everyone connected with it.

WARDER: Nope. Don't think so. Seems I know more 'bout yer Mr. Girard than ye do, Mary.

MARY: I doubt that anyone in your position would know anything at all about the likes of Mr. Girard. But your superiors will.

WARDER: All I know is that it was Mr. Girard hisself who

said yer lunatick an' asked most kindly that ye be put here. That's all I know.

MARY: That's a lie! How dare you impugn my husband's name with such a lie!

WARDER: Some says ye done some of that impugnin' yerself, Mary Girard.

MARY: *(Striking at him)* How dare you!

(Warder ducks her blow and slips out of the cell. He closes the door)

MARY: What are you doing?

WARDER: Lockin' the door to yer new home. It's customary.

MARY: You can't keep me here. You cannot. Where am I? Is this a prison? What authority do you have to do this? I want to go home. Please. Don't do this to me! Please! Please!

WARDER: I'm only doin' what I gets paid for doin'. It's my job. I only takes orders from 'em what's higher up, Mary.

MARY: But surely you can see this is wrong.

WARDER: There yer wrong, Mary. I'm not paid to see what's right or wrong. It's not my business. My business is lockin' ye up. The rest is not my business.

MARY: You will drive me mad.

WARDER: It's not my business. My business is lockin' ye up. The rest is not my business.

MARY: You will drive me mad!

WARDER: It's not my business. My business is lockin' ye up. The rest is not my business.

MARY: Answer me! Is this a prison?

WARDER: That's real insultin', that is. This is the Pennsylvania Hospital. Founded by Mr. Franklin hisself, for treatment of sick poor folks. Lucky fer him he died this year, otherwise he might be highly offended by the way yer talkin' 'bout his fine hospital. An' ye are in the ward fer the mentally deranged. The place fer lunaticks, in plain speech.

MARY: But I'm not a lunatic.

WARDER: That's not fer ye or me to say. That's fer Mr. Girard to say. He be yer legal guardian an' he's the one who put ye here.

MARY: Stop saying that! I won't permit you to lie about

him that way. He . . . he would never do . . . do anything
. . . I don't believe you . . . but even if he did, he hasn't the
authority. He's no doctor. He's not medically qualified to pro-
nounce me either sane or insane.

WARDER: He's yer husband, ain't he? This Stephen
Girard?

MARY: Yes.

WARDER: Well then, thar ye be. He don't got to be no
doctor. All he gotta be is yer husband. That makes him yer
legal guardian an' by law whenever a legal guardian says the
one they's guardian over is lunatick then we picks 'em up and
puts 'em here. We got lots of women folks here whose
helpmates has writ out a little letter saying' they's lunatick.
You'll see 'em. They's crazy, too. Seems to happen more to
women folks 'count of the delicacy of thar minds.

MARY: Look at me, sir. You can tell I am not . . . like those
others.

WARDER: Oh, lots of crazy folks looks jus' fine when they
come in here. I jus' give you 'bout a month. I bet I won't be
able to tell you from any of those others. Wait an' see if I can.

MARY: For God's sake, sir, look at me! Do I appear to be
without my reason?

WARDER: Have ye not heard the wive's tale, niver judge a
book by its cover?

MARY: But I tell you I'm sane.

WARDER: Yep. That's what most of 'em thinks, too.

MARY: Listen to me. Even though Mr. Girard is my legal
guardian, surely someone, someone must make out some
legal document declaring me insane. Isn't that true?

WARDER: Right as rain.

MARY: Well, this has to be a dreadful mistake because no
one has examined me. My husband said I was to come with
you to see a doctor.

WARDER: Yep. That's what we tell most of 'em. "Jest goin'
to the hospital to see the doctor." Works nearly every time.
Sometimes tell 'em they're goin' to see the dentist. Jest for
variety's sake. An' I got the legal an' bindin' written document
from Mr. Shepherd, hisself, one of the managers of the whole

hospital. He's got a little letter from Mr. Girard sayin' straight out that ye, his wife, Mary Girard, is lunatick an' requestin' that ye be held here fer treatment fer the rest of yer natural life. Lest a course ye be cured.

MARY: For God's sake don't jest with me, sir!

WARDER: Oh, no, it's no jest. *(He closes the lock)* Ye can be sure the locks here are the finest and the realest locks ye'll ever see. Also, yer companions. They're the genuine thing. Out an' out lunyticks, ever last one. I'll jest get the good Dr. Rush's Tranquilizin' Chair fer ye. I think yer sorta subject to excitations. Ye'll feel better then. See if ye don't. *(He exits)*

(The Furies enter)

FURIES: Don't be. Upset. Mary. Mary. That one's past. You can forget. All about that one, Mary.

MARY: I have to get out of here. I have to see someone, talk with someone. When will they let me see someone?

FURIES: But we can let you. See anyone. You choose. Just tell us who it is. Name the name. And instantly you'll see them.

MARY: Will you truly or am I only imagining this?

FURIES: What does it. Matter, Mary? Give us the names.

MARY: I want to see my mother.

FURIES: Her mother! Oh, how funny! Little Mary wants to see her mother!

MARY: Yes. Let me see her. Please

(Furies exit. Mrs. Lum enters)

MRS. LUM: Madam, you sent for me?

MARY: Mother? Mother, you've come to me?

MRS. LUM: Rise, Madam. Of course I would come at the bidding of Mrs. Girard. I could hardly do otherwise, could I? Although I cannot pretend to understand why you wanted me here.

MARY: Oh, I need you, mother.

MRS. LUM: Need me, Madam? You never needed me very much, and now I'm sure you need me not at all. You mustn't speak extravagantly. Surely there is nothing I can do for you that you haven't the wherewithal to do much better than I.

MARY: It isn't money that I need from you.

MRS. LUM: I should think not.

MARY: It is comfort that I need of you, now

MRS. LUM: Comfort? You live in the very heart of comfort, Madam. Never have I seen a house this fine, furnishings this rich. The shine on these floors makes me afraid to take a step, lest they prove to be glass and crack underfoot. Everything here shines like lights from a great tower. You must be quite happy here.

MARY: What are you saying? This is not my house. This is a cell for lunatics in the cellar of the great hospital. Do not mock me, Madam! Surely you see it is cold and damp and horrid here.

MRS. LUM: I see only that when you married above your station it brought you great rewards. I see also why you did not want your family coming here, traipsing the dirt from workmen's feet across the polish of your fine wood floors.

MARY: My family was not welcome here. Neither were my friends. And now I myself am not. I told you whenever I visited you what things were like for me. You must have believed me, didn't you?

MRS. LUM: A poor excuse beats none, they say.

MARY: You didn't believe me. You never did, did you! You thought I didn't want you here because I was ashamed of you.

MRS. LUM: Something like that, yes. It's all right. We understood. We knew that it would happen. Happens all the time. It's all right. It's to be expected.

MARY: But it wasn't me at all. It was Mr. Girard. He didn't want you here.

MRS. LUM: That's all right, too. Why should he? We wasn't kin to him, and I won't listen to you berate Mr. Girard. He was a prince to your father. An absolute prince. Kept him working on his ships as long as your father was alive. I'll not listen to any bad words about Mr. Girard.

MARY: Mother, my husband abuses me.

MRS. LUM: For shame that you should give him cause. And double shame that you be brazen enough to tell it. You should have learned by now that there is nothing unusual in a husband's abusing his wife. It is the woman's place to be clever enough to seem to do his will whether she do or no. If you have been married this longish time, Madam, and still not learned that, I do not doubt that you have made a sorry time for yourself and for poor Mr. Girard as well.

MARY: And must the wife always bend to her husband's will, whether it be right or wrong?

MRS. LUM: Most assuredly, for it is the husband's place to rule his wife. The woman's to obey her husband.

MARY: And why must it be so?

MRS. LUM: Because it is the Law.

MARY: Whose Law?

MRS. LUM: God's Law. When you married you vowed to honor and obey your husband, Madam, 'till death do you part. Do you dare question the Law of God Himself?

MARY: If it is unjust . . .

MRS. LUM: It is not possible for God's Law to be unjust.

MARY: If this is God's Law, as you say it is, why didn't you explain this Law to me before I married Mr. Girard?

MRS. LUM: You were a woman, Madam.

MARY: I was sixteen years old. I was a girl.

MRS. LUM: It was your wish to marry.

MARY: It was Mr. Girard's wish to marry me.

MRS. LUM: You were not so innocent as that, Madam. Your marriage was a financial transaction. Your father and I . . . You knew that Mr. Girard had money and that you would never have to work another day in your life if you married him.

MARY: Then why did you speak to me about love and home?

MRS. LUM: Because I knew it would be easier for you if you loved him.

MARY: But you know I didn't. I was a servant. I wanted a home of my own.

MRS. LUM: You knew what you were doing. You got the home you wanted and much more. The shine of this house blinds the eye.

MARY: Look about you. Nothing you see here is mine. I have nothing, Madam, nothing.

MRS. LUM: Then you can only blame yourself. A wise

woman never lets her husband know the distaste she may feel
for him. You should have dissembled more and hidden whatever loathing you may have felt behind a display of feigned
affection.

MARY: I would have been a liar.

MRS. LUM: You would have fared better.

(Pause)

MARY: I asked you here because I have desperate news.
(Pause) I am with child.

MRS. LUM: Polly! This is wonderful!

MARY: No . . .

MRS. LUM: Nothing in all the world can do more to please
a childless man. Mr. Girard must be overjoyed.

MARY: No.

MRS. LUM: You mean he is not?

MARY: I haven't told him.

MRS. LUM: But you must, at once.

MARY: I cannot.

MRS. LUM: What do you mean you cannot?

MARY: I fear for my safety, mother. I fear what he might
do to me.

MRS. LUM: Do to you?

MARY: It is not Mr. Girard's child.

MRS. LUM: Polly! No!

MARY: I have informed Mr. Girard that I intend to leave
his house. I want to come home again. I can bring you nothing but my gratitude and a still fond regard for you.

MRS. LUM: I cannot help you, Madam. It would have been
well for you to have had his child.

MARY: Don't you think I tried to have a child by him?

MRS. LUM: All I know is that you have stupidly jeopardized
not only your own welfare but . . . but everything else . . . as
well. If Mr. Girard repudiates you, so must I. If Mr. Girard
repudiates you, so must I.

(Mrs. Lum exits)

MARY: No! Don't leave me! Don't leave! *(To Furies)* She
didn't even see me here. She thought that I was still mistress
of my house. But I wasn't.

FURIES: You never. Were. Were you, Mary?

MARY: What? Leave me alone. You cheated me. I want to see my mother here.

FURIES: Do you think? Do you imagine? Do you suppose? That it would make. The slightest bit. Of difference?

MARY: Yes. Yes, it would. I know it. When she sees me here, sees what they have done to me.

FURIES: But she. Won't! Mary. She won't. Why should. She? She'll get. From Mr. Girard. The little help. She's always. Wanted. She'll not come. Here. Again.

MARY: You're lying to me. Lying!

FURIES: We? You're doing it. To yourself. We want you to see. How things are. With you. How things are. Are. Are. With you.

(Lights up on Mr. Phillips and Stephen Girard)

MR. GIRARD: "How things are with her." What do you mean by that?

MR. PHILLIPS: Dr. Rush asked that I speak to you personally, Mr. Girard, to make known to you certain surprising developments that have only now come to our attention regarding the state or condition of your wife, sir.

MR. GIRARD: I do not know, sir, if you value your time, but I do mine. Please be brief.

MR. PHILLIPS: I will try. May I sit, sir?

MR. GIRARD: By all means, sit or do whatever you wish, only let us get this bothersome business settled. If there is some question as to the adequacy of the monthly payment of her expenses I shall naturally increase the allotment to whatever sum is necessary, although I will remind you that both you and Dr. Hutchinson assured me the amount settled on was more than sufficient.

MR. PHILLIPS: Oh, no, Mr. Girard. Let me assure you that it is not a question of costs. The generosity of your settlement is well-known by all concerned in this matter. No, the hospital could not wish for a more beneficial arrangement. No, sir, it is not a financial matter that brings me here but rather one concerning your wife's mental and . . . physical condition.

MR. GIRARD: As I am quite familiar with the one and not at all interested in the other, I doubt that anything you have to tell me could be of the least interest to me. Nonetheless, as she yet remains my wife, and as you have taken it upon yourself to interrupt my affairs with this matter, I am willing to listen to you, only briefly.

MR. PHILLIPS: I have rather surprising news for you and for all of us at the hospital. Mrs. Girard is with child.

MR. GIRARD: Yes.

MR. PHILLIPS: Do you mean, sir, you have been cognizant of that fact?

MR. GIRARD: I have.

MR. PHILLIPS: And were you so aware when you had her brought to us?

MR. GIRARD: Yes, sir, I was.

MR. PHILLIPS: And yet you brought her to us to be confined with the mentally insane?

MR. GIRARD: Most certainly. I find it curious that I need point out to you that physical conditions have nothing whatsoever to do with the state of one's mind. I brought my wife to you because she is insane. That has nothing to do with whatever physical condition she may be in.

MR. PHILLIPS: Mr. Girard, I am happy to tell you that is not always the case. Although it is true that the mind functions separately from the body which supports it, there is one major exception to that general rule.

MR. GIRARD: And what is that?

MR. PHILLIPS: The state of pregnancy. It is not uncommon for a woman with child to exhibit many of the signs we ordinarily ascribe only to the insane. You see, many of the irregularities you spoke of are quite possibly due to nothing more than the naturally flighty state of mind brought on in many women by the physical changes in the female body during the pre-natal period. When a woman is with child she is wont to have imaginings, to suffer strange cravings, certain outbursts of temper and language that one does not expect. In other words, her behavior may become erratic in a fashion that is often alarming to those who are used to a more sedate and stately behavior on the part of the lady. Consequently, under these circumstances, the board of directors and I agree that it is in everyone's best interest for you to remove Mrs. Girard from our care, allow her the confinement usually recommended for the later stages of a pregnancy, and, after her deliverance of your child, she will most probably prove to be as sane as she ever was. What I am trying to tell you, sir, is the happy news that Mrs. Girard is quite possibly, even probably, as sane as you or I.

(Pause)

MR. GIRARD: My wife, sir, is insane.

MR. PHILLIPS: Mr. Girard . . .

MR. GIRARD: *(Interrupting)* I said, she is insane.

(Slight Pause)

MR. PHILLIPS: Your wife suffers from severe headaches. She is extremely nervous. Upon occasion she has exhibited erratic behavior, and outbursts of abusive language. If she were not pregnant, there might be cause to think an extended rest, close care, and quiet might not be enough to restore her normal faculties. However, as she *is* with child . . .

MR. GIRARD: That is a fact I wish you and the members of the board to disregard. Whether she is, as you say, with child or not need be no concern of yours. Nor of anyone else's. I tell you in all candor it is not a fact I wish ever to be known. Nor do I feel kindly disposed toward you, sir, for your having pressed this loathsome fact to my consideration. True, I was previously aware of . . . her condition. But I have chosen of my own free will to ignore it. It is my wish, sir, that you and all the members of the board do likewise.

MR. PHILLIPS: Sir, I am amazed. I have just told you that your wife is soon to be delivered of your child, a child you seem determined will be gestated and born in a madhouse, amidst scenes of the most horrid chaos, amongst madmen and madwomen, and you advise me to ignore it?

MR. GIRARD: Precisely.

MR. PHILLIPS: Mr. Girard, I am trying to tell you that given these newly discovered circumstances we cannot permit you to leave Mrs. Girard in these conditions. Indeed, to place such a woman in such surroundings at such a time is to pose the greatest possible threat to her sanity, no matter how sound of mind she might have been beforehand.

MR. GIRARD: I see. *(He writes out a draft)* Perhaps this will be sufficient.

(He hands the check out to Mr. Phillips, but Phillips does not take it)

MR. PHILLIPS: Mr. Girard. It is not a question of money, sir.

MR. GIRARD: Is that fact?

MR. PHILLIPS: It is, sir.

MR. GIRARD: Come, come, sir. I am a loyal and an active supporter of our new Republic, and I am a businessman. In both capacities it has been my experience that everything in life is a question of money. I have found no friendship, no love, no loyalty, and no fact that cannot be altered by a large enough draft or a tidy enough sum of money.

MR. PHILLIPS: Surely you can't believe that, Mr. Girard.

MR. GIRARD: Believe it? I know it. It is fact, sir. I have staked my career on it, and, as you can see, I have prospered. *(Thrusting the check at him)* Look at this!

MR. PHILLIPS: *(Taking the check)* Three thousand dollars. But this is made out . . .

MR. GIRARD: To you, sir. That is payment in advance which I hope you will be gracious enough to accept from me. You see, I do not choose to be concerned any further with any difficulties that may arise due to my wife's . . . confinement. Therefore, I humbly ask that you personally see to it that whatever needs be done is done to keep all references to her, her child, if it should live, and any other difficulties concerning her, beyond my awareness. As to the board of trustees, tell them I will assume all responsibility for this matter, in writing, of course. Tell them, also, that within a month of my unfortunate wife's demise the hospital shall receive a check identical to the one you hold now. You need not ever mention this check. I feel a man's finances are no one's affair but his own. Tell them, also, that upon my death, I will bequeath Pennsylvania Hospital no less a sum than ten times the amount written there. All this, of course, to be above and beyond the sums already agreed to for her daily care, and given in deepest gratitude for the superb treatment accorded the insane woman who unfortunately still bears my name.

MR. PHILLIPS: I don't know what to say.

MR. GIRARD: Answer only this: can it be done?

MR. PHILLIPS: Yes.

MR. GIRARD: Good! See to it then. I believe you know your way out?

MR. PHILLIPS·   But, sir . . .

MR. GIRARD: Sir?

MR. PHILLIPS: What of the child?

MR. GIRARD: That, sir, is no concern of mine.

MR. PHILLIPS: I would not have a child of mine born under such conditions for all the money in the world.

MR. GIRARD: And I can assure you, sir, neither would I.

MR. PHILLIPS: Mr. Girard. Do you mean the child . . .

MR. GIRARD: I bid you good day, sir.

MR. PHILLIPS: Sir.

(*Lights fade on Girard and Phillips. Furies set Mary free*)

MARY: No, Mr. Phillips, don't go! Please don't go!

FURIES: He can't. Hear you. Mary.

MARY: He can. I know he can. He looked right at me.

FURIES: He can't hear you. Because he doesn't. Want to. Men lose all their faculties. If the profit's sound.

MARY: Mr. Phillips!

FURIES: He can't hear you, Mary. He won't hear you. No. Body. Will. Poor Mary. Poor Mary Girard.

MARY: What will become of my child?

FURIES: Whose baby is it, Mary? Yes, tell us, Mary. Tell us who the father is. Tell us. Tell. Tell.

MARY: The father is unimportant. He was someone warm and affectionate to me.

FURIES: You were untrue, Mary. You cuckolded your husband. You betrayed him. And broke your marriage vows. For shame. Shame, Mary. You will give birth to an evil thing. Only evil comes from evil. Something dark and horrid comes from evil. Darkness bred in darkness gives forth darkness.

MARY: I don't believe it. I don't believe you. You're trying to drive me mad.

FURIES: You should have been like. Polly. Kenton. Yes, definitely. Like Polly. Then you would have. Been all right. Had your baby. And your home. Your mother would have.

Been so. Grateful. Mrs. Lum would have. Loved. Having a. Daughter like. Polly.

MARY: What are you saying?

FURIES: Polly. Polly. Polly.

MARY: I am Polly.

FURIES: Polly. Polly Mary. Polly Mary Girard. Crazy Mary Girard. Yes, now. But not soon. No, not soon. Soon the whole city will know. Mr. Girard's Polly. They will have. Forgotten you. Mary. Even your mother. If she were alive. Would favor. Polly.

MARY: What are you talking about?

(The Furies exit, leaving Polly Kenton)

POLLY: They were talking about me, Mrs. Girard.

MARY: Who are you? What are you doing here? I don't know you!

POLLY: My name's Polly, Polly Kenton. There's no reason why it should be important to you. I'm only one of a long line of housekeepers who'll replace you, Mrs. Girard.

MARY: You admit that to my face?

POLLY: I'm not important really. Only one in a long line of girls and women he will turn to, has turned to already. You know that.

MARY: Yes, I know it. I know that Sally Bickham, the slut. He brought her into my house. Called her his housekeeper. Tried to keep me out of town so I couldn't see she'd taken over my room. And you! You're just like her, is that it?

POLLY: In a way, just like her.

MARY: And there will be others, too, I suppose.

POLLY: I'm sure there will be.

MARY: And so you're a whore just like all the others.

(Pause)

POLLY: I'm his housekeeper, Mrs. Girard. The difference is that I will be more successful and longer lasting than the rest. He will even come to care for me a little, as much as he is able to care for a woman, anyway.

MARY: I don't believe you.

POLLY: I wouldn't lie to you, Mrs. Girard, because I have no need to do so.

(Pause)

MARY: Why didn't he care for me?

POLLY: In the beginning he did. You should have had his child.

MARY: But it wasn't my fault we didn't have children. Oh, I thought it was. And I knew he blamed me. He didn't say anything, but sometimes as I was sewing I'd suddenly feel cold, as though a draft of icy wind had pierced me, and I'd look up and see him staring at me. Only that. Only staring. And I knew he was looking at me as though I were a column of figures that didn't quite balance in his cash books. Later, he started taking me to doctors. They said that I was a "nervous woman." So he would send me into the country to cure my "nerves." Then I began to have these terrible headaches. And I hated to be around him, for I knew he felt I'd swindled him because I couldn't give him a son.

POLLY: You sound as though you wanted him to care for you.

MARY: Is that so strange?

POLLY: It isn't practical. You should have known what you could get from him and what you could not. You should have known what he expected in return and seen to it that you gave it to him.

MARY: His affection was all I wanted.

POLLY: But he had none to give. Wealth was what he had to give you.

MARY: That was nothing to me, nothing.

POLLY: If you had given him a baby you would have completed your side of the bargain. He, in turn, would have given you his undying gratitude. And if you could have managed to have a son, you would have won his affection as well.

MARY: But we could not have children. We tried and we could not.

POLLY: You should have seen to it that you had a child, even if it was not his. He would have thought it his, and the bargain would have been complete. You would have won his affection.

MARY: Must it be like a business transaction?

POLLY: All relationships are. Everyone expects to get

something in return for what they're giving. And if you misjudge the stakes or barter foolishly, offer what you cannot give, take what you do not want, the relationship won't last, or else, what is far worse, it will last for a long time, with each bitterly believing he was cheated, but too ashamed to admit it even to himself.

MARY: But you've not had his children have you?

POLLY: Of course not. A man expects his wife to bear his children and his mistress to bear none.

MARY: Yet you've won his affection.

POLLY: Yes, I have.

MARY: Why? How?

POLLY: By not even wanting it. I have always been honest with him. He knows all I want from him is a comfortable home. In exchange I've shown him a solicitous care. I've babied him, become his mother, his mistress. And I've always known the mistress was only incidental. I've let him become with me the little boy he wanted from you. When he was a boy his mother went insane. He saw in you that which had closed him off from her. The more outrageously you tried to gain his attention and sympathy, the more he turned away in loathing. Your behavior has made him come to hate you.

MARY: Has he said that to you?

POLLY: I can tell you his words exactly. "I hate her like the devil, and I note with pleasure that this feeling increases daily."

MARY: I don't believe you. He wouldn't say that. He wouldn't feel that.

POLLY: "I hate her like the devil, and I note with pleasure that this feeling increases daily."

MARY: I won't believe you! I can't!

POLLY: "I hate her like the devil, and I note with pleasure that this feeling increases daily."

MARY: What intolerable wrong did I do him?

POLLY: Perhaps he does not know himself. The fact is, however, you were not sensible. You see, it is never sensible to expect a man to understand or to tolerate the dreams of his wife.

(Polly exits)

MARY: And they told him that I suffer from dreaming.

FURY #1:   Oh, we got us some cures for dreamers here, Mary.

FURY #4:   Dr. Rush gives special care to dreamers, Mary.

FURY #3:   Some icy baths in winter.

FURY #5:   Splinters under the thumbnails.

FURY #2:   A white-hot iron on the soles of the feet for sanity.

MARY: But they would not do that to me, for they know I'm sane.

FURIES: How could they. Possibly. Know that?

MARY: They know it because it's true.

FURIES: Did they. Tell you. You are. Sane? Mary?

MARY: I know it. One can tell. Surely one can tell for one-self?

FURIES: No. They have to tell you. Tell you, Mary. Tell you.

MARY: Who can do that? The doctors? The Board of Managers?

FURIES: You can, Mary. It's easy as pie, Mary. Mary. Crazy Mary Girard. You can tell. If you really. Want. To. It's easy as pie, Mary. Easy as making your bed. Gathering flowers. Listening. As simple as praying to God, Mary. God. God. Where are you God?

FURY #5:   Do you ever pray, Mary?

MARY: What do you mean? Of course, I . . .

FURY #5:   No, no, no, no. To really, really pray to Almighty God with all of your mind and all of your heart and all of your soul. To pray until His heart and His mind and His soul open out to you until you are riding there. Until you are riding there like crystal. Riding on beams of the purest, whitest, celestial crystal. O Jesus. My Saviour. Sweet, Sweet, Jesus . . .

FURIES: Jesus. Jesus. Sweet, Sweet Jesus.

MARY: And because of that you have . . .

FURY #1:   Have ye never locked up a lock, Mary?

FURIES: Clickety-clack. Clickety-lock. Lock up the lock.

FURY #1:   I have. Many times. Ye turns the key right in the lock big as a pie. Takes 'em with this hand, like this, an' puts 'em in, like this, an' turns the key in the lock, like this, big as a pie. Big as a pie. You turn the key right in the lock, big as a pie. Takes 'em with this hand like this, jus' like my daddy tole 'er, and puts 'em in, like this, an' turns the key in the lock, like this, big as a pie. Ye turns the key right in the . . .

FURIES: Lock big as a pie. Takes em with this hand. Clickety-clack. Lock up the lock.

MARY: I don't understand what . . .

FURY #3:   I would have understood. Exactly, Mary. Have you ever made your bed, Mary? It must be done, exactly. At the proper time. Not too late or improperly or too soon. Not just any way. The sheets must be smoothed and straightened well until no single line or wrinkle. Until no single line or wrinkle disturbs the weight of the counterpane that touches. . . . And if the covers are spread straight. Pillows fluffed up soft. Smoothest straight then. But if it is not as neat and as smooth as hair. It must be. It must not . . . it must be torn apart. One must begin . . . again. The sheets must have . . .

FURIES: No. Wrinkles. Mary. Smooth, Mary. As smooth as. Hair, Mary.

MARY: But how can you possibly . . .

FURY #4:   Have you listened, Mary. On the docks, I lifted . . . I lifted with the sweat . . . Hold. And listen. Listen to the robin . . . Bales and . . . thrush. Heave for the nonce, lad. Listen for the. Lift. Laugh. Laugh. No. Hold . . . Heave with the crank on. Hold. Falls all. No. Heave. Lips. Speak. Heave. No. Cry. Thunder. Asks. Why? No. Hold. No.

(Mary screams)

FURIES: Don't cry. Mary. You mustn't. Cry. Mary. Or listen. You mustn't scream, Mary.

FURY #2:   You never gathered flowers, did you, Mary? I gathered more flowers than anyone has ever dreamed of. I had to hide them. Have you ever held a flower, Mary. Your very own flowers, Mary. Tender and secret and gentle. Hide it in your arms. You in your secret place. Did you rock with it, Mary. Rock until one by one the petals fall and the stem dries up and the cradle rocks. By yourself, Mary. . . . Rock yourself, Mary.

FURIES: What can you tell, Mary. Tell us, Mary. Tell us about your. Self. Mary. Tell us. Tell. Us.

MARY: Afterward. The sounds of water lapping in the pail through the streets. And before. As I drew it from the well, for my arms were always strong.

FURIES: Yes. Mary? Mary? Yes. Yes?

MARY: The sounds of empty spaces in the water made by the dripping. By the sucking of the bucket. Brim-full. Lifting, lifting . . .

FURIES: Yes, Mary.

MARY: And . . . and sometimes as a little girl I stood beside my father to watch him working. The sound of his hammer hammering. Nails . . .

FURIES: That's right, Mary. Yes.

MARY: The sound of the nails being driven and him . . . and him . . . Bring him to me!

FURIES: *(Afraid. Weeping. Trembling)* We don't know. Who you. Mean. We daren't step. On any toes. We cannot . . .

MARY: *(Interrupting)* Bring Stephen Girard! Bring him now into this cell.

FURIES: No, no. Oh, no, we must. Not. We can. Not. No, no, no.

MARY: Bring him!

(Girard enters. He does not know where he is for a moment. The Furies surround him and then hide behind him)

GIRARD: How did you get here?

MARY: I am where you placed me, Stephen.

GIRARD: Where I . . . I shouldn't be in this place.

MARY: No, Stephen?

GIRARD: No, I . . .

MARY: *(Laughing)* Do you think I'm a vision?

GIRARD: No. Of course not. I . . . no.

(Mrs. Hatcher enters with Mr. Phillips)

MRS. HATCHER: Is it true as they say that the baby is that of Mary Girard's?

MR. PHILLIPS: The baby's origin is a matter of no importance, Mrs. Hatcher. You and Mr. Hatcher will receive the set sum for nursing the child just as you have with all the other children you have cared for in the past.

MRS. HATCHER: Yes, Mr. Phillips. I do appreciate your calling on me again. My health is ever so much better now than it used to be.

MR. PHILLIPS: The past is past, Mrs. Hatcher.

MARY: Why have you done this to me?

GIRARD: I had no choice. You are insane.

MARY: Don't lie to me, Stephen. Even if I were insane you could have spared me this. Both you and I know what my behavior was. You know as well as I that I am sane.

GIRARD: I hope that is true.

MRS. HATCHER: Oh. Such a pretty little baby. And a girl. What is her name?

MARY: Her name is Mary!

MR. PHILLIPS: Call her whatever you wish. It is immaterial.

MRS. HATCHER: Oh, I shall take good care of this one, Mr. Phillips. There won't be no repeats of my old mistakes. I'm ever so much better now.

MR. PHILLIPS: I told you not to speak of the past, Mrs. Hatcher. Both for your sake and for the sake of the Hospital it is best if you keep hidden from your neighbors the source from which you've received this child.

MRS. HATCHER: (*Exiting*) Oh, I shall love having her. I am truly grateful. I've never had a little girl before. I think I'll call you . . . Rose. Rose is my name, you see, and you will be my little girl.

MR. PHILLIPS: (*Calling after her*) Mrs. Hatcher!

MARY: She told me you hated me like the devil. I didn't believe her until this moment.

GIRARD: Who told you that?

MR. PHILLIPS: (*Calling*) Mrs. Hatcher!

MRS. HATCHER: (*Returning*) Yes, Mr. Phillips?

MR. PHILLIPS: Mrs. Hatcher. I would caution you against becoming too fond of this child. It is, after all, a child born under unpropitious circumstances.

MRS. HATCHER: What do you mean, Mr. Phillips?

MR. PHILLIPS: I am asking you to treat it the same as you would any other child.

MRS. HATCHER: Oh, I will sir.

MR. PHILLIPS: Yes? Well, good. Yes, I would have you treat it just as though it were a . . . a normal child.

MRS. HATCHER: Isn't it a normal child, Mr. Phillips?

MR. PHILLIPS: Oh, I didn't mean to alarm you, Mrs. Hatcher. This baby seems normal, doesn't it? It needs all the care and attention other children require. Only there is a difference.

MRS. HATCHER: What difference, Mr. Phillips? Tell me, please.

MARY: Don't let him do this!

MR. PHILLIPS: Its mother is a patient among the insane.

MRS. HATCHER: Oh, no!

MR. PHILLIPS: The baby has been born by and among those possessed of devils.

(The Furies dance)

MRS. HATCHER: God preserve us!

MR. PHILLIPS: Born by and among those possessed of devils.

MRS. HATCHER: God preserve us.

MR. PHILLIPS: By and among those possessed of devils.

MRS. HATCHER: God preserve us.

(Mrs. Hatcher and Mr. Phillips exit)

MARY: Is that what I am to you? When we met I was sixteen, a servant carrying water through the streets. I laughed at everything then. And I was happy without even knowing it. Do you remember that girl, Stephen?

GIRARD: She does not exist, Madam.

MARY: No. We destroyed her, you and I. Destroyed her utterly. Didn't you ever love her?

GIRARD: She was pretty. People noticed her. She was innocent, a trait few women have.

MARY: Innocent! And then she married you and she thought she had gained the whole world, and in reality gained only this little room.

GIRARD: She had everything she could have wanted.

MARY: The cost was too great.

GIRARD: It cost her nothing.

MARY: Nothing! *(She laughs)* What is the value of nothing, Mr. Girard? What is its price? Can you estimate the enormity of nothing? I can tell you it is beyond calculation. I was prepared to give you everything, but you wanted only nothing. So it is fitting that you have placed me here in this room with nothing.

GIRARD: You had everything a woman could reasonably have wanted.

MARY: What good is reason without some little affection?

GIRARD: If you wanted affection you should have told me instead of making a public display of yourself.

MARY: Stephen, I made no attempt to hide my behavior from you. We differed in only one way. I didn't bring my lovers under your roof. You cannot fault me for that. I always maintained a respect for you and a regard for your feelings and your pride. Perhaps I should not have done the things I did. But in that I am not alone. Don't lock me up in this poor house. Send me away, Stephen. I will go wherever you wish. Take me back to one of your houses and lock me in a room for the rest of my life. Give me my father's tools, nails and a hammer, and I will drive the demons away from me. Lock me in a room; allow me there to suffer my conscience and dream my dreams alone.

GIRARD: Alone! A seclusive wife pleases no one. The needs of my sex are fewer than those of yours, Madam. Men are more self-sufficient. Consequently, it is all the more important for a man's wife to see to it that his needs are met. Your acknowledgment of me as your husband never went beyond the duties of the flesh.

MARY: You mean to say my thoughts were my own?

GIRARD: I mean to say you failed to be a dutiful wife. When I found you you were a peasant. Your mother remains one. I had hoped you would develop a sense of who you had become in becoming my wife. I had hoped you would rise above your origins sufficiently to modify an overly tolerant nature. It is well-known that the wife of Stephen Girard converses indiscriminately with persons of no consequence as readily as she does with persons of some social standing. In these ways, and others, you have failed me.

(Pause)

MARY: Yes, you are right. In these ways I have failed you, Stephen.

(Mary turns from him and starts to exit)

GIRARD: If only you could . . .

MARY: What? Be a dutiful wife? *(Slight pause)* No!

GIRARD: I can make your life a hell on earth, Madam!

MARY: When I was childless you blamed me. I, too, thought I was barren. I felt I had cheated you out of a son. But it wasn't me. You couldn't put life in my body because you had none in your own. I got more warmth from a stranger in a little hour than you could ever give. It isn't my child that is loathsome to you, Mr. Girard, but the freedom of my mind and my love of life itself. May God have pity on you, sir.

GIRARD: God? *(Pause. Very calmly)* I do not know if God exists. If I thought He did I would pray that He keep you here for ever so long a time. As I cannot be sure of Him, I will see to it myself that you endure a hell on earth. And I will pray to a possible God that it may endure forever.

(Girard exits)

MARY: All right. All right. But my baby will live.

FURIES: She thinks her baby . . . She thinks her infant . . . She thinks her child . . . Will give her comfort. Will give her solace. Will bring her relief. Not so, Mary. Oh, no, no. No. You were untrue, Mary. You cuckolded your husband. You betrayed him. And broke your marriage vows. For shame. Shame, Mary. You will give birth to an evil thing. Only evil comes from evil. Something dark and horrid comes from evil. Darkness bred in darkness gives forth darkness. As we have shown you the head. As we have shown you the heart. As we have shown you the past. As we have shown you what the far future holds. So we will now show you what is yet to be.

(Furies place the bundle in Mary's arms)

MARY: She is so . . . so very lovely. If I ever doubted that you were worth so much suffering forgive me. *(To Furies)* Why are you looking like . . . laughing . . . laughing? Tell me. Tell me. She will live, won't she?

FURIES: Oh, yes. Doubtlessly. Most definitely.

MARY: And she will be happy? Tell me. Will she be happy?

FURIES: Most certainly. Decidedly. Assuredly. Quite as happy as she could be. Most decidedly happy.

MARY: Then I shall live for that if you will promise me that.

FURIES: Oh, yes. We can do that. Yes. The question. However. Is. How long?

MARY: How long?

FURIES: It will not be. A longish. Life.

MARY: Will she die young?

FURIES: *(Taking the bundle from her)* She will. Yes. Quite. Quite young.

MARY: Quite young? Will she live twenty years?

FURIES: Twenty! Heavens! What an age!

MARY: Fifteen years?

FURIES: Goodness, no! Certainly. Not!

MARY: Then ten years, surely ten?

FURIES: Gracious goodness, no. Nothing like it. Far from it.

MARY: Then five? A little five?

FURIES: Yes, Mary. Yes, indeed. You've hit on it.

MARY: My poor dear little child. Only five brief years of life.

FURIES: Oh, wrong! Years? We said nothing. About. Years.

MARY: But you just now said five . . .

FURIES: Months. Mary. Yes. Months. Five. Five months. Yes. Yes.

MARY: No! Oh, no! My little one.

FURIES: Five months. Is. Quite enough. Then buried. In an unmarked grave. That you will have in common. Mary. You, too, will be buried in an unmarked grave. Here. On the hospital grounds. You'll never leave these walls. Mary. And no services. Oh, no, Mary. No hymns nor prayers for you. A burial. No services.

MARY: Good! That at least I delight to hear. And tell me

when. The sooner the better will best suit me. If God has any mercy it will be soon. Tell me.

FURIES: Guess! We couldn't just say. Oh, no, you'll have to guess.

MARY: A year?

FURIES: So short a time? Heavens. No.

MARY: Two? Three? Five? Surely no more than five.

FURIES: Yes, five! Five is right again! So clever is our Mary. Five. And twenty. Twenty. Twenty. More.

MARY: Twenty more? Five and twenty years? I could not stand it!

FURIES: Well, most of it. Will be. There. In this chair. The Tranquilizing Chair. The restraining chair. Bound down. Like the evil. Thing you are.

MARY: No! No! God would not permit it. He would not keep me living here in this hell hole for five and twenty years. I couldn't bear it. He will be merciful to me and let me die soon. Soon! Please dear God, sweet, sweet Jesus, be merciful to me and let me not stay here for such an age.

FURIES: Oh, isn't she funny! Sweet, sweet Jesus! Jesus! She's starting to froth at the mouth in prayer. God won't hear you either, Mary. No more than Mr. Phillips. Why should He? He's too busy. Besides He's set you up for it. It's God's jest, Mary. And the fool is. You!

MARY: Get away from me! I won't listen to you. Please God, please!

FURIES: He made you beautiful. God did. And you made the mistake of believing in your own beauty. It's played you a devilish trick. It's been your doing. And your undoing. It's played you a devil of a trick. God did it to you. Too. Mary.

MARY: God, help me! Help me!

FURIES: Look at her. Oh, I love it when she prays to dark corners and damp walls! To empty spaces between the stars. If she could see any stars. Can you, Mary? Can you. See. Any stars?

MARY: I don't know. My eyesight is so dim.

FURIES: It always happens. After long confinement. In dark places.

MARY: Where are you God? Please answer me.

FURIES: Please answer me! Oh. Where. Are. You. God. God. God.

MARY: Stop it! Damn you! All of you. Where is He? And who is He? Is He another man? Then I'll have nothing to do with such a God. And I damn you, God! I damn you!

FURIES: Do you hear? She's now giving proof. That she's. Insane. Insane. Insane folks always deny God. They have to. They're the Devil's own. His handiwork. His cohorts. His consorts. Maybe she's the Devil's bitch. The Devil's whore. Maybe she's sucked bile from the Devil's own tit. And filled her belly with his swollen prick. Mary, the Devil's trick. Mary Girard, the Devil's harlot, the Devil's cat, the Devil's bat, the Devil's meretrix! When they discover how she's cursed God . . .

MARY: Leave me alone!

FURIES: And turned on Him . . .

MARY: Don't touch me!

FURIES: And denounced and damned Him . . .

MARY: Stop!

FURIES: Then maybe they'll tear the babe from her bleeding belly. Condemn it for a cursed thing. Pull it with pinchers from her Devil's doorway. Kick it. Tromp on it. Spit on it. Damn it. Curse it. Pull it. Tear it. Bury it living. Burn it with firesticks. Break it with stones.

MARY: STOP!

FURIES: Now she's caught our scent. Like hounds behind the fox. Let's hope. She's quick. To. Make the. Leap. At last. She. Understands!

MARY: Yes. At last I do understand. *(Pause)* What if I were insane and didn't even know? I think I wouldn't care. The bed is firm. There is a window there that I could look from if I stood atop the bed. If I were calm they would not always keep me in this chair. If I were to accept you as my companions and not resist you . . . I could walk about. Take some few steps. Look from the window. Sometimes I might see the sky. Smell the air. Give birth to my poor, pitiful child. Isn't that true?

FURIES: *(Softly)* Yes. Mary. Yes. Yes. Indeed.

MARY: And if I were to turn my back on that world, and

scorn all the values it adores, denying myself the luxury wealth can provide, then that must stand as proof that I am insane, wouldn't it?

FURIES: Yes! Oh, yes! Yes. Yes.

MARY: For here is only poverty, solitude, and deprivation, where there, in the great world, is wealth, endless self-indulgences, and the society of ordinary people such as him, Mr. Stephen Girard. And if I were to prefer all this to all that, then the world would know me to be mad, wouldn't they?

FURIES: Yes, certainly. Most assuredly, Mary. Definitely so, Mary.

MARY: Then if I am not mad already, I soon shall be. For there is a point in my mind, a point of absolute stillness where hatred, jealousy, and greed cannot come. A point of feeling, of being, which longing and unhappiness cannot touch. And when I pull myself into that place I feel as though I'd reached something like God, but greater, far greater than God. And going there I can look out on my little life as though it were a shadow shown upon a wall. And all is quiet and gentle and peaceful there for no human being can enter. And by comparison the world outside is horrid with greed, and heartless and cruel.

So let them come to the windows to point and laugh at me. I will show them the respect they warrant. Dare let them come. I shall give them the show they expect and deserve. I will greet them with venom, caress them with violence and address them with words obscene and gestures which are vulgar. I shall look them boldly in the eyes to curse them and spit on them from the depths of a well of hatred, for I shall teach them that they are nothing more than a fart in the face of God. And tear off my clothes to show them my netherparts so they can plainly see how completely I repudiate their world in order to enter this. And I shall have nothing to lose. And it shall be no capitulation or surrender. For, from this day, I, Mary Girard, shall be truly and happily insane. Insane. Insane. Insane. Insane. Insane. Insa . . .

(During the latter half of the above speech, the Furies have very cautiously placed Mary in the restraining chair. On the line, "And

I shall have nothing to lose," the bells of the churches peal throughout the city.

In the midst of Mary's final word, one of the more daring of the Furies drops the box down over Mary's head, so the sound of the word is cut off.

The Furies exit.

Lights stay up on Mary in the restraining chair, then they slowly begin to fade and suddenly blackout. Bells continue chiming and grow in volume, then stop)

Curtain

Stanley Taikeff

AH, EURYDICE!

To sounds of heav'nly harps she dies away,
And melts in visions of eternal day.

ALEXANDER POPE

Stanley Taikeff

Stanley Taikeff makes his debut in *The Best Short Plays* series with his imaginative comedy, *Ah, Eurydice!* First presented as a staged reading by the Joseph Jefferson Theatre Company, New York City, it later was given a workshop production farther downtown at the Off-Broadway Vandam Theatre, a playhouse that has been consistently hospitable to outstanding new playwrights.

Mr. Taikeff was born in Brooklyn, New York, in 1940, and holds an M.A. in Theatre from Hunter College (City University of New York). A recipient of a Shubert Foundation Fellowship and a John Golden Award for playwriting, he has been widely represented on stages in the Off-Off-Broadway area and in regional theatres in various parts of the country.

His comedy, *The Sugar Bowl*, was presented at the Eugene O'Neill National Playwrights Conference in Waterford, Connecticut, during the summer of 1976, and in December, 1977, at Off-Broadway's Circle-in-the-Square.

The premiere of another Taikeff comedy, *Don Juan of Flatbush*, was held at the Missouri Repertory Theatre, Kansas City, in July, 1976.

Mr. Taikeff, a resident of Brooklyn, is a member of The New Dramatists and the Playwrights Workshop of the Joseph Jefferson Theatre Company.

Characters:

PLUTO
ORPHEUS
EURYDICE

Scene:

Before Pluto's palace in the Underworld. Grey mists, long shadows, dead flowers, the occasional cry of a lost bird.
The stage is in semi-darkness when Pluto is discovered asleep in a beach chair before the palace door. As the lights come up full, he awakens abruptly, rubs his eyes, stares out at the audience and then slowly rises and addresses it.

PLUTO: This is the third time in an hour that I've been awakened from my sleep. The first time, Jove sent a thunderbolt down that nearly destroyed everything, including my palace. The second time, the Bull, the Lion and the Scorpion had it out over territorial rights, and now the lights. And every time the lights come on, my ghostly kingdom becomes a stage and I have to make a speech. So, good evening, ladies and gentlemen. The author of this play has asked me to explain a few things to you before the play begins. Tonight, he's given us a comedy, or a tragedy—we don't know what it is and we're not sure he knows either. It's about those two unlucky lovers of legend, Orpheus and Eurydice. It's an old story and Lord knows why he's dusted the cobwebs off the tale, but here it is. Three characters act the drama: Pluto, that's me, Master and King of the Underworld, and of course, Orpheus and Eurydice. Now some of you might get the impression that I'm the villain of the piece but I want to make it clear that there are no villains in this play anymore than there are heroes. But if you're not happy with that and feel you need a villain, then look elsewhere, in the passions that move our lovers across the stage, in a word, gesture, or movement or even, as some writers are fond of calling it, the frailty of human nature. But I've already told you more than you have to know. A word about the ending. It's shocking and bloody and violent. And if there are some of you out there who don't have a tolerance for that kind of stuff then I urge you to leave the theatre now. Thank you.

(He returns to his beach chair and closes his eyes. A faint melody is heard on the flute, and presently, Orpheus enters. He's a man of forty, short, paunchy, with a kind, affable face. He carries an assortment of musical instruments, some which he pulls along on a small wagon, and others which are strapped to his back)

ORPHEUS: *(Calling)* Eurydice! Oh, Eurydice!

PLUTO: *(Starting up)* What? Who's there?

ORPHEUS: It's me, Orpheus.

PLUTO: Who?

ORPHEUS: Orpheus, the musician, the songwriter.

PLUTO: You woke me. Do you always sneak up on people and wake them right in the middle of a delicious dream?

ORPHEUS: I'm sorry. *(Resting his instruments)* But I'm looking for my wife, Eurydice. Sisyphus told me I might find her here.

PLUTO: I was dreaming of moonlit forests and wild-eyed creatures with gossamer wings who fly through the trees looking for wood nymphs. *(Suddenly standing and looking him up and down)* What do you want with your wife?

ORPHEUS: I want to take her back home.

PLUTO: *(Laughs)* Might as well change these ghostly flowers to brilliant blossoms, my boy. Nobody leaves the Underworld, you know that.

ORPHEUS: I know but I've got our passports and marriage license and Prometheus, the guy chained to the rock, assured me you'd give her back to me. I can't bear to be without her anymore.

PLUTO: A familiar tune.

ORPHEUS: It's no joke. I'm going out of my mind without her. I lost weight, I get palpitations in the middle of the night, I roam the streets like a lost soul and everything I play is flat and empty.

PLUTO: What'd you say her name was?

ORPHEUS: Eurydice, like in the Greek myth.

PLUTO: There's no one here by that name.

ORPHEUS: We were married only a few hours. At the wedding reception she choked on a chicken bone and died before anyone could do anything for her.

PLUTO: That's a pity. Some girls are blessed with good fortune from birth, and others know grief in a wedding dress.

ORPHEUS: We didn't even have a chance to consummate our marriage, it was that quick. We were going to go to Bermuda for our honeymoon. We had everything arranged. Her mother had all the color schemes picked out for our new apartment. *(Breaking into sobs)* I wouldn't have come down here, except that she was so young and pretty, not even thirty, and like spring herself.

PLUTO: What does she look like?

ORPHEUS: She's short, bleached blonde hair, a small nose, deep brown eyes—

PLUTO: A girl with a pretty smile and dimples?

ORPHEUS: Yes, that's her! That's Eurydice!

PLUTO: Teaches kindergarten in Yonkers?

ORPHEUS: Oh, yeah, she loves kids. Her school district voted her teacher of the year for two consecutive years.

PLUTO: *(Pause)* Listen, Orpheus, take my advice and go back home. She probably forgot all about you anyway. Two months in the Underworld and nobody remembers how it was back there, believe me.

ORPHEUS: For once in my life, I was happy and the next thing you know, I'm standing over her grave. I must have her back!

PLUTO: Don't raise your voice to me! I'll turn you and all your instruments into three-throated cats, you arrogant toad!

ORPHEUS: Please, Pluto, don't turn me away. I risked everything to come here. It wasn't easy for a guy my age—

PLUTO: You just can't walk into the Kingdom of the Dead and make demands like that! For one thing, you're nobody special, and for another, you're not even dead! And even if you were, you'd have to wait a long time before I could consider your request. Men like Tristan and Romeo and Othello have been waiting years and years to see their sweethearts again. Why, Pyramus waited three decades to see his Thisbe, and even then she was just a phantom of her former self.

ORPHEUS: But I haven't got three decades! I'm forty years old!

PLUTO: Then get the hell out of here if you can't wait!

ORPHEUS: I love her, Pluto! I love her more than my music, more than my Stradivarius and Buffet clarinet!

PLUTO: (*Waving him away*) Ah, you all give me an ulcer with your love, love, love!

ORPHEUS: I've waited all my life for a girl like Eurydice. I'll never find anyone like her again. She's sweet and good and she makes a great quiche. I'll do anything to get her back. I'll play until my fingers fall off and sing until my throat's burned dry.

PLUTO: I hear enough songs all day. Harps, flutes, birds—my ears are numb from the racket. Go back to Yonkers or wherever you come from and leave me alone! (*He turns back to his chair*)

ORPHEUS: (*Catching his arm, pleading*) I'm not an ordinary musician. I was All-City Orchestra in high school and I played with the East Yonkers Symphonic Wind Ensemble for five years before I turned professional. I was one of Maurice Eberhart's students. I've got no rival on the harmonica, unless you count the gods, who count me as one of their own.

PLUTO: Go blow your harmonica for the old ladies back home! I want to go back to sleep.

ORPHEUS: I soothed the Sirens and saved Jason and the Argonauts from the harpies.

PLUTO: Oh, yeah? How'd you do that?

ORPHEUS: I played *Claire de Lune* on the bagpipes. (*Pluto looks at him, unimpressed*) I made Cerberus roll over on his back and even Sisyphus had to rest his rock when he heard me play.

PLUTO: (*Astonished*) My three-headed dog rolled over?

ORPHEUS: Yeah, and Prometheus cried like Niobe when

he heard my melodies and Charon ran his ferryboat aground, he was so touched by my voice.

PLUTO: *(After a moment, impatiently)* Go ahead and play something for me.

ORPHEUS: What do you want to hear?

PLUTO: Do you know Verdi's *Requiem?*

ORPHEUS: No, but I can sing some English madrigals and Irish ballads. Or I'll play the Grand Pas De Deux from the second act of *Giselle.*

PLUTO: What's that?

ORPHEUS: Ballet music, very beautiful.

PLUTO: I've got enough balleteers down here—Offenbach, Delibes, Tchaikovsky, no thanks.

ORPHEUS: How about *Besame Mucho, Golden Earings, The Anniversary Waltz?*

PLUTO: Masses, Gregorian Chants, Funeral Marches. Don't waste my time with sentimental eyewash. *(Turns to go)*

ORPHEUS: *(Stopping him)* Wait! Here's a song I wrote on the way down. *(Sings)*
Ah, Eurydice,
Dear ghostly shade,
Do you hear me?
I've looked everywhere
From Alaska to the
Murky Everglade,
Even asked a black, she-bear.
Ah, Eurydice,
My honey, my sweet,
I'm out of money
And falling off my feet.
I'm no longer myself,
I'm no longer me:
I'm just a harmonica player
Pining for thee:
Ah, Eurydice!

PLUTO: *(After a long moment, in tears)* I haven't been moved like that since the Muses sang to me when I was a baby. Tell me, who were your parents?

ORPHEUS: I'm not sure. But I think my mother was a

gypsy. She played the castanets and sang gypsy songs on trans-Atlantic ocean liners. I can't say who my father was but I know he was a singing waiter in a Paris bistro during the war.

PLUTO: *(Drying his eyes)* Anyone who can turn a phrase like that, who can disarm my watchdog and charm the Sirens with a tune, deserves a second chance. I'll tell you what. I'll let you have your wife back but with one little condition: that you don't look at her as long as you're both down here in the Underworld—

ORPHEUS: But why the condition?

PLUTO: Let me finish! If you should turn around and sneak a look at her, you'll lose her forever, and the higher gods'll never let you back here again. I promise.

ORPHEUS: But that's crazy! It's insane!

PLUTO: And she must never find out about this condition either because if she does then she'll melt just as quickly into the mist and you'll embrace the vapor. As for the condition—well, just let's say the higher gods are a little jealous of your musical talent and they'd like to see you sweat a little.

ORPHEUS: But I'm not—

PLUTO: One other thing I must warn you about. If you do weaken and give her so much as a furtive glance, then that one look will set off a whole chain of events culminating in your own untimely and very violent end.

ORPHEUS: *(Terrified)* What!

PLUTO: That's right, Orpheus. Give her half an eye, and a million hands will tear you apart, limb from limb.

ORPHEUS: But that's how it was in the myth! I'm not a myth! I'm real!

PLUTO: Down here we all have some of that mythic quality about us. Of course, you have feelings and thoughts and passions and desires but don't forget that we're in the twilight of a dream world here and there's just the right amount of fantasy and reality to keep our footing.

ORPHEUS: I don't know about reality and fantasy! I didn't come down here to make trouble or start a revolution. I want my wife back!

PLUTO: Look, if it was up to me, I'd give you a ranch house

and a swimming pool in the Elysian Fields, all right? But it's what the higher gods want, so don't give me a hard time. I've got a pretty good deal here—a beautiful palace, a coupla hundred slaves, a nice wine cellar, some very valuable Hepplewhite pieces. If the higher gods see that I can't handle this situation, there's no telling what they'll do to me—change my ears into horses' tails, turn my hair into creeping vine—I don't know. So just be careful on your way out and see that you eyes don't stray.

ORPHEUS: God, you don't seem to understand! I know about that other Orpheus. I know he was torn apart by a bunch of drunken women, but he was a god and I'm a man, a mortal. He came from Thrice or Thrace or someplace like that. I'm Orpheus from Yonkers, New York!

PLUTO: You're an old worn-out myth that some writer pumped new blood into. Now that's what you are.

ORPHEUS: I went to Ambrose Bierce High School and played at the prom at the Hotel Dorchester. I went steady with Laurie Briggs for two years when I was sixteen. Her father owned a dry-cleaning store on Continental Avenue. You ask him about me, he'll tell you.

PLUTO: Orpheus—

ORPHEUS: I went to Community College to study hotel management but my heart was always in music so I became a musician. I played weddings and bar mitzvahs and all kinds of celebrations. I met Eurydice at a dance and we got married. God, don't you see what you're doing? You're confusing me with that other Orpheus character. Maybe we look and talk alike and we even have the same name, but that's a coincidence. How many Smiths do you have in the phone book, for Crissakes!

PLUTO: For Demeter's sake, will you shut up! Do you think I care a scorpion's tail for your personal history? We're in the Underworld, buddy, all shadow, no substance; everything's real and nothing's real. Women with snakes in their hair, men with lions' heads, seas the color of gold, ghostly flowers that disappear in your hands when you pluck them from the ground! Now that's where you are! It's mist and mystery here, my friend, and whether you were breast-fed or wet your bed is no concern of mine! Now do you want your precious wife or not?

ORPHEUS: *(Not answering at once)* How far to the sunlight?

PLUTO: About three hours, depending on which path you take.

ORPHEUS: Will Charon give us a lift back on his ferry boat?

PLUTO: If she was properly buried, he will.

ORPHEUS: *(Suddenly feeling a great weight upon him)* Oh, boy! *(Troubled)* Mind if I sit down for a minute?

PLUTO: Are you having second doubts?

ORPHEUS: *(Worriedly)* No, no, of course not. *(He moves to the beach chair and sits)*

PLUTO: Stay here, I'll go and get her. *(Starts for the palace door, stops)* Cheer up! When Socrates got here a few years ago, he was worried he'd have nobody to talk to. Now he talks non-stop, twenty-four hours a day and you can't shut him up. So there you are. *(Smiling benevolently)* The happiness rope is full of knots but in the end they all come undone. *(Turning to go inside)* Go ahead, toot your flute. She'll be right out. *(He goes inside)*

(Orpheus lingers a moment in the chair then slowly rises and sings)

ORPHEUS:
Oh, gods of the Underworld,
You good-for-nothing so and so's,
What if she wants to dance
And I sneak a glance?
Or demands a kiss
And I turn in bliss?

Oh, cruel demons of Hades
Avert my eye
From her pretty face
And lead us out
Of your Kingdom of Shades
Past the three-eyed dragons
And bearded maids
On monkey-drawn wagons

Through icy glades,
Around bubbling streams
And bone-crackling screams
Behind those hairy lizards
You call the ghostly gizzards
And the caverns of death
Where the dead draw breath.

Show us the way
And we'll be back some day:
I promise.

(Enter, Eurydice, thirty years old, a bleached blonde, with warm, liquid brown eyes; she wears a frayed, soiled wedding gown, and carries a bouquet of dead flowers)

EURYDICE: Well, here I am, Orpheus! White and pure and ready to go!

ORPHEUS: *(Almost turning around, but checking himself)* Oh, Eurydice! My wife! My wife!

EURYDICE: I never thought you'd get here. What took you so long?

ORPHEUS: A lousy travel agent who didn't know north from south, terrible connections, crowded terminals . . . don't ask!

EURYDICE: Turn around. Let me look at you.

ORPHEUS: *(Terrified)* No! I can't! I mean—I got a stiff neck. Caught a draft on the ferry.

EURYDICE: *(Going up to him)* I can't wait to get out of here. Nothing but nymphs chasing satyrs and satyrs chasing nymphs. And those groaning cows all day, they never shut up. I'll be glad to get out of this wedding dress, too, and slip into something more comfortable. *(She is behind him now and slips her arms around his waist)* Did you miss me?

ORPHEUS: Of course—but not now, Eurydice. Later.

EURYDICE: What's the matter with you? I just want a kiss.

ORPHEUS: Please, Eurydice, just let's get out of here. I've got a chill in my bones, so just take my hand and follow me.

EURYDICE: *(On the verge of tears)* You act as if you're not even happy to see me. *(Bursting into tears)* You don't love me anymore! *(Orpheus is silent, sweating)* You don't!

ORPHEUS: I came all the way from Yonkers and I don't love you anymore! Do you know what kind of trip that was with the Sirens screaming in my ears and the three-headed hydras shouting obscenities at me and all those maniacs with the snakes in their hair? My God, Eurydice, if that's not love, then I can't sing a note!

EURYDICE: *(Sobbing)* You used to hold me and kiss me and now you won't even look at me. All I want is one look. Just one lousy look!

ORPHEUS: God, we'll never get out of here!

EURYDICE: I don't care! I hoped and prayed you'd come for me and now that you're here, you're colder than a clam. *(Crying)* I'm your wife and all you give me is the back of your head!

ORPHEUS: For Crissakes, Eurydice, you'll get the front as soon as we leave this hellish place!

EURYDICE: Don't yell at me!

ORPHEUS: I love you, Eurydice! Trust me, dear, trust me!

EURYDICE: Trust you! You know I don't like to nibble on chicken bones but you said, "Everybody's nibbling a little, so nibble." I nibbled and nibbled and I choked to death!

ORPHEUS: Are you blaming me because you swallowed a little chicken bone?

EURYDICE: It was a little piece of ice that sank the Titanic, wasn't it?

ORPHEUS: We got a three-hour trip ahead of us and Charon doesn't run that damn ferryboat all night, you know! Let's go, please!

EURYDICE: Maybe if you and everybody else, including my family and relatives, didn't panic, I might be alive today. But nobody knew what to do for me. Everybody shoved something else down my throat—lettuce, stale bread, fingers! God, to die like that on my wedding day! And now all you do is stand there like the dumb rock Sisyphus pushes up the mountain! Look at me, Orpheus, I'm talking to you!

ORPHEUS: It's going to be dark soon and I don't even have a flashlight or a map—

EURYDICE: Oh, I had plenty of time to think about that day and everything that happened. The way you acted toward my family and the way you treated my aunts and uncles from California. My Uncle Fred and Aunt Dorothy were very hurt. They gave us a very nice wedding present—three hundred dollars—and you were nasty and abrupt with both of them all night.

ORPHEUS: Your Uncle Fred spits when he talks and your Aunt Dorothy sounds like a buzz saw!

EURYDICE: And you didn't even have the common decency to thank my cousins Bob and Beverly for the blender they got us. Okay, so they don't know the first thing about music but they've always been good and generous to me. When I was a kid they always brought me games and coloring books when I was sick. They don't deserve the cold shoulder from you or anybody else!

ORPHEUS: Okay, next time I see them I'll play a Roumanian rhapsody for them. Anything else?

EURYDICE: I know you don't want my mother to help us with the apartment but I do.

ORPHEUS: I thought we agreed that she was only going to pick out the colors for the kitchen and bathroom?

EURYDICE: I died before we could agree upon anything.

ORPHEUS: Well, she's not picking out our furniture!

EURYDICE: I want her to feel that she's not completely excluded from my life just because I'm married now!

ORPHEUS: Who's excluding her from anything? I just don't want her to interfere and tell me what kind of bed to sleep on!

EURYDICE: Is that what you think of her? That she's an interference?

ORPHEUS: She picked out my barber for the wedding, didn't she?

EURYDICE: That's because you were going to a boy's barber and not a hair stylist!

ORPHEUS: If she furnishes our apartment the way she furnished her home, then I'd rather sleep on a park bench for the rest of my life!

EURYDICE: She happens to have a very quick eye for detail. Maybe some of the colors in her living-room don't match and the ones in the master bedroom clash but there's no law—

ORPHEUS: Why do you always say that?

EURYDICE: Why do I always say what?

ORPHEUS: "There's no law." Every time we have an argument about something, you always say, "But there's no law that says we have to do it that way."

EURYDICE: It's just a figure of speech.

ORPHEUS: Well, find a new figure. My ears feel like Chinese gongs every time you say that.

EURYDICE: Yes, I forgot, you have very sensitive ears, like tuning forks. Remind me to buy you a pair of ear warmers for Christmas!

ORPHEUS: Save the sarcasm for your students!

EURYDICE: Look, I'll talk anyway I want and if you don't like it, you can go back to Yonkers without me!

ORPHEUS: I'm tired, honey. I didn't come here to fight. The flight was a killer and the ferry ride across the River Styx wasn't exactly the Leonardo Da Vinci with front and rear stabilizers!

EURYDICE: And I suppose you think I've been living it up here, drinking nectar with the gods and picking boysenberries in the Elysian Fields? Well, let me tell you something, darling, I've had my hands full here. A swan wanted to rape me, that's right, a swan! And when I first got here, they didn't know what to do with me. Juno wanted to turn me into a horse with wings, like Pegasus; Persephone wanted to make me one of Tantalus's mistresses and some other genius, Poseidon, I think, wanted to put me inside a seashell, don't ask me why. In the meantime, I've been living here in Pluto's palace working as a wine-jugger. *(Pause; sobbing)* I want to go home. Oh, Orpheus, I missed you so. I was so lonely without you, so miserable, and here we are, fighting. Let's make up. Let's kiss. *(She puts her arms around his neck and moves to face him)*

ORPHEUS: *(Moving away from her, with great self-control)* Oh, God, Eurydice, don't do that! Please, sweet, not now.

EURYDICE: Everytime I heard a flute, I thought of you. Everytime a lark sang, I looked up and thought you were coming to take me back. *(Running her hands across his face, through his hair)* I want to make you happy and be a good wife . . .

ORPHEUS: Don't, Eurydice. . . . Don't do that.

EURYDICE: *(Continuing to move her hands softly and seductively)* We'll be so happy together in Yonkers. We'll have a big family, with lots of pets and two stationwagons and when you make more money and become rich and famous we'll buy a little house upstate in Orange County and we'll go there for the Christmas holidays and roast chestnuts in the fireplace and ice-skate on frozen lakes, and in summers, we'll hike in the mountains and go antiqueing and swim in warm ponds and pick blackberries and make our own brandy . . . *(Kisses his neck)*

ORPHEUS: Don't, please, don't . . .

EURYDICE: We'll have five children, three girls and two boys and we'll name the girls Cassandra, Electra and Helen and the boys we'll call John and Jerry, and the girls will become schoolteachers like me or interior designers like my mother, and I want our sons to go to military school and then to college so they can become diplomats or bankers, because men should have a little adventure in their lives and be successful . . . *(Kissing him more and more passionately)*

ORPHEUS: Eurydice, don't do that. I'm begging you . . .

EURYDICE: And I want you to learn how to cook because I think it's important that we both know our way around the kitchen, because then if one of us gets sick then the other can prepare nutritious dinners. And let's never fight before we go to sleep because one of us may die in the night and then the other one will feel guilty, and we'll always sleep with nothing on because it's more romantic that way—

ORPHEUS: *(Melting)* Oh, God, Eurydice, don't, don't . . .

EURYDICE: *(Caressing him)* And we'll buy scented oils and massage each other and then we'll shower together and sponge each other down with aromatic soaps. In the mornings, I'll cook breakfast and it'll be something different everyday: bacon and eggs on Mondays, waffles on Tuesdays, French toast on Wednesdays, lox, eggs, and onions on Thursdays, grilled cheese and tomato sandwiches on Fridays, oatmeal and bananas on Saturdays, and anything you want on Sundays, and while I'm in the kitchen, you can make the bed or read the morning paper or practice your kazoo or just dream about our wonderful life together . . . *(Caressing him more and more passionately)*

ORPHEUS: *(Exercising great self-control)* No, Eurydice! Don't!

EURYDICE: And on weekends you'll vacuum the apartment and wash the windows and dust all the bookshelves while I do the shopping and the laundry and return the library books and buy flowers and go to the beauty parlor for a trim and a facial—

ORPHEUS: *(Moving away)* No more, Eurydice! No more!

EURYDICE: *(Pursuing him)* And you'll teach me how to read music and I'll learn to play the tuba and the bassoon so we can play romantic duets by Wagner and Gershwin, and I'll read the romantic poets to you in bed when you get the flu, and when our birthdays come around, we'll always surprise each other with something different, and we'll go out to eat in the best French restaurant, while on our anniversaries, we'll really splurge and go to a Broadway play and then to one of those rooftop restaurants where they have soft music and candlelight and you can see the lights from the little tugboats blinking on and off in the water—

ORPHEUS: *(Surrendering)* Oh, Eurydice! Oh, dear God, you feel good!

EURYDICE: *(Holding him from behind)* And on New Year's Eve, we'll go to Times Square and watch the ball come down or we'll fly to South America and go on a boat ride down the Amazon. Oh, Orpheus! We'll be so happy together! We'll travel the whole world looking for rare books and campaign buttons and we'll shop for winter coats and go for annual heart check-ups together and we'll walk our two St. Bernard dogs in the rain and snow and sleet and when we're old and fuzzy and grumpy and gray, and all our darling grandchildren are running around the house with balloons and firecrackers, you'll sit in a nice, soft, leather chair and smoke a sweet pipe, and I'll sit across the room looking at you and knitting a mohair cardigan for your old, arthritic bones—

ORPHEUS: *(Suddenly facing her, explosively)* But we didn't even go on our honeymoon yet! *(Eurydice, hurt and about to cry, looks uncomprehendingly at him)* I mean you've got the whole menu planned out in your head already! Life should be *à la carte*, not a *prix fixe* dinner for two! *(He stares at her trembling with anger, while Eurydice, shrinking away from him ever so slightly, bursts into tears. With horror)* Oh, my God! *(Brief pause, then joyously)* Eurydice! *(Laughing)* Oh, my Eurydice!

EURYDICE: What's so funny?

ORPHEUS: You were supposed to disappear, to vanish like smoke. But you're still here, alive and beautiful! I told that guy I wasn't part of that stupid, old myth! *(Ecstatic)* I told him! *(Goes to embrace her)* Oh, my Eurydice, my—

EURYDICE: *(Suddenly crying out)* Orpheus, I'm melting! I'm going back!

ORPHEUS: No, it can't be! It's a trick! An optical illusion! Eurydice!

EURYDICE: Hurry, Orpheus, I'm drowning in the mist!

ORPHEUS: *(In a panic)* I can't move! I'm stuck!

EURYDICE: Take my hand! Oh, God, don't let me go again! *Not twice!* Orpheus!

ORPHEUS: *(Bursting into tears)* Eurydice!

EURYDICE: Do something! Strum your harp! Blow your trombone!

ORPHEUS: *(Fumbling through his pockets)* I can't find the mouthpiece! I lost the goddamn mouthpiece! *(In a wild panic)* Hang on, Eurydice!

EURYDICE: *(Her voice fading as she melts into the mist)* Tell my mother she was right; sky blue's the perfect color for the ceiling in the bathroom . . .

ORPHEUS: *(Desperate)* No, Eurydice! Wait! Come back!

EURYDICE: *(Blowing him a kiss)* Good-bye, Orpheus! Maybe we'll meet again sometime, somewhere, in Elysium or in the depths of a dazzling dream . . . I love you, Orpheus! *Au revoir,* my crooner! *(She disappears, blowing him soft kisses)*

ORPHEUS: *(Running to embrace her)* Eurydice! *Eurydice!* Oh, my beautiful bride! *(Sobbing)* Oh! . . . Oh! . . . Oh! *(But he's too late and he's left embracing the shadowy mists. A pause. Enter Pluto)* She's gone! *(Shaking his head in disbelief)* For the second time, she's gone! I can't believe it!

PLUTO: What do you mean, you can't believe it! Take my

word for it, Orpheus, she's not coming back tonight or any other night.

ORPHEUS: You didn't even give us five minutes. A turn of the head and she vanished!

PLUTO: How can you be so stupid? You could've walked right out of here, straight to the sunlight without a rest. Everybody was pulling for you, too, some of the biggest gods up there and a coupla immortals, too, like Rudy Valentino and Florence Nightingale, the whole crowd cheering for you and you had to go ahead and botch it up. I bet a whole garden of sweet herbs and a hundred of my best-looking gargoyles on you!

ORPHEUS: I didn't even have a chance to explain. It's not fair! it's unjust!

PLUTO: You're no better than Antigone or Medea or that other lunatic who wanted to murder his mother, what the hell's his name—Orestes! You're all from the same cut of meat—prime hotheads! Sure, let the juices flow, what do you care? Unleash the passions, and then cry foul when something tragic like this happens! Well, maybe you finally learned something. Maybe it won't be a total loss, going back to Yonkers.

ORPHEUS: I don't want to go back! I want to die!

PLUTO: Don't be a fool!

ORPHEUS: *(Sobbing into a tissue)* I do! What's my life without her? I want to spend the rest of my life with her even if it means living in this dreary dreamworld for all eternity.

PLUTO: But the gods don't want you yet. They want you to go back to Yonkers where you belong.

ORPHEUS: Yonkers! I'll run amok—

PLUTO: Take it easy! All right, so you're a little upset: things didn't work out. You got a pang in your heart and you feel guilty. But in a few days, you'll hear a robin outside your window and you'll leap out of bed with a whistle and a song.

ORPHEUS: I'll kill myself first!

PLUTO: Don't play the tragic hero, Orpheus. You don't have that dimension, and besides, you're middle-class.

ORPHEUS: I'll throw myself in front of a train or bang my

head against your palace door. *(He runs headlong to the palace door)*

PLUTO: *(Stopping him)* Will you calm down! Now relax! Do you want a drink? A little nip of ambrosia? *(Orpheus shakes his head)* Do you know what'll happen if you kill yourself? You'll have your Eurydice again but you still won't be able to look at her. You'll be together all the time but she'll always be one step behind you, and you'll never be able to look back at her, never! Is that what you want? *(Orpheus, silent, sobbing, shakes his head)* Now listen to me. Tomorrow's supposed to be a beautiful day up above, one of those balmy Indian summer days that makes you drunk with life. Get up early, scramble a few eggs, and then go out and get drunk! Your life's up there with the living, not down here with blood-drained ghosts!

ORPHEUS: What do you know about the living, about anything?

PLUTO: I know that after the owls hoot all night, the skylarks sing the next morning. *(Putting a paternal arm around him)* Anyway, you can count yourself among the more fortunate mortals. At least you got a look at her, and that's more than most guys get in this shady realm.

ORPHEUS: What's one look, for Crissakes! I want her in my sight forever!

PLUTO: Yeah, if she were a painting, you'd want her forever. Look, pretty soon you'll see a nice pair of legs and you'll forget all about your Eurydice. *(Confidentially)* And just between you and me, Orpheus, you can do better. She had a mouth like an overseas operator, and you would've been strapped down with a live-in mother-in-law.

ORPHEUS: I'm nothing great myself. I snore, I eat in bed, and I hate to socialize. But we loved each other, and now she's gone and I'm left with nothing.

PLUTO: Nothing! You call your poetry and music nothing? God, I wish I had your talent! After all, it's not every day that the Furies cry and a six-eyed dog rolls over and whimpers like a sick puppy. Even Midas, with all his gold and rose gardens, envies you.

ORPHEUS: But what good is my talent if I can't share it with the woman I love?

PLUTO: Stop talking like a melodrama! You could get a girl anytime but a gift like yours doesn't happen every day and the gods know it.

ORPHEUS: Yeah, they know it! I bet they got a big kick out of my little ordeal, letting me come down here and then closing the trap in my face!

PLUTO: Pack up your instruments and go home. Find yourself another bride and write some catchy songs. The world up there could use a good tune.

ORPHEUS: Just like that! Go back, live on tears and sorrow and compose snappy songs! Boy, for a god, you think like a flea!

PLUTO: Live on that divine madness that sings in your heart, Orpheus!

ORPHEUS: *(Incredulous)* What divine madness! Eurydice sings in my heart! She's my aria, my song! So why don't you just kill me here and now and save me the trip back some day?

PLUTO: Because your music would empty all the tombs and drive the apparitions wild with ecstasy! Because the Four Winds told Jove they'd blow the earth to ashes and if that happened there'd be no light, no music, no beauty—only a great void, deeper in its silence than the depths of the sea! Because in spite of your loss, Orpheus, you're luckier than any of the gods down here who must live in eternal darkness and who've lost the most beautiful poem of all—that world upstairs. *(Turns away with a tear in his eye)* Now beat it! The stage lights are hurting my eyes.

ORPHEUS: *(Not answering at once, gathering his instruments)* I don't know which is better, to be alive and wretched or dead and happy.

PLUTO: *(Thundering)* Nobody's happy dead! Now get out of here, before I change you into a weed-grown swamp!

ORPHEUS: I bet my friends fifty bucks and my seventeen-jewel Swiss watch that I'd come back with Eurydice. Now I'm going back with empty pockets and a memory. *(Throws the tissue away in disgust)*

PLUTO: Hey, come on, I got a clean Underworld here. Don't mess it up.

ORPHEUS: *(Retrieves the tissue and stuffs it back in his pocket)* I never even held her in my arms or touched her lips . . .

PLUTO: Don't look so sad. Pretty soon it'll be apple-picking season up above and if that doesn't lift your spirits, nothing will.

ORPHEUS: *(Flatly)* Yeah, I'll kiss a Rome beauty. *(He starts to go)*

PLUTO: Oh—a warning for the future, Orpheus: keep your eyes open for the Maenads.

ORPHEUS: Who?

PLUTO: Those frenzied, drunken women, the same ones who ripped Pentheus apart. They might come for you, too, one day.

ORPHEUS: Thanks for telling me. Haven't I suffered enough already?

PLUTO: Nobody ever suffers enough, Orpheus. There's always a little more. But don't think about it. In the meantime, make music. Now hurry, before Charon locks up his ferryboat for the night. *(Orpheus struggles with his load of instruments, finds his harmonica and cleans it on his pants)* Oh, Orpheus, if your new bride eats chicken at the wedding, tell her to be careful with the bones.

ORPHEUS: Don't worry, I'll make sure they fillet it for her next time. *(He sets his harmonica to his lips, and with his musical instruments rattling on his back and bouncing in the wagon, he goes out playing a soft, plaintive melody)*

PLUTO: *(Addressing the audience)* I want to apologize. I promised some violence earlier and now you're probably all sitting there feeling cheated and disappointed. Actually, the Maenads were supposed to appear in the last scene and tear Orpheus apart, limb from limb. They were going to eat his heart and liver, drink his blood, toss his head in your lap and make a bonfire of his bones. But at the last minute, contrary to the author's wishes, we, the gods, decided against that. The theatre has certain honorable conventions, and wanton, bloody violence isn't one of them. And so, if only to accommodate some of your more refined sensibilities, we dispatched Orpheus to the other world without further insult or pain. You see, even in their jealousy, the higher gods admire some-one of Orpheus' courage; they like a man who'll risk every-thing, especially when it's all for love.

(Pause)

Well, I wish I could tell you that Orpheus got over his Eurydice, that he married someone else and became a famous musician and songwriter. For a while, nobody knew what happened to him after he left the Underworld. Some say he went mad and drowned himself in a canal. Others say he went to New Hampshire and lived a hermit's existence, playing only to the trees and forest animals. And still other report that he became an organ grinder and died of food poisoning in Istanbul. But from what I've been able to learn, he returned to Yonkers and remained there in virtual seclusion, going out only for sheet music and groceries. He spent most of his time writing poems and composing love songs for the soprano to-nette, a small, plastic instrument of limited range, but one which remotely reminded him of Eurydice's voice. Whenever he sang or played, traffic came to a standstill, stray cats stopped foraging in garbage cans, and office workers de-manded more coffee breaks. Then, quite unexpectedly, the music stopped. He began to drink, and as the days grew shorter and colder, he sank deeper and deeper into utter lone-liness and despair. All he could do was stare at his wedding picture and listen for the echo of Eurydice's voice that cried faintly from afar. *(Beat)* One night, in a drunken rage, he destroyed all his instruments—the valuable fiddles and cellos, the priceless harps and guitars, the silver flutes and gold harmonicas—all shattered and splintered until nothing was left but the howling wind outside his window.

(Pause)

On New Year's Day, quite early in the morning, he was struck down by a speeding car and was killed instantly. There were five women in the car returning from a party; all were drunk. No one came to claim the body, and so Orpheus was buried in an unmarked grave in a cemetery for the unknown.

I'm told that whenever somebody steps on the spot where he died, he hears music sweeter than all the harps of heaven. But then, what do I know about heavenly harps? Well, I'm giving a little party of my own tonight in honor of Themis, goddess of justice, and I better go inside and shave. Somebody kill those lights! *(He goes inside)*

Blackout

John Harding and John Burrows

FOR SYLVIA

John Harding and John Burrows

An enormously popular British play, *For Sylvia* appears in print for the first time in the United States in *The Best Short Plays 1978*.

Written and performed by John Harding and John Burrows, the work opened to exceptional praise in the London press. The correspondent for the *Sunday Telegraph* advised readers that "It should not be missed. It's moving and very funny." According to Irving Wardle in *The Times*, "*For Sylvia* is an obvious winner; as deft and accurate a piece of work as the cult of wartime nostalgia has yet produced."

The Observer's representative termed it ". . . a gentle but very funny satire on some flying movies of the Forties," while others described it as "superb" and a conspicuous "triumph" for the creators, the Messrs. Harding and Burrows.

In summation, *Time Out* magazine reported: "It's a history of the Second World War in forty minutes, not so much the facts, but the way in which the actuality affected people. It's fast, funny and fluid: between them they conjure up any number of pilots, officers, their wives, home guard, surgeons and newsreel presenters. . . . *For Sylvia* probably gets closer to what it was like to be a young man in the war than has anything else not conceived by people who were there."

John Harding and John Burrows are two young English actor-writers who first met as undergraduates during the late Sixties in the drama department of Manchester University. As with most of their work, *For Sylvia* was originally written for performance by themselves, which they did principally as a lunchtime entertainment at British fringe and pub theatres, and subsequently at the Edinburgh Festival, in Holland, and on BBC television and radio.

The team's other short pieces are the television play *Do You Dig It?*, a satire about homemade fall-out shelters, and *The Manly Bit*, a comedy about male sexual obsessions, performed in 1976 at the Open Air Theatre in London's Regents Park. Their best known full-length works are the largely autobiographical *The Golden Pathway Annual*, which transferred to the West End in 1974, and *Loud Reports*, a three-man musical history of the British Empire 1900–1975, written and performed with composer Peter Skellern at the Royal Court Theatre Upstairs.

In addition to their collaborative work, Harding and Burrows pursue independent theatre careers. Mr. Harding was in the original London casts of *My Fat Friend* and *Donkey's Years*, while Mr. Burrows has appeared in a number of television plays and maintains close links with the Sidewalk Theatre Company, a London-based community group for whom he scripted and directed *Son of a Gun*, which toured Europe in 1977.

Characters:

For Sylvia is a play for performance by two men. The following characters appear:

FIRST LECTURER*
SECOND LECTURER
FLYING OFFICER JOHNNY SUTTON DFC*
LIEUTENANT HANS BADEN-BADEN
SPECIAL CONSTABLE EPHRIAM C. SPOON
SYLVIA
THE SQUADRON LEADER
THE WARRANT OFFICER*
WARD ORDERLY BROWN*
MCKINDOE
FLYING OFFICER "BUSTER" SHAW-JONES
A POPSIE
"SPOOF" FRISSOM
BATMAN CORPORAL SMITH
GINGER*

Parts marked with an asterisk are played by actor A. All other parts are played by actor B.

The play is divided into scenes for convenience but the action is continuous. All props are mimed with the exception of the map/diagram. Basic costume of cricket whites is worn throughout.

Scene One:
Stand By!

The two lecturers, dressed in comfortable cricket whites, are on stage. They appear to be discussing tactical details around a map/diagram of "Invasion Corner" which rests on a small table upstage. The only other furniture is two wooden chairs, either side of the table. They turn to face the audience.

FIRST LECTURER: When one thinks of the summer of 1940—The Battle Of Britain—the intense fighting that took place in the air, over the Southeast of England during those months—one finds it difficult to imagine, I think, that anything like it ever happened.

SECOND LECTURER: "Like running the mile as a series of 100 yard sprints, then bloody doing it again," was a pilot's summing up.

FIRST LECTURER: But however one tries to describe it, it was, without doubt . . .

SECOND LECTURER: . . . Britain's finest hour.

FIRST LECTURER: What was it all about? What enabled young man after young man to hurl himself against the enemy, do his bit, and if his number came up, die proudly and fly west?

SECOND LECTURER: The answer lies, I think, in one word: survival. Not personal survival, the survival of an entire nation's way of life. For this is just what Hitler threatened in those dark days of 1940. He stood poised, ready, waiting.

FIRST LECTURER: But waiting for what? Well . . . *(Throughout the rest of this speech, the second lecturer demonstrates the tactical manoeuvres etc., on the map/diagram, which is suitably animated for the purpose)* . . . the German seaborne invasion of England, Operation Sealion as Hitler called it, awaited two things. One was favourable weather conditions. The other was the total destruction of the Royal Air Force. And this is the task Hitler now set Herr Göring and his Luftwaffe. For Hitler knew he dare not let the Sealion slip into the channel and attempt to squat heavily on this island of ours while the Hurricanes and Spitfires of Fighter Command defiantly flew the skies and challenged him on every quarter.

Scene Two:
Choose Your Weapon

This scene takes the form of a duel with pistols.

JOHNNY: I'm Flying Officer Johnny Sutton, on a routine patrol along the South coast of Kent somewhere. I'm keeping an eye out for Gerry. I'm enjoying the early morning sunshine, and I'm thinking about breakfast.

HANS: I am Lieutenant Hans Baden-Baden, attempting to cross the Southeast coast of Kent at a point whose exact location I am not at liberty to disclose. I, too, am keeping an eye out, as you say, for you English. However, I am not thinking about breakfast, and the sun is too hot. My machine is the Messerschmitt BF *109 E* Series 111.

JOHNNY: The kite I'm flying is a Supermarine Spitfire Mark 1A.

HANS: Power plant: Daimler-Benz *DB601A*.

JOHNNY: Up front's a 12-cylinder Rolls Royce Merlin aero engine.

HANS: Range: 656 Kilometres.

JOHNNY: With 85 gallons of 100 octane aboard, she'll take me 475 miles.

HANS: Maximum speed: 568 k.p.h.

JOHNNY: With a top speed of 365 m.p.h.

HANS: Armament: Two 7.9-mm MG17 machine guns and two 20-mm MGFF cannons.

JOHNNY: She's got four Browning machine guns nestling in each wing. So bloody exact is Gerry, so bloody sharp. He comes down out of the sun from 20,000 feet, firing as he comes. I'm hit. I get him in my sights. I fire. His port wing belches smoke. He fires again, but this time his aim is wide. I let him have another burst. I hit him fair and square. His cockpit becomes a ball of flame, and down he goes into the drink, leaving behind a thin black column of smoke. Now I'm losing height fast. Don't think I'll make home. Better put her down where I can.

(Hans lies dead. Johnny kneels, wounded, nearby)

Scene Three:
E. C. Spoon's Finest Hour

SPOON: *(North country)* Oh, there you are, son. Got over here as fast as I could when I saw you coming down. *(He pulls Johnny to his feet)* All right, are you?

JOHNNY: Yes, I'm all right, Constable. But the plane's a bit of a sieve.

SPOON: Nothing new to me, son. Used to watch the Royal Flying Corps boys bringing 'em down in France, 1917. Course, you've got to be a bit loony to fly one of them things, haven't you?

JOHNNY: Well, I don't think I'm ready for the asylum yet, Constable.

SPOON: No offense, sir. No offense. Course, we've got to be pretty careful about what comes down out of the sky these days, you know. But I think I'm prepared for any contingency.

JOHNNY: I'm sure you are, Constable.

SPOON: Total vigilance, sir! Gas attack, fire drill, first aid, painting out road signs, throwing pepper. I've read all the pamphlets that come down from the Ministry, you know, about what to do when they come over, dropping stealthily out of the azure, attempting to spread panic and infiltrate the countryside. That's the trouble with Gerry, you see, sir, doesn't obey any rules. He could come over here not wearing any uniform, dressed as our boys, trained in our ways, speaking faultless English, *(Growing suspicion)* nonchalant, blasé. . . . Is that your five pound note down there, sir? *(Takes rifle from shoulder and levels it at Johnny)* Don't move!

JOHNNY: I say! Are you all right?

SPOON: It's all right now, mate, you can drop it. I've tumbled you. You're under arrest. All tricks are useless and verboten! Besides which, there's a machine gun at your back.

JOHNNY: I can't see it!

SPOON: Camouflage! What do you think we are, mate, amateurs? Ich bin ein ex-marine, mate. I can smell danger! All right, Charlie! George! Keep him in your sights!

JOHNNY: Look here! I'm Flying Officer Johnny Sutton stationed at Biggin Hill. If you don't believe me, phone them and check. Really!

SPOON: Are you telling the truth, the whole truth, and nothing but the truth?

JOHNNY: Yes, of course I am.

SPOON: Say "Up Hitler's arse."

JOHNNY: Up Hitler's arse.

SPOON: *(Relieved, puts rifle back on shoulder)* Oh, all right then, sir. I'm very sorry about that, but one can't be too careful these days, you see.

JOHNNY: That's all right, Constable. I understand. You and your lads are doing a great job.

SPOON: I am all the sons of my father's house, sir.

JOHNNY: I beg your pardon?

SPOON: I'm on me tod, sir. There aren't any others. It was a ruse. Charlie and George are mere fictions, sir. Did I fool you sir? Did I really? Did I?

JOHNNY: Well, yes, you did.

SPOON: You've made an older man very happy, sir. I may have the wisdom of years, but I'm past me prime, and a long way from home.

JOHNNY: Yes, you're not a native of Kent, are you, Spoon.

SPOON: Well spotted, sir; those eagle eyes, the boys in blue! No, you're quite right sir, I'm a newcomer, sir, settled here in 1918. Got the wrong train when I was demobbed, sir, and sort of stayed on. Of course, you won't remember Armistice night, will you sir?

JOHNNY: I was a mere babe in arms, Spoon.

SPOON: 'Course you were sir, course you were. What a night that was! I come home, sir, covered in it.

JOHNNY: Covered in it, Spoon?

SPOON: Glory, sir.

JOHNNY: Oh, yes! What a time you must have had. Well, old chap, I think I better be getting back to the squadron. I think I'll just hitch a lift.

SPOON: Hitch a lift, sir, hitch a lift. I'd never live it down, sir; when I've got a perfectly good puncture repair outfit in my saddlebag, sir? I'll soon have you airborne, sir. Just a jiffy. *(He lifts Johnny up into the air on his shoulders)* How's that, sir?

JOHNNY: Incredible, Spoon. Thank you very much.

SPOON: Not at all, sir. And don't forget. You can always count on the total support of the other boys in blue.

Scene Four:
Taking the Leap

Johnny jumps down from Spoon's shoulders, flying his Spitfire, and la-la-ing the Dam Busters March. Meanwhile, Sylvia is below him picking apples. They see one another, she takes up the song and they wave. Sylvia bends over in an attempt to lift a particularly heavy basket of apples. Johnny sees her difficulty and bails out to help her. While Johnny is busy with the sound and mime of the parachute descent, Sylvia, unaware, continues to pick apples. Johnny arrives just in time to pick a high one. Now they face one another and hum the song. During the following dialogue whoever's not speaking continues the tune.

JOHNNY: Hello. My name's Johnny—Johnny Sutton. What's yours?

SYLVIA: I'm Sylvia.

JOHNNY: Pleased to meet you.

SYLVIA: How do you do.

JOHNNY: Don't tell me you spend all your day picking apples?

SYLVIA: Yes, it's part of my war effort.

(Johnny stops humming and la-la's again. He indicates his plane still flying overhead with his hand. Sylvia follows Johnny's hand and makes the plane drone. In this way, Johnny makes her look into his eyes. He kisses her. She slaps his face. The song has stopped. The plane has crashed)

JOHNNY: What the devil was that for?

SYLVIA: For ruining a perfectly good Spitfire.

(The song begins again)

JOHNNY: Marry me, Sylvia.

SYLVIA: Johnny, yes. I'll write to you, Johnny.

(The song swells up. They wave and take their leave of one another)

Scene Five:
Skunks!

While the Warrant Officer stands to rigid attention and glowers at the audience, the C.O. addresses them.

SQUADRON LEADER: I have been C.O. of this squadron exactly a month and have several comments to pass on to you all. My NCO's are slack and slipshod. They have allowed the men to get lazy and out of hand. The Station Warrant Officer has complained to me that they are blatantly arrogant and so conceited that they refused to take orders from anyone but their own officers. This will stop immediately, or I shall be forced to take drastic action.

I have studied my officers behaviour with concern and frankly I think it stinks. You are the most conceited and insubordinate lot I have ever had the misfortune to come up against.

Admittedly you have worked hard and got a damn good score in the air—in fact a better score than any other squadron in Fighter Command—but your casualties have been appalling. These losses I attribute to the fact that your discipline is slack; you never by any chance get some sleep; you drink like fishes, and you've got a damn sight too good an opinion of yourselves.

Now, your billets. It appears that you have turned the living quarters which were allotted to you to provide a certain amount of security and rest into a night club. It also appears that you ask your various lady friends down to spend weekends with you whenever you please.

This will cease. All women will be out of the house by 2300 hours sharp.

Your clothes—I can scarcely call them uniform. I will not tolerate check shirts, old school ties, or suede shoes. While you are on duty, you will wear the regulation dress. Neither will I tolerate pink pajamas under your tunics.

You all seem to possess high-powered automobiles. None of these appear to be taxed and insured, but I hear from the Adjutant that you have an understanding with the local police. Well, that may be, but how do you explain where you get your petrol from? Your cars reek of 100 octane, and I can assure you you're not fooling the Station Commander.

Finally, I want to see an all-round improvement. At the moment I think you're a lot of skunks!

Scene Six:
Scramble!

FIRST LECTURER: So, no more pink pajamas under uniforms. Things were getting serious.

SECOND LECTURER: On August 13th, Eagle Day as Göring named it, the German Air Force began a new phase of bombing attacks. The objectives of these air raids would no longer be coastal shipping and ports, but the aerodromes of the RAF.

FIRST LECTURER: Before this the confidential Reichsmarshal had merely been sounding out his valiant but foolish foe. Now in four days he declared he would smash the British Air Force. By early September, "mopping up" operations would be complete. By mid-September the Sealion would sail on the tide beneath a moonless sky, empty of all but German aircraft.

SECOND LECTURER: Fighter Command dug in its heels. Men and machines prepared to take the strain.

FIRST LECTURER: "Men and machines prepared to take the strain." What of that machinery? Not for the moment the Hurricanes and Spitfires, but the complicated web of ground control that linked radar station with operations room and operations room with airfield. For instance:

(The following speech is demonstrated on the map/diagram by the first lecturer while the second lecturer addresses the audience)

SECOND LECTURER: You are Sector Ground Controller at Biggin Hill. You are ordered to intercept an enemy raid approaching Dungeness at 15,000 feet. The enemy's sixty miles away and moving towards you at a speed of four miles a minute with the sun behind it. You decide to use a squadron of Spitfires already over Biggin Hill at 19,000 feet. They can fly at six miles a minute. There is no wind and the sky is cloudless. You don't want your chaps to be dazzled by flying into the sun. What would you do? What orders would you give? What course to steer? Where would you expect your boys to engage the enemy?

FIRST LECTURER: And this type of decision you face a

hundred times a day. Yes, men and machines prepared to take the strain. The question now was, "Could they take it?"

Scene Seven:
Maestro McKindoe

Though McKindoe was in fact a New Zealander, he should be played here as a dour Edinburgh surgeon.
The mime for this scene is focused on the burn victim who Brown wheels in, singing. The preparations and work of the surgeon are seen in detail: dressing in gown and cap, hand scrubbing, donning of rubber gloves, sterilization of instruments, exploratory surgery, heart massage, etc. Brown assists in his own particular way.

BROWN: O there ain't no fighter pilots down in hell,
O there ain't no fighter pilots down in hell.
The place is full of queers,
Navigators, Bombardiers,
But there ain't no fighter pilots down in hell.

MCKINDOE: Fiovoranti! I don't suppose you've heard of him?

BROWN: No, sir. I can't say I have.

MCKINDOE: Fiovoranti, my friend, was a particularly bombastic Sixteenth Century surgeon.

BROWN: Didn't realize they had any, sir.

MCKINDOE: To whom, I feel, I owe a certain amount of gratitude. In 1551, Fiovoranti was witness to a duel between two Italian gentlemen in Africa. In the course of the duel, one of the duelists had his nose cut off and Fiovoranti, showing great presence of mind, I think, picked it up out of the sand, urinated on it . . .

BROWN: Urinated on it, sir?!

MCKINDOE: Aye, urinated on it, man.

BROWN: Whatever for, sir?

MCKINDOE: To clean it laddie, to clean it. And put it back on the unfortunate fellow's face.

BROWN: I wouldn't have thought urine was much good for that, sir.

MCKINDOE: A week later, when he removed the bandage, he was astonished to find that instead of the gangrenous mass he expected, he was looking at a nose well attached and in its correct place.

BROWN: Sounds rather far-fetched to me, sir.

MCKINDOE: What particular bits and pieces have we got under here, then?

BROWN: These bits 'n pieces, sir, have sustained standard Hurricane burns and belong to a certain Flying Officer by the name of Buster Shaw-Jones.

MCKINDOE: I mention Fiovoranti because his experience and mine happen to be similar.

BROWN: You mean you've done the same thing, sir?

MCKINDOE: Done what same thing?

BROWN: Pissed on someone's nose, sir.

MCKINDOE: No, I have not. Nor, before you ask, have I witnessed a duel, Ward Orderly Brown, except, perhaps, for our daily attempts at communication.

BROWN: Don't quite follow your gist, sir.

MCKINDOE: No, I don't suppose you do. Never mind, is there a photograph?

BROWN: Yes, sir. (Gives photo)

MCKINDOE: That's how he was. Let's see how he is.

BROWN: Nasty.

MCKINDOE: Very nasty. If it were food I would not bother to eat it. Is this all there is?

BROWN: There are some other bits in the tray underneath, sir.

MCKINDOE: It's very difficult to do the puzzle without having all the pieces, Ward Orderly Brown.

BROWN: I realize that, sir, that's why I told you about the bit underneath.

MCKINDOE: And the time that elapses before one particular piece is reunited with another particular piece is extremely critical. Remember Fiovoranti! No sooner was the nose in the sand than he was urinating on it, and reuniting it with the face.

BROWN: Sorry, sir. It's just that I found your story about the Eyetie so engaging.

MCKINDOE: Aye. Did you bring the uniform?

BROWN: Yes, sir.

MCKINDOE: Without removing any attached matter, I hope?

BROWN: I did give it a bit of a brush down, sir.

MCKINDOE: Ward Orderly Brown, when I set about to do a jigsaw puzzle, I start off with the pieces with the straight edges, the pieces on the outside. In the case of the human body that has sustained standard Hurricane burns, the pieces on the outside are invariably forming an additional lining to the uniform. If I have'na got the uniform, life gets pretty difficult.

BROWN: Beg pardon, sir.

MCKINDOE: The skin, man, the skin. Where did you do your brushing down? Can you find the missing pieces?

BROWN: I'm afraid I flushed them, sir. Down the toilet. Best place I thought.

MCKINDOE: You're making it very difficult for me.

BROWN: You can do it, sir. I believe in you. You've got all my trust.

MCKINDOE: In future make sure I get all the pieces as well.

BROWN: You could turn burnt toast into Christmas cake. I've seen 'em coming in here looking like piles of old cinders and going out like Errol Flynns. Is that the acid, sir, the tannic?

MCKINDOE: Aye.

BROWN: I believe putting cold tea on sunburn involves the same principle. Is that right, sir? Tea, having tannin in it?

MCKINDOE: I think you missed your vocation, Ward Orderly Brown.

BROWN: Don't quite follow your gist, sir.

MCKINDOE: No, I don't suppose you do. Never mind.

BROWN: Is he done for now, sir?

MCKINDOE: Aye. Take all of Flying Officer Buster Shaw-Jones to the salina, Ward Orderly Brown.

BROWN: Right, sir. Do 'im the world of good. It always surprises me how effective the salt water is. How did you get onto it, sir?

MCKINDOE: Fiovoranti!

BROWN: Don't quite follow your gist, sir.

Scene Eight:
Buster Goes Out

Buster pulls on batting gloves and takes his place at the wicket, back to audience. Johnny is the bowler, and the whole scene a game of cricket. As Buster plays strokes, Johnny provides the whack of leather on willow with an oral click.

JOHNNY: Hello, Buster. What the devil have you been doing with yourself?

BUSTER: Hello, Johnny. Had a row with a German, old boy. Burnt my fingers. Kind of nice to look at, aren't I? Made an offering to the Gods, you see, Johnny. Sent half of me up in smoke as a sort of thank you for the half that fell back down again. Not got a cigarette, have you? They won't let you smoke in here. Got an aversion to anything that burns.

JOHNNY: Has the Maestro had a look at you yet?

BUSTER: Thanks. I believe so.

JOHNNY: And?

BUSTER: Nothing. No-one's said a damn thing.

JOHNNY: I'm surprised they let me see you. I thought you'd be drugged up to the eyeballs. You've been out every time I phoned.

BUSTER: Social commitments, old son.

JOHNNY: What?

BUSTER: Social commitments.

JOHNNY: Oh, I see. You're a difficult man to replace, Buster.

BUSTER: What! Squadron not managing without me?

JOHNNY: We've had to get an arrangement with Gerry not to fly our way till you're back.

BUSTER: That's the spirit! *(Pained)*

JOHNNY: What's up?

BUSTER: Only hurts when I laugh.

JOHNNY: Don't laugh then.

BUSTER: Who's laughing?

JOHNNY: Is there anything you need?

BUSTER: How about a new face? Sorry, Johnny, what a fool I've been. How did I buy this lot? You'd think I'd have known better.

JOHNNY: Come on, Buster. It could have happened to anyone.

BUSTER: I was so bloody sure there wasn't a Hun around for miles.

JOHNNY: I thought you'd seen him. He came out of the sun.

BUSTER: Yes. Oldest bloody trick in the book.

JOHNNY: Could have been worse.

BUSTER: You think so?

JOHNNY: The whole lot of you could have gone up in smoke.

BUSTER: What a bonfire that would have been!

JOHNNY: There's nothing you want then?

BUSTER: *(Cleans his crease)* You might have a word with someone—find out how long I'll be in here.

JOHNNY: Sure.

BUSTER: And tell Peter to use the bike.

JOHNNY: Right.

BUSTER: You've no idea how hot it is being a mummy, Johnny. That's something you could get me—a nice cold draught. A bed in a wind tunnel. That'd be heaven right now. Yes, and ice cream by the seaside. That'd be nice. Riding on a donkey, with shorts on. Feeling the wind on your legs. Turning brown. *(Johnny delivers a final ball. Buster slashes at it, turns to see his bails fly off, pulls off his gloves and tucks his bat under his arm)* I've had a good innings, Johnny. *(As Buster leaves the field, Johnny is staring at the fallen wicket)*

Scene Nine:
Under Stress

c.o.: Come in, Johnny. Sit down.

JOHNNY: Thank you, sir. I'd rather stand.

c.o.: Good to feel your feet on terra firma for a change, eh? Drink?

JOHNNY: Thank you, sir. Scotch if you have it.

c.o.: Oh yes, I have it, Johnny. That's the one thing they can't ration if they want us to win the war. Well, Johnny, how are you? Don't see nearly enough of you these days, nor of anybody else for that matter. If you knew the bloody paper work a dicky engine causes! So. Everything all right after that stunt landing?

JOHNNY: Yes. Fine, thank you, sir. The new kite's just as good as the old one.

c.o.: How's Sylvia?

JOHNNY: Fine. I'm pleased to say, sir.

c.o.: What's your score now?

JOHNNY: About average, sir.

c.o.: Don't be ridiculous. What is it?

JOHNNY: 14 confirmed. 6 probables, sir.

c.o.: You'll be getting a bar to that *DFC* soon. The Squadron's proud of you, Johnny.

JOHNNY: Is it, sir? Proud of the number of men I've killed? Proud of the bloody carnage that's going on? Well, I'm not proud. You know what you can do with your DFC!

c.o.: Johnny! Take hold. That's fool's talk and you know it. When did you last have leave?

JOHNNY: It's not leave I want, sir. It's out. I'm sick of their bloody war. God, can't you understand? I don't want a ringside seat to watch schoolboys blown out of the sky every day. Do you know how many of the original squadron are left now, sir? I'll tell you. Eight! Which means one hell of a lot of men gone west. The boys deserve better treatment. It's weeks since the Mark 11's should have arrived to re-equip the squadron. If we'd had those *glycol* clovers and bullet-proof screens, Buster wouldn't have gone down a flamer!

c.o.: Shut up! You think you've got all the answers, don't you? You think because I'm not up there every day I don't know what's going on? I've got a squadron of Boy Scouts! Yes, it's nasty! It's not for children, Johnny. It's for men. And you *are* a man. You still are. I've seen the way the other chaps look to you, and I know you're worthy of their trust. You may as well know you're to get your own squadron soon. Oh, have another drink and sit down for Christ's sake! Johnny this isn't us. This isn't real. We're behaving like hysterical women.

JOHNNY: You're right, sir. I'm sorry. I suppose everything just caught up with me all of a sudden.

c.o.: It's forgotten.

JOHNNY: But morale is a bit low, sir. We're taking a hammering. The mess isn't what it used to be.

c.o.: Well, I'm doing everything I can on my end. Those Mark 11's have definitely been promised for within a week. But you're right. The boys do need something. There's fresh blood coming into the squadron from Uxbridge tomorrow—shiny new wings and heads full of tales of what a cracking lot we are. We can't let them down. There's got to be something we can do.

JOHNNY: Yes, sir, but what? We're working flat out as it is.

c.o.: Um. Now think, Johnny, think hard. What can pull us out of a flat spin?

JOHNNY: Well, sir, how about a party?

c.o.: I was hoping you'd say that! Right, Johnny, a party they'll know about from here to Bentley Priory. An almighty drunk.

JOHNNY: It'll cost a bit, sir.

c.o.: Well, I'm good for a tenner, and I'll tell you what, I want five of it spent on that barmaid from the Fox.

JOHNNY: How do you mean, sir?

c.o.: Well, I have it on good authority that before the war she took her clothes off, for money.

JOHNNY: A stripper, sir?

c.o.: Yes, Johnny. And if she did it before she'll do it again! If she doesn't get her knickers off, I'm a German.

JOHNNY: Right sir, I'll put it to her as part of her war effort.

C.O.: Good. And we must get the cooks to rig up some sort of cake for her to burst out of . . .

JOHNNY: An icing sugar Spit or something.

C.O.: Yes. God knows, it will be an improvement on the last strip I saw in the Mess. Some idiot blind drunk crawling out of a sidcot and making obscene gestures with a flying helmet. Completely blotto?! Who was it now . . . ?

JOHNNY: Buster, sir.

C.O.: Oh. Oh, I'm sorry Johnny . . .

JOHNNY: It's alright, sir. Happens to all of us.

C.O.: Yes. Right then. You can see to all that can't you, Johnny?

JOHNNY: Yes, sir. I'll cut along, sir. And thank you, sir.

(They shake hands, then salute)

Scene Ten: Ragtime

Johnny and the Popsie dance for the most part on the spot, rotating so that, in best film tradition, the speaker faces the audience over the partner's shoulder. When they do dance round the room, it is an awkward silent waltz.

JOHNNY: Would you like to dance?

POPSIE: Oh, all right then.

JOHNNY: There. I haven't seen you before, have I?

POPSIE: No, it's my first time here.

JOHNNY: Do you like it?

POPSIE: Oh, yes! I mean it's a bit strange. I think everybody's had quite a lot to drink, haven't they?

JOHNNY: I suppose they have. Would you like something?

POPSIE: No, thanks. I've got one back where I was sitting. My friend will look after it for me. Anyway, we're dancing.

JOHNNY: Yes.

POPSIE: You're a pilot, aren't you? I can see that by your wings. Are you married?

JOHNNY: That's right.

POPSIE: I don't know many pilots. Well, only one really, and I only went out with him once or twice. He's funny. Oh, very nice—but—you know—I didn't understand what he was talking about half the time! My friend says that all pilots are a bit mad from being up there in the sun all the time. That's silly, isn't it?

JOHNNY: Perhaps we're all a bit mad in our different ways.

POPSIE: Oh, yes. I see what you mean. *(She doesn't)* I don't think I could do it.

JOHNNY: What?

POPSIE: Go up in an aeroplane. I shouldn't feel safe. I mean, at least a boat's on the water, isn't it? But I suppose you get a lovely view.

JOHNNY: Yes. But there's a bit more to it than that.

POPSIE: Oh, I'm sure there is. I'm sure it's very difficult, like driving a car.

JOHNNY: Yes. Why isn't your friend dancing? She doesn't look very happy.

POPSIE: Oh, she's always like that. Anyway, she's waiting for someone she met before. He's a pilot. She's mad about him, and she only met him once, in a pub. I don't know what she sees in him myself. He was very aristocratic. If you know what I mean. Don't expect he'll come now, do you?

JOHNNY: What's his name?

POPSIE: Buster somebody-or-other.

(They stop dancing)

JOHNNY: Oh.

POPSIE: What's the matter?

JOHNNY: I'm afraid your friend's in for a bit of a shock. You see, Buster was shot down. He's dead.

POPSIE: Oh, my God!

JOHNNY: Would you like to tell her?

POPSIE: I couldn't. She set everything on him being here. Perhaps I could say he's been transferred, could I?

JOHNNY: Yes, I think that would be best. Say he's been transferred. Now if you'll excuse me. I think I need a drink.

Scene Eleven:
How Do They Do It?

Johnny and Spoof are at the bar and drunk enough to say:

JOHNNY: God! Look at all those flies! You know they must be bloody good pilots landing on the ceiling like that. I wonder how they do it?

SPOOF: Quite simple, old man. *(The following discussion is accompanied by elaborate hand demonstrations)* They cruise along at the correct height below the ceiling and then half loop, landing upwards at the top.

JOHNNY: That's all very well, but they'd have to be pretty good judges of distance not to nose dive on the way round. Presumably they're not fitted with altimeters working inversely downward from the ceiling. I think you're talking a load of bull.

SPOOF: No, no. They wouldn't nose dive, Johnny, just the opposite. As soon as they lost enough flying speed to effect a good 3-point landing, they would stall in an upside down position and go into an inverted nose dive. To get out of that they'd have to pull out into a loop again and then they'd go on and on for some time, especially the inexperienced ones who'd just joined the squadron from *OTU*.

JOHNNY: Think about it, Spoof, if they do land out of a loop they'd end up facing the wrong way, which is going to be pretty confusing for the ceiling staff. No, what they'd do is come in close up under the ceiling and then instead of looping they make a slow half-roll. I seem to have spilt my drink all over your mess uniform.

SPOOF: Oh bugger it, so you have. I reckon the really experienced flies with plenty of ops behind them just zoom up and put out a sticky foot.

JOHNNY: That'd be against *fly* flying regulations. It would put a terrific strain on the undercarriage.

SPOOF: Ah. But then he has got six sets.

JOHNNY: No, old man. Eight.

SPOOF: Six, I tell you.

JOHNNY: *Mustica domestica* has eight.

SPOOF: I'm talking about flies. They've got six.

JOHNNY: I'll bloody settle this!

SPOOF: Look out flies! Red Leader is about to buzz you! Break left, Red Leader! Bandit on the port wing! One on your tail, Red Leader. I'll see if I can get him for you. *(Spoof kicks Johnny on the backside)* That one's in a power dive. Where the hell is ground control? Never there when you want them, are they, Johnny?

JOHNNY: I'm out of ammo Blue Two. Let's scrub this Rhubarb!

SPOOF: Righto, Red Leader. Not a very good score I'm afraid, though you sent one for home with smoke streaming from the starboard engine. Want to claim him as a probable?

JOHNNY: Certainly not! I am going to probe deep into the enemy airfield and carry out a reconnaisance. I shall need your close support in this venture. Switch on the lights over the bar will you, to give me a proper flare path.

SPOOF: I think I'd better warn you there's an electric light pendant barrage balloon flying in the centre of their 'drome, Red Leader.

(Spoof lifts Johnny up towards the ceiling. Johnny tips over Spoof's shoulder and heads towards the floor falling head over heels onto his back)

JOHNNY: Christ, I'm stuck to the ceiling. I've pancaked on their 'drome. Hang on and I'll jump down. Don't seem able to move. Pull me down, will you? Chuck up a rope or something. What a moment for Sir Isaac to fail me! Hope this ceiling's strong or I shall break through and head straight out to the stratosphere. Goodnight sweet earth! *Ave atque vale*. I love you all.

(He passes out)

Scene Twelve:
Preparations for War

BATMAN: Now come along, sir. Wake up. Wake up, sir. *(Johnny groans)* Now then, sir. This won't do at all. I've already let you have an extra half hour.

JOHNNY: Go away.

BATMAN: No sir, I'm not going to go away. I'm afraid I'm going to pester you until you get up, sir.

JOHNNY: What time is it?

BATMAN: 4:30. Which means you have exactly half an hour to get out to dispersal.

JOHNNY: Go away. I'm sick.

BATMAN: Shall I call the Medical Officer, sir?

JOHNNY: Oh, for goodness sake, Smith, just let me die on my own! I've got a bit of a head.

BATMAN: I'm not surprised, sir, after last night. I've got just the thing for it, but not a drop will pass your lips till I see your feet touch the floor, sir.

JOHNNY: All right, you win. Oh, my head!

BATMAN: Yes, sir. *(As Johnny's head comes up to a sitting position)* The first thousand feet are the worst. Now, sir, drink this.

JOHNNY: *(Drinks it)* What in God's name?

BATMAN: One of my specials, sir. Never fails. Brandy, sour cream, Bovril and two raw eggs.

JOHNNY: Are you trying to kill me? God, we could use that as a secret weapon!

BATMAN: No sir, I'm not trying to kill you. Just the opposite. I'm thinking of you up there in just over an hour breathing pure oxygen, sir.

JOHNNY: Point taken, Smith.

BATMAN: Now, sir, as we're a little delicate this morning, I thought we might like to be shaved, sir. I've got the hot water right here, sir, and if you'll just keep still . . .

JOHNNY: You're a wonder, Smith. Carve away. *(He begins to shave him)* Were you at the party last night, Smith?

BATMAN: I was behind the scenes, sir. A very pleasant time seemed to be had by all. I enjoyed your stories particularly, sir.

JOHNNY: What stories?

BATMAN: Don't want to nick you, sir. The ones you were telling the new chaps about flying for the squadron . . .

JOHNNY: I don't remember.

BATMAN: . . . though I did think one or two were a little far-fetched.

JOHNNY: All right, Smith. I don't remember. Did you see the striptease?

BATMAN: I didn't think it proper, sir, though judging from the general uproar, I imagine the young lady in question was as comely as expected.

JOHNNY: I seem to remember she was, Smith. She certainly had guts.

BATMAN: Yes, sir. Now what about a cold bath, sir?

JOHNNY: Are you serious, Smith?

BATMAN: Yes, sir. Just the thing. My gentleman in the last war always had a cold bath before going on patrol, sir.

JOHNNY: I suppose it takes all types, Smith.

BATMAN: It does indeed, sir.

JOHNNY: Did he survive?

BATMAN: Oh yes, sir. No one has ever come to any harm while I've been doing for them, sir. That's why they call me Lucky Smith, sir.

JOHNNY: Do they really, Smith? I didn't know. I feel honoured.

BATMAN: I don't pay too much attention to it myself, sir. Probably all explainable by the laws of coincidence.

JOHNNY: Lucky Smith, eh? Do you only bring luck to others, Smith, or are you lucky yourself?

BATMAN: I reckon it's the same thing, sir. We've got to look out for one another. That's what it's all about, isn't it, sir?

JOHNNY: The war you mean?

BATMAN: Yes sir, and the Force. Gives you a sense of belonging.

JOHNNY: Yes, I think there's a lot in what you say. Well, Lucky, you certainly shake a mean cocktail. That potion has worked wonders.

BATMAN: Don't know how you could drink it, sir.

JOHNNY: What, you mean you never tried it? Well, you old blighter, Smith.

BATMAN: Yessir. Well, I think I'll leave you to it now, sir. Have a pleasant day.

Scene Thirteen:
15th September 1940

FIRST LECTURER: A pleasant day? Not really. But a decisive one. A month had passed since Eagle Day, August 13th, and the Luftwaffe hadn't managed in four weeks what it had set out to do in four days. Now it was the morning of the 15th September and time was running out for Göring.

SECOND LECTURER: As the Reichsmarshal's private train rumbled towards the French coast from where he would direct that day's operation, Göring remembered his promise to Hitler. Air supremacy by the middle of September when, for the last time before winter, weather conditions would be favourable for the invasion. *(They turn to the map)* What would bring up Fighter Command in its entirety? What would precipitate the final all-out battle that the Germans so desperately needed if victory was to be theirs? Nothing but an all-out Blitzkreig on London.

FIRST LECTURER: On the 15th September 1940, this is what London had to bear. Wave after wave of German aircraft homing menacingly on the capital, raining its bombs on a defiant people.

SECOND LECTURER: The formations were twice met over Kent, Sussex and the greater London area by almost as many fighters as the Luftwaffe Intelligence staff credited the British with possessing in the whole of the United Kingdom. Two days later, Hitler noted that the Royal Air Force was still undefeated and issued a directive postponing Operation Sealion "until further notice." The Battle of Britain had been won.

Scene Fourteen:
We'll Meet Again

Johnny sits in a chair. Sylvia sits at his feet with her head on his knee.

SYLVIA: Darling, do they really look after you at the Station?

JOHNNY: Yes, of course they do, much too well. You've met Corporal Smith, haven't you?

SYLVIA: Corporal Smith! Every time I think of him I have to laugh. He's such a dear, like an old mother hen fussing over you.

JOHNNY: Well, then. Anyway, you're the one who needs looking after. I'm worried about you, Sylvia.

SYLVIA: Don't be silly, darling. People have babies all the time. Aren't you happy we're having a baby?

JOHNNY: Of course I'm happy. It makes me the happiest man in the world. We'll call her Sylvia.

SYLVIA: Oh, so it's a girl already?

JOHNNY: Or Buster. I think it would be nice to call him Buster.

SYLVIA: Don't upset yourself darling. I think it would be just as nice to call him Johnny. It really doesn't matter what we call him as long as he's like you. *(She starts crying)*

JOHNNY: There. Now don't be silly, love.

SYLVIA: I can't help it, Johnny. I try to be brave, but every time you have leave I can't help it. I know it's silly, but it wouldn't be me if I wasn't dreadfully frightened that one day you weren't going to come back. I never know what to say to you and yet there's so much. Just as long as you love me and know I love you. Darling Johnny. *(She starts crying again)*

JOHNNY: Yes, come on now.

SYLVIA: I must look a sight.

JOHNNY: You look beautiful.

SYLVIA: I was at Sevenoaks yesterday. I went to see Betty. It's funny you know, it still feels like summer, but the plants know. The leaves are just beginning to go hard. Soon they'll turn brown. Only the roses are really still full and alive. Oh! This summer. So much has happened, and now it's nearly over. Perhaps the bombing will stop now, Johnny. They can't go on with *their* losses, can they? Can they, Johnny? I don't think they can. It's funny, being here in London I almost forgot that people were in danger anywhere else. But one of your chaps brought down a bomber very close to Betty's and the hill behind the cottage is all charred. Isn't that a horrid thought: all that wheat burned down. Somehow it almost seems worse than people. I know it isn't but I think the war does put funny ideas into people's heads. Don't you think so, darling? You mustn't mind my chatter. You must say "shut up" or I shall go on and on, and really I'd much rather listen to you. What are you thinking?

JOHNNY: Nothing. Just enjoying being warm here with you. The war's a long way away. It doesn't exist. All that matters is you and the fire and being warm here together. That's the most important thing. Oh, Sylvia, Sylvia, Sylvia. Aren't we lucky to have found each other in the middle of all this and to be so happy?

SYLVIA: Yes . . . I really think you should be smoking a pipe to complete the picture. I shall buy you a pipe. And you must make Bonzo curl up at your feet and fetch your slippers, and when the war is over he can bring your evening paper when you get off the train with all the other bowler hats.

JOHNNY: I shan't be a bowler hat, darling! I shall be an airline pilot and bring you back precious spices and perfume from the Orient and lion skins from deepest Africa and keep you in fine style.

SYLVIA: Then I shall always be a passenger in your aeroplane, or a stewardess. Do you think I'm pretty enough to be a stewardess? And fly with you everywhere. Wouldn't that be exciting?

JOHNNY: Yes, but I should be terribly jealous of all those fat business men getting all your attention. Perhaps I'd better be something in the City after all, then you can be my secretary. But then I shouldn't get any work done. You see what an impossible creature you are! . . . Darling, I hate to say it, but it's getting awfully late. (*Johnny stands. Sylvia is kneeling. They are holding hands*) Now come on. Just imagine I'm in my pinstripes and catching the 8.15 up to the Bank. Just a nice wifely peck on the cheek. Please. For me. No more tears. Promise?

SYLVIA: I promise. (*She kisses him*) But tomorrow?

JOHNNY: I shall be gone.

SYLVIA: But not for ever.

JOHNNY: No, not for ever. I promise.

SYLVIA: I shan't stop loving you.
JOHNNY: No, don't stop, ever.
SYLVIA: I'll write to you, Johnny.
(Slowly, Johnny backs away. Sylvia is still kneeling. Their hands part. They begin to sing "We'll Meet Again." During the song Johnny reverses his parchute mime from scene four and gets himself back into the cockpit of his Spitfire. They wave goodbye and the last note of "We'll Meet Again" becomes the drone of the plane's engine)

Scene Fifteen:
The Bright Star

Sylvia places her hands over her face. A voice comes over on Johnny's intercom—"Break right, Red Leader, break right, break right!" Johnny turns as directed. Then his engine and intercom stop. He freezes. Sylvia lowers her hands and reads the telegram.

SYLVIA: "Immediate. Air Ministry. Kingsway. Regret to inform you that your husband, Squadron Leader John Sutton DFC . . . " *(She clutches the telegram to her. Ginger enters)* Hello, Ginger.
GINGER: Hello, Sylvia.
(He takes the telegram from her and reads John Pudney's poem)
Do not despair
For Johnny-head-in-the-air,
He sleeps as sound
As Johnny underground.

Fetch out no shroud
For Johnny-in-the-cloud;
And keep your tears
For him in after years.

Better by far
For Johnny-the-bright-star
To keep your head
And see his children fed.

Curtain

Martin Halpern

TOTAL RECALL

Martin Halpern

Martin Halpern is the author of more than a dozen plays, as well as being a widely published poet and critic. His plays have been produced by the Circle Repertory Company and the Judson Poets' Theatre in New York; the Arena Stage, Washington, D.C.; the Image Theatre and Poets' Theatre, Cambridge; the Berkshire Theatre Festival; and a number of university theatres, including Brandeis University, where he has taught since 1965.

His poems have appeared in leading journals for over two decades, and have been collected in two volumes: *Two Sides of an Island and Other Poems* and *Selected Poems.* He also has published many articles on literature and the drama and a book-length critical study of the turn-of-the-century American poet-dramatist William Vaughn Moody.

Born in New York on October 3, 1929, Mr. Halpern grew up in the West Bronx, attended DeWitt Clinton High School, and took his B.A. and M.A. degrees in English at the University of Rochester. From 1951 to 1953, he served in the U.S. Army Signal Corps and as a broadcaster for the Armed Forces Radio Service. He then resumed his graduate studies at Harvard University, where he was a teaching fellow and received his Ph.D. in English in 1959. He taught at the University of California at Berkeley and the University of Massachusetts at Amherst before returning to the Boston area in 1965 to accept a position in the Brandeis Theatre Arts department. From 1972 to 1976 he was chairman of that department and presently is the Shulman Professor of Playwriting and Dramatic Literature.

Mr. Halpern has held both a Fulbright Scholarship and a Howard Foundation Fellowship in Writing. His plays have received awards from the Corporation for Public Broadcasting and the California Olympiad of the Arts. Besides his activities as a writer and educator, he has worked both professionally and non-professionally as a musician and actor.

Total Recall, along with its companion play, *What the Babe Said,* was presented in a showcase production at St. Clements, New York, in the spring of 1978. It is published for the first time anywhere in this anthology.

Characters:

WILFRID PORTER, *middle forties*
ELEANOR MANNING, *early thirties*

Scene:

A one-room studio apartment below Fourteenth Street in New York, shabbily furnished and very cluttered. Down right, the only window, with a threadbare easy chair and standing lamp beside it. Up left of the chair, a dresser. On the dresser a cassette tape recorder, several boxes of cassette tapes, scattered piles of paper, and a clutter of books including, prominently, a large King James Bible. Left of the dresser, a closet. Left of the closet, the front door, with a police safety lock attached. Left of the door, a kitchenette with an eating table and a sink piled high with dishes. On the eating table, a box of donuts. On the stove, a coffee pot heating up. Down left, a daybed with a small table beside it. On the small table a lamp, telephone, pad of paper, and pencil. Scattered around the apartment, a number of ashtrays, all fairly full, plus two opened cigarette packs, one opened pack of small cigars, one box of large cigars, several pipes, and a tobacco tin.

Time:

The present. Late October. About 10:15 AM

Wilfrid Porter, in pajamas and bathrobe, is putting a cassette into the recorder, puffing rapidly on a small pipe. He picks up the recording microphone, presses the "Record" buttons, taps the microphone to make sure it is on, picks up one of the sheets on the dresser, studies it a moment with a scowl, drops the paper back on the dresser, crosses to the armchair and sprawls in it, holding the microphone before his mouth. He puffs more rapidly on the pipe, finds it has gone out, scowls again, rises, tosses the pipe on the dresser, pulls a cigarette out of an open pack, lights it, inhales deeply, and sprawls back in the armchair, blowing smoke into the microphone as though intending an affront to it. He closes his eyes, sighs, opens his mouth to speak into the microphone, stops, shakes his head, scratches his hair, rubs his face as though trying to stimulate the blood, takes another puff of the cigarette, blows out the smoke, and is about to speak when the telephone rings. He tilts his head toward the telephone with a "You again?" look, sighs, rises slowly, drops the microphone on the dresser, turns off the recorder, and crosses to the small table by the daybed. He stares down at the ringing telephone another moment, then picks up the receiver.

PORTER: Yes? *(His voice brightens but his face does not)* Ah, good morning, Reverend, good morning . . . . Fine thank you, fine. And you? . . . . Good, good. *(Puffs on the cigarette while listening)* Well, I'm glad you liked it. . . . Ah, that's always good to hear. It isn't every day that one . . . *(Blows smoke into the receiver as into the microphone before)* affects other human beings. . . . Oh, yes, I got the check. Thank you. *(Sits on the daybed, listening)* Ah, yes, well I have a bit of a backlog now, but . . . Uh, when would you need it by, Reverend? . . . Mm. Well, I have two others to get off by *Thursday,* but it's possible by Friday. Would that be . . . ? Ah, good. Any particular text? *(Drops the cigarette in an ashtray, picks up the pencil from the small table, and scrawls on the pad of paper)* Nehemiah, Chapter Four, Verse Ten. Ah, yes. "And Judah said, the strength of the burden-bearers is decayed, and there is much rubbish." *(Small, "modest" laugh)* Ah, yes—yes, I suppose almost total recall. *(The doorbell rings. He calls, without turning from the receiver)* Yes? . . . Uh, excuse me a moment, Reverend. My doorbell. *(Calling more loudly)* Come in! . . . Oh sorry, I didn't mean to shout right into the phone. I'm expecting something from my typing service. *(Calling, away from the receiver)* Come on in, the door's not locked!
(The door opens slowly, part way, and Eleanor Manning— wearing an old but clean trenchcoat and shoulder purse and carrying a manila envelope and cassette box—looks in)
MRS. MANNING: Does . . . Wilfrid Porter live here?
PORTER: Who are you?

MRS. MANNING: *(More insistently)* Does Wilfrid Porter live here?

PORTER: *(Seeing the cassette box and envelope)* Ah, there they are, at last!

MRS. MANNING: *(With surprise, coupled with esteem)* You're Wilfrid Porter.

PORTER: So it seems. Well, come in, come in, I'm on the telephone.

MRS. MANNING: Oh. Excuse me.

(She enters, closing the door behind her. As Porter speaks into the telephone again, she stares rather intently at him)

PORTER: Hello? Sorry . . . , Uh, well yes, I'll do my best to have it by Friday. *(Turns his eyes to Mrs. Manning. She returns his stare briefly, then looks around at the rest of the apartment. It is not what she expected)* Yes, fine, fine . . . . Oh, no trouble at all. . . . Oh, well yes, thank *you*. . . . Bye-bye. *(Hangs up, half snuffs the cigarette out in the ashtray, and rises)*

MRS. MANNING: *(Holding the envelope and cassette box out to him)* I know this was promised yesterday . . .

PORTER: Indeed it was. *(Takes them. Tosses the cassette box onto the dresser, opens the envelope, and draws out a typescript)*

MRS. MANNING: It's not the agency's fault. I was supposed to get it into the office by four o'clock so they could deliver it to *you* by closing time. But one of my children took sick, and . . .

PORTER: *(Scanning the top page of the typescript)* Ah, too bad.

MRS. MANNING: Nothing serious as it turned out, thank heaven.

PORTER: Amen to that. *(Takes the paper clip off the typescript, flips the top page to the bottom, and scans the second page)*

MRS. MANNING: But I had to get him to the doctor, and there was a long wait, and by the time I got home to my typewriter it was past closing time. Then . . . *(Seeing his cigarette still smoking in the ashtray, crosses to it and carefully snuffs it out)* when I brought it to the agency this morning, there were no runners on hand. So I . . . volunteered to run it over to you myself.

PORTER: *(Flipping to the third page)* Well, that was good of you. You've proofread this?

MRS. MANNING: Oh, yes!

PORTER: And you're sure it's all correct?

MRS. MANNING: Quite sure. I re-read it four times last night, along with the tape.

PORTER: *(Flipping to the fourth page)* Four times? Well, you're conscientious. *(Quickly scans the rest)* Yes, it looks fine. *(Drops the typescript, without re-ordering the pages, on the dresser)* You're a very neat and, it seems, accurate typist.

MRS. MANNING: Thank you. *(Crosses to the typescript, re-orders the pages, neatens the stack, and replaces the paper clip)*

PORTER: And you take pride in your work. . . . Is it you who does all my things?

MRS. MANNING: *(Laying the typescript carefully on the dresser)* No. This is the first of *yours* they've given me.

PORTER: Well, I must see to it that they give you *more* of mine.

MRS. MANNING: Oh, I'd like that very much.

(Short pause. Then both speak at once)

   PORTER: You're not . . .

   MRS. MANNING: You see . . .

(Both smile. Porter "yields" to her with a gracious gesture)

MRS. MANNING: I was going to say . . . . Uh, is it *Doctor* Porter? Or Reverend? Or . . . ?

PORTER: Oh, Mister is quite sufficient, thank you.

MRS. MANNING: Oh. Well, I was going to say, Mr. Porter: I read this *that* many times because . . . well, because I thought it was very beautiful.

PORTER: Well! Thank you so much, Miss . . . Mrs . . . Ms . . .

MRS. MANNING: Mrs. Manning.

PORTER: Ah. Mrs. *what* Manning, if I may ask?

MRS. MANNING: Eleanor.

PORTER: Ah.

MRS. MANNING: *(Touching the cassette tape gently)* It really . . . reached me, deeply.

PORTER: Ah. *(Short pause)* Lucky you. *(Quickly, as she looks puzzled)* "When I tell any truth, it is not for the sake of convincing those who do not know it, but for the sake of defending those who do." William Blake.

MRS. MANNING: Oh. . . . Yes—yes, I understand that.

PORTER: You did "know"—that is, believe—what it says already.

MRS. MANNING: Well . . . yes.

PORTER: Otherwise, it could not have so . . . reached you.

MRS. MANNING: But you did strengthen that belief, Mr. Porter.

PORTER: Ah. Defended it, as it were.

MRS. MANNING: Yes.

(Short pause. Then both speak at once again)

   PORTER: You're not . . .

   MRS. MANNING: As a matter of . . .

(Both smile again. This time she "yields" to him with a gracious gesture)

PORTER: I was going to say: you're not a native New Yorker.

MRS. MANNING: No. I'm from Ohio.

PORTER: Ah.

MRS. MANNING: I . . . *we* . . . moved here five years ago when my . . . uh, husband was relocated.

PORTER: Ah. Your "*uh,* husband."

MRS. MANNING: You could tell from the way I speak.

PORTER: Well, that *too.* Also, few *native* females would venture, so fearlessly, into a strange man's apartment, in *this* city.

MRS. MANNING: *(Small laugh)* Oh, well, neither would *I,* ordinarily.

PORTER: Ah. That's a relief. *(Short pause)* Uh . . . you were going to say? "As a matter of . . ."?

MRS. MANNING: Oh. Well, as a matter of *fact,* I . . . wasn't entirely truthful before.

PORTER: Oh?

MRS. MANNING: There *was* a runner on hand.

PORTER: Oh!

MRS. MANNING: But I confess: I couldn't resist a chance to meet the . . . person behind the voice.

PORTER: Ah. *(Short pause)* And now that you have, you're disappointed.

MRS. MANNING: Well, what makes you . . . ?

PORTER: Coffee? *(Turns quickly toward the kitchenette)*

MRS. MANNING: Oh! Well . . . yes, thank you.

PORTER: *(Pouring coffee into a cup)* If not yet with *me*, at least with the . . . *(Gesturing at the apartment)* environment.

MRS. MANNING: Oh. Well, I'm used to clutter.

PORTER: Ah. Yes, of course. Your . . . children. *(Brings her the cup. As she takes it, he gestures more generally at what is outside the apartment)* But . . . the *surrounding* environment . . .

MRS. MANNING: Well, I confess I was a *little* surprised, and a little uneasy, in the hall and on the stairs. But . . .

PORTER: Once inside *that* door . . .

MRS. MANNING: Yes.

PORTER: The uneasiness passed.

MRS. MANNING: Of course. *(Short pause)*

PORTER: Uh . . . would you care for some cream and/or sugar in that?

MRS. MANNING: No, this is fine, thank you.

(She sips her coffee. He watches her a moment, then crosses back into the kitchenette and pours a cup for himself, dumping in two heaping teaspoons of sugar)

PORTER: I take it you're not in some rush to be somewhere else?

MRS. MANNING: Well, I do have to be *home* by *noon.* My youngest comes home from kindergarten then.

PORTER: Ah. Well, It's not even ten-thirty. *(Crossing back to her with his cup)* You live far from here?

MRS. MANNING: Just twenty minutes or so by subway.

PORTER: Well, then. . . . I, uh, never ride the subways myself. . . . In that case, perhaps you'd like to take your coat off and enjoy your coffee in comfort. *(Indicates the armchair)*

MRS. MANNING: Oh. Yes, all right.

(She lays her cup and purse on the arm of the chair and takes off her coat. She wears a plain skirt and sweater)

PORTER: How many children do you *have*, Mrs. Manning?

MRS. MANNING: *(Sits, carefully pulling down her skirt, and picks up the cup)* Three. One boy in second grade, one in first—he's the one who took sick yesterday—and a little girl in kindergarten.

PORTER: Ah. One per year.

MRS. MANNING: Yes . . . for a time.

PORTER: Ah. Yes. *(Short pause)* You're Catholic.

MRS. MANNING: Yes.

PORTER: Nevertheless, you do not wear a wedding band.

MRS. MANNING: *(Instinctively reaching for her ring finger)* Oh, you do notice things. No, I don't.

PORTER: I take it you're widowed?

MRS. MANNING: No. I'm divorced.

PORTER: Oh? Really?

MRS. MANNING: I wasn't Catholic *then.* Only *since.*

PORTER: Ah! A convert!

MRS. MANNING: Yes.

PORTER: In the . . . wake of a failed marriage, you . . .

MRS. MANNING: Yes.

PORTER: . . . sought consolation in . . .

MRS. MANNING: Yes.

PORTER: And found it.

MRS. MANNING: Yes. Yes, I did, and do.

PORTER: Mmm. *(Short pause. He picks up an open pack of cigarettes)* Cigarette?

MRS. MANNING: Thank you, I don't smoke.

PORTER: Ah. Lucky you. You don't mind if I do?

MRS. MANNING: Not if you don't.

PORTER: *(Laughing "appreciatively")* Ah, yes, I see what you mean. *(Lights the cigarette, inhaling deeply)* How long?

MRS. MANNING: Ten months.

PORTER: Since your divorce.

MRS. MANNING: No. Since I . . . completed my conversion.

PORTER: And since you . . . completed your divorce?

MRS. MANNING: Well, let's see now . . . . Nearly two years.

PORTER: *(Short pause)* I take it you get—if I'm not becoming too personal—adequate alimony?

MRS. MANNING: No, none. Not even child-support.

PORTER: None? Why not?

MRS. MANNING: I didn't want anything from him. Just my freedom, and the children.

PORTER: Ah. Lucky him. It was that bad, was it? Oh, sorry.

MRS. MANNING: That's all right. It *was* that bad.

PORTER: Alas. *(Short pause. Both sip from their coffee)* But surely, with three children and . . .

MRS. MANNING: I manage. I do take in a lot of this typing work. And my husband did leave us the apartment, rent-controlled.

PORTER: But there's much . . . scrimping and saving in that apartment? Much doing without.

MRS. MANNING: Of course.

PORTER: None of the amenities. For you *or* your children.

MRS. MANNING: Not many.

PORTER: Ah. Well, that's good for the soul.

(Pause. He stares fairly hard at her as she sips her coffee, then turns away, puts out his cigarette, drops his coffee cup on the dresser, and takes a small cigar from an open box)

MRS. MANNING: I kept . . . wondering, Mr. Porter, while I was listening to the tape, just which denomination *you* were.

PORTER: Denomination. Ah, yes. *(Lights the cigar)* Well, as a matter of fact, the same as you, Mrs. Manning.

MRS. MANNING: *(Surprised but pleased)* You are?

PORTER: Only by birth, not conversion.

MRS. MANNING: *(Indicating the Bible on the dresser)* But that isn't a Catholic Bible you have.

PORTER: Ah, you do notice things. *(Picks up the Bible)* Well, you might say, I do tend rather toward the . . . ecumenical.

(Drops the Bible) Say! Have you heard the one about this very ecumenical Catholic bishop trying to comfort his Methodist colleague? "After all," he said, "you and I both worship the same God—you in your way and I in His."

MRS. MANNING: *(Short pause. Then smiling and breaking into a pleasant laugh)* That's . . . very good! "You in . . ."

PORTER: *(Laughing with her)* "Your way . . ."

MRS. MANNING: "And I in . . ."

PORTER: "His!" *(Both laugh fairly hard for a moment. He stops first and stares at her until she gradually stops)* Yes, Mrs. Manning, I may be a renegade, but a renegade from the *true* Church.

MRS. MANNING: A renegade?

PORTER: Alas, yes.

MRS. MANNING: In the sense that . . . you no longer . . . ?
You're . . . lapsed?

PORTER: Lapsed. Yes, I think that's just the word. Lapsed,
yes.

MRS. MANNING: But . . . why?

PORTER: I'm allergic to incense. *(As she looks at him dubiously)* Uh, that was also a little joke.

MRS. MANNING: *(With a touch of annoyance)* Well then, what
church *are* you affiliated with now?

PORTER: Affiliated with? Well, you might say, whichever is
applicable at the moment.

MRS. MANNING: I'm afraid I don't understand that.

PORTER: Mm. No, of course not. *(Snuffs out the cigar and
turns to her)* You see, Mrs. Manning, I am, as it were, a scribe.
A scribe *and* something of a Pharisee to boot. But by *profession*
the former. You see . . . *(Picks up the cassette tape she brought)*
This sermon you were kind enough to read four times last
night—on sainthood and the beauty of self-sacrifice?—is of
the high Episcopal denomination. For a very charming minister in Connecticut. *(Drops the cassette and picks up another one
from the dresser)* The one before that—which someone else at
your agency typed, and has already been mailed off—was
rather low Unitarian. Brooklyn. Just as you came in . . .
*(Drops the tape, crosses to the small table, and holds up the pad of
paper)* I was taking an order for a sort of middle Presbyterian
sermon. Staten Island. *(Drops the pad)* All *very* ecumenical, as
you see.

MRS. MANNING: You mean you're . . .

PORTER: A scribe. Or, in the parlance of today, a ghost
writer.

MRS. MANNING: I see.

PORTER: You're shocked.

MRS. MANNING: Well, I . . . confess I never knew there *was*
such a thing.

PORTER: But of course there is! Surely you realize how
busy men of the cloth are nowadays. Caring for their flocks,
fighting for political and social causes, fund raising? You can't
expect very many of them to compose a whole, new, original,
effective sermon every week in addition.

MRS. MANNING: No. I suppose that's true. *(Short pause)* You—uh—do this . . . full time?

PORTER: *(Picking up a pipe and stuffing tobacco into it)* Oh, yes. *More* than full time since my second divorce.

MRS. MANNING: You've been divorced *twice?*

PORTER: That's right. Two times. And heavy—I might say monstrous—alimony, as well as child-support, in both settlements. Two children by the first disaster, one by the second. My wives, of course, got custody. *(Lights the pipe)* At all events, this has fed them and my children and kept this modest roof over *my* head. Once, I had *other* literary ambitions—poet, novelist, all that, you know. But not really worth the struggle. *You* know: "the critics' contumely, the editors' delay," and all that. I—uh—parody *Hamlet. (Puffs on the pipe, finds it has gone out, throws it down with a touch of self-rage, and turns to her)* Well, now you know, Mrs. Manning. And I trust you *are* sufficiently shocked, disappointed . . . and uneasy.

MRS. MANNING: I do not judge other people, Mr. Porter. Lest I be judged.

PORTER: Ah! Mm! Yes, that was nicely put. Very nicely put.

MRS. MANNING: *(Rises, crosses to the dresser, and picks up the typescript she brought)* Besides, just because you wrote this sermon for someone else to speak, and for pay, doesn't make it any less . . . true, and beautiful.

PORTER: Oh, it doesn't, does it?

MRS. MANNING: Of course not!

PORTER: Well, suppose I told you that to *me* there is neither truth nor beauty nor anything in that document but a routine job done, as quickly, as efficiently, as mechanically as possible. By rote, right off the top of my . . .

MRS. MANNING: If you did tell me that, I wouldn't believe you.

PORTER: You . . . ? Well, I like *that!*

MRS. MANNING: Remember: it wasn't just your *words* I heard last night, but your *voice. I* could feel how much you meant, and felt, what you were saying. There were tears in your voice . . .

PORTER: *"Tears* in my *voice"?* Good God!

MRS. MANNING: *(Firmly)* And in my eyes as I listened. All four times.

PORTER: *(Starts to expostulate, but is at a loss for words. Then grudgingly)* Well, all *right!* Of *course* once I get *into* something, once the . . . Muse is warmed up and . . . lubricated as it were, a *kind* of fake passion does sort of rise up in me sometimes . . .

MRS. MANNING: Oh, how easy it is to be cynical, Mr. Porter.

PORTER: What?! *Easy* to . . . ?

MRS. MANNING: *I used* to be that way.

PORTER: How dare you? How dare you patronize me?

MRS. MANNING: Oh, no, I wasn't. Believe me . . .

PORTER: Yes, you were! What do *you* know of *me* anyway? What do *you* know of what's easy or hard for me? You come marching in that door there with your phony story about a sick child and no runners on hand, and in no time at all you're telling *me* what *I'm* like!

MRS. MANNING: I'm sorry if I offended you. I didn't mean to.

PORTER: Well, you have! And now, if you've finished your coffee, I'm sure you have better things to do with your morning than patronizing *me.* Surely you have some shopping to do? Cothes to wash? Floors to scrub? Another typing job? Some . . . rendez-vous?

MRS. MANNING: *(Regretfully)* Well . . . I suppose *you* must have work to do . . .

PORTER: That's right. Some rush orders here.

MRS. MANNING: *(Picking up her coat and purse)* Well . . . thank you for the coffee, Mr. Porter. And for last night.

PORTER: *(Exaggeratedly ironic)* Oh, last night was *my* pleasure . . . Eleanor.

MRS. MANNING: I do hope you'll still see to it that *I* get to type your sermons.

PORTER: Oh, by all means. You *are,* as I said, a very efficient typist. And I'm sure you could use the cash.

MRS. MANNING: Yes, that *too.* Well . . . goodbye then. And . . . thank you again . . . *(Starts for the door)*

PORTER: Uh . . . just a minute.

MRS. MANNING: Yes?

PORTER: I just got a . . . notion.

MRS. MANNING: Yes?

PORTER: *(Short pause)* But I don't suppose you take shorthand.

MRS. MANNING: I'm a fully trained stenographer.

PORTER: Oh, you are? Well, in that case, perhaps you'd like to stay and take some direct dictation.

MRS. MANNING: Oh! Well, I . . .

PORTER: *(Picking up the sheet of paper he had been looking at when the play began)* I can speak this order to *you* instead of the machine. Show you how I do it, how I just knock these things off. You'll have a chance to see a real live hack at work. Then you can take it all home to type and I'll pay you direct, for both jobs. You'll make twice what that exploiting agency pays you.

MRS. MANNING: Well, I'd certainly like that. But . . . *(Looking at her watch)* do you think there's time? I do have to be home by noon. That means I'd have to leave *here* by eleven-forty at the latest. Would that give us enough time to . . . ?

PORTER: Of course! I've been known to knock off a whole hour-long sermon in less that *half* an hour. You'll see: once that Muse is warmed up and lubricated, it just comes gushing out. Well, are you game, Mrs. Manning?

MRS. MANNING: *(Short pause)* Yes!

PORTER: Good!

MRS. MANNING: And it's not just for the money, Mr. Porter. I still say, no one can just "knock off" something like . . . *(Picking up the cassette she brought)* this.

PORTER: Ah! A little challenge as it were! All *right!* Now . . . *(Crosses quickly to the small table, picks up the pencil and the pad, and tears the top sheet off the pad)* Here's a clean pad and pencil, and you can sit right here. *(Pulls the small table around in front of the daybed and lays the pad and pencil on it)* This will be your desk. Let me have your coat. The bathroom is just down the hall, by the way.

MRS. MANNING: I don't need a bathroom.

PORTER: Ah. Good. . . . Never?

MRS. MANNING: *(Ignores this, laying the cassette back on the dresser, crossing to the daybed, dropping her coat and purse on a corner of it, sitting behind the small table, and picking up the pencil)* I'm ready, Mr. Porter.

PORTER: More coffee?

MRS. MANNING: No, thanks. I think we should get right to work.

PORTER: It's all right. I'm paying you for every minute since you stepped through that door, coffee breaks included. *(Crosses with her cup into the kitchenette, fills it, crosses back to her, and lays the cup down next to the writing pad)* How about a donut? I have some . . .

MRS. MANNING: No, thank you.

PORTER: Ah, calories, is it? Well, then . . . *(With a clap of the hands)* to work. *(Takes the sheet of paper from the dresser again and scans it)* Mm. Yes. Next order, due Thursday. Congregationalist minister, New Jersey. Sermon on Matthew 12, verses 38 and 39. *(Drops the sheet, clasps his hands behind his back, and quotes)* "Then certain of the scribes and of the Pharisees answered saying, Master, we would see a sign from thee. But he answered and said unto them, An evil and adulterous generation seeketh after a sign; and there shall no sign be given to it."

MRS. MANNING: You know all that by heart?

PORTER: Oh, yes. Almost total recall when it comes to Scripture.

MRS. MANNING: That's very impressive.

PORTER: *(Picks up another pipe and stuffs tobacco into it)* Well, I *was* raised on this stuff. Rather deeply into it for a period, too, before I . . . lapsed. *(Lights the pipe)* I did have this college classmate, though, who later became pastor of some Lutheran church in Westchester. Phoned one day and asked if I'd help him out on a big sermon he had to give. I obliged. In fact, I ended up writing the whole thing *for* him. It went over so big he started paying me to do this regularly, and passed my name on to others with similar needs. Before too long, this labor had completely displaced pornography.

MRS. MANNING: Pornography?

PORTER: Oh, yes, I used to write *that* too—for the income. But the wages were shockingly low—at least compared to *this* labor. Apart from that, though, the two are not so far removed, are they? Both, after all, require an indulgence in, shall we say, unfettered fantasy with as little concern as possible for the reality principle? Eh, Mrs. Manning?

MRS. MANNING: I know that you . . . *think* you believe that, Mr. Porter.

PORTER: Ah. "Think?" Only "think" I do, hm? *(They stare at each other a moment. He averts his gaze first)* Well, now! The scribes *and* the Pharisees, hm? *(Walks around, pondering)* Mmm. Hmm. *(Draws deeply on the pipe)* Hmmmmm. *(Drops the pipe on the dresser and lights another small cigar)* Mmm . . . Not sure I'm quite up to faking *that* one this morning. *(Picks up the sheet of paper, scans it again, and tosses it away)* Mmm. Never *could* warm fast to *that* item. They asked Jesus for a sign—any little old supernatural demonstration—just so they'd *know*. And he turned them down flat.

MRS. MANNING: Of course. They were hypocrites. They'd hardened their hearts to any *real* faith.

PORTER: Ah! *Brava*, Mrs. Manning! You're pretty up on all this yourself.

MRS. MANNING: Well, I may not have your total recall, but I *have* come to know my Gospels pretty well.

PORTER: Now *I'm* the one who is impressed. *(Draws on the cigar and blows out the smoke slowly)* Then you know that to his *apostles* he gave *oodles* of signs. Or so it is written. Turning water to wine, walking on the waves, dragging poor Lazarus back from the dead, et cetera. *They* didn't *have* to believe out of mere *faith*, did they?

MRS. MANNING: They had that already. Otherwise they wouldn't have *been* apostles.

PORTER: So then these signs were merely a means of strengthening that faith—defending it as it were.

MRS. MANNING: Yes.

PORTER: Nevertheless, *they* are the ones who denied and betrayed him! The apostles!

MRS. MANNING: Oh, but Judas *wasn't* a *true* apostle . . .

PORTER: I refer not merely to Judas, my dear, but even—yea, even to Peter himself! Peter, the dearest of his apostles, who got to see all those miracles with his own eyes! Why, he even got to walk on those waves him*self*! Yet in the end, when the going got tough, he, Peter, denied the maker of those miracles no less than three times in one night!

MRS. MANNING: *(Short pause)* The flesh is weak, Mr. Porter. Peter was only a man.

PORTER: You mean, as distinguished from . . . a woman?

MRS. MANNING: No, of course not. I meant, as distinguished from . . . Him.

PORTER: Ah. Yes, yes. From *Him*. *(Draws on the cigar)* Yet this same weak Peter, it is written, was chosen, *by* Him, to be the rock on which His Church would be built. While those poor maligned scribes and Pharisees, who merely asked, quite politely . . . *(Snuffs the cigar out in an ashtray)* Ah, well, it does seem a bit unfair, if you ask *me*. *(Turns quickly back to her)* Do such enigmas never trouble *you* . . . Eleanor?

MRS. MANNING: If you can't "warm fast" to *that* item, Mr. Porter, maybe you can try another.

PORTER: No, of course not. With three children to raise, without even any alimony, you can't exactly *afford* to be so troubled any more, can you?

MRS. MANNING: *(Looking at her watch)* Time *is* short. You were going to show me how easily you . . .

PORTER: All right, okay, okay! I *will* do another one! *(Picks up the sheet of paper again)* No, this one even *I* can't fake. Think I'll just send it back and tell him so. *(Starts to throw the sheet down, then turns and holds it out to her)* Or perhaps I'll turn it over to *you*. *You* seem to . . .

MRS. MANNING: *(With a small laugh)* Oh *you're* the "hack writer," not *I*.

PORTER: Mm. Hmmm. *(Throws down the sheet and picks another one off the dresser)* All right, okay, let's try this one. *(Scans the sheet)* Ah, yes, this should come very easily. First Book of Genesis. "Stress verses 25 to 27, on the creation of man." Also due Thursday. For a rabbi in Great Neck. You ready?

MRS. MANNING: *(Poising the pencil over the pad)* Ready.

PORTER: *(Scanning the sheet again)* Mm . . . let's see. "Stress

man as apex of creative miracle." Uh-huh. "Consciousness.
Freedom to choose between good and evil." Yes . . . uh-huh.
(Tosses the sheet aside) This should come in record time. Let's see
. . . *(Gestures for her to begin writing)* Uh . . . "Dearly beloved"
. . . . Uh, no, I don't suppose that's the style of opening. Uh
. . . "Brothers and sisters" . . . . No, no. I've never done one
for a rabbi before. Must check into how they start off. Well, for
now we'll let *him* supply the salutation. Right into the body of
the thing! *(Walks around, stops, turns, raises a finger, and gestures
for her to write)* "Consider the . . ." Uh, make that . . . "Imagine the . . . " "Imagine . . . the . . . " Mmmm . . . *(Walks
around some more, pondering; then stops near the kitchenette table)*
I'm hungry. Sure you wouldn't like a donut?

MRS. MANNING: No, thank you.

PORTER: Come! Let us, as it were, break bread together.
(Holds up the donut box) All kinds and shapes in here.

MRS. MANNING: All right, half of one.

PORTER: Good! *(Opens the box)* Plain, cinnamon, jelly, black
raspberry, or crumb?

MRS. MANNING: Plain.

PORTER: Plain it shall be. *(Takes out a plain donut, holds it
aloft, and intones as he breaks it in half)* Hoc est corpus meum, quod
pro vobis . . .

MRS. MANNING: *(Rises; reprimanding but not angrily)* Mr.
Porter!

PORTER: Oh, sorry. I thought, what with the services in
English nowadays, you wouldn't . . .

MRS. MANNING: It's so easy to blaspheme, Mr. Porter.

PORTER: Ah, *that* tune again. *So* easy! *(He crosses to her with
half a donut in each hand and holds one half out to her)*

MRS. MANNING: Yes, it is. *(She takes her half, drops it on the
small table, and starts to sit again)*

PORTER: Oh, you mustn't cast that away. We have broken
bread together, and this sacred act must be consummated. A
human communion, as it were—with a small "c", of course.
*(She looks at him a moment, then smiles, picks up her half donut, holds
it out to him as in a toast, and takes a bite)* Good, hm? *(He gobbles
his half in one bite)*

MRS. MANNING: *(Lays the rest of her half on the small table, sits, and picks up her pencil)* Now, where were we? *(Reads from the pad, with pointed irony)* "Imagine . . . the."

PORTER: Yes. Well . . . make that . . . *"Let* us imagine." *(Crosses to the dresser as she makes the change, lays his hands on its corners as at a pulpit, and addresses an imaginary congregation offstage)* "Let us imagine on this Sabbath morning . . ." *(Turns his head to make sure she is writing; then turns back to the "congregation")* ". . . that last in the acts of divine creation. Conceive if you can . . ." *(Turns back to her with a laugh)* No, no, cross that out. Sounds like Gilbert and Sullivan. *(Sings, with a parody of Gilbert and Sullivan movements)* "Conceive me if you can/A commonplace young man/A steady and stolidly/Jolly bank holiday/Ev-er-yday young man." *(Takes a very large cigar out of a box on the dresser)* You don't mind if I smoke one of *these,* do you?

MRS. MANNING: No.

PORTER: You're sure?

MRS. MANNING: My husband smoked them. I'm used to . . .

PORTER: Oh, well, in that case . . . *(Drops the cigar like a hot potato)* I wouldn't want to remind you of *him.*

MRS. MANNING: It's all right!

PORTER: Ah, well . . . thank you. *(Picks up the cigar and starts to light it)*

MRS. MANNING: You're not doing very well, are you?

PORTER: Oh, I'm always a slow *starter. (Finishes lighting the cigar, blows out the match, and tosses it away)* All right, here I go! Ready? *(She poises the pencil. He takes a breath and starts dictating rapidly)* "Conceive what it means to have created, out of nothingness, out of pure void, a sun, moon, stars on the firmament . . ." Uh, that's f-i-r . . .

MRS. MANNING: I know.

PORTER: ". . . stars on the firmament, fish in the sea, and all manner of beasts on the dry land; and then, as the culmination of all that, at the apex, a *conscious* being, *man,* capable of contemplating his own existence and choosing freely—freely, mind you—between good and evil . . ."

MRS. MANNING: You're going a bit too fast.

PORTER: Ah! There, you see?

MRS. MANNING: Oh, yes, the *speed* is there, but otherwise I could hardly compare it to *that*. *(Indicating the cassette she brought)*

PORTER: Well, give me a chance! Where did I lose you?

MRS. MANNING: At the apex.

PORTER: Ah, yes. "At the apex, a *breed* of conscious beings, male *and* female, who . . . a breed of *conscious* beings, male and female, who . . . who . . ." *(Sighs, puffs on the cigar a few times, lays it in an ashtray, and turns to her)* It must be you. Can't seem to pick up any momentum.

MRS. MANNING: Maybe it's because you don't *feel* any of this the way you . . .

PORTER: It's got nothing to do with feeling! It's you. You're . . . making me self-conscious.

MRS. MANNING: Oh. *(Short pause; reluctantly)* Well, then, I suppose you want me to leave . . .

PORTER: No! I mean, I'll get used to you, I'll adjust. Even you're better company than that machine.

MRS. MANNING: Well, thank you.

PORTER: I admit, it does get to be a bore having only it to talk to fifteen, sixteen hours a day.

MRS. MANNING: Oh, you don't work *that* much.

PORTER: Yes, I do. Quite often. My wives, and children, are very voracious. *(Takes a cigarette out of an open pack and lights it)* Besides, I'm not much of a sleeper. Four or five hours is all the oblivion I can expect on the *best* night.

MRS. MANNING: *(Short pause; slyly)* Lucky you.

PORTER: Lucky?!

MRS. MANNING: It gives you that many more hours to . . .

PORTER: Endure—yes. *(Snuffs the cigarette out and turns abruptly to her)* Did I tell you why I never ride the subways any more?

MRS. MANNING: No.

PORTER: It's this very interesting nightmare I have, often, when I do sleep. But I don't suppose you'd want to hear about it.

MRS. MANNING: *(Indicating the pad and pencil)* Well . . .

PORTER: *(Plunges right into it, with a sudden intensity)* I'm in this subway car, see? Rush hour. I'm packed in on all sides by people bigger and taller than me. Can't see beyond all those backs and bellies and buttocks. Then all of a sudden the train stops—just stops—in the middle of a one-track tunnel. And everyone just stands there waiting—for somebody out there to get things going again. You get the picture? All of us waiting for that little lurch, that motion underneath, back toward fresh air, sunlight . . . . But it doesn't come. The train never lurches, you see. We're all in that one-track tunnel forever, slowly suffocating. And the worst of it is, you see, that I know there'll be no end to it, the suffocating. It will just go on and on and on, because none of us, you see, can ever even die. *(Short pause)* Then I wake up. It's like that every time. *(Short pause)* And you know what? You're the only person I've ever . . . shared this dream with.

MRS. MANNING: *(Pause; affected but keeping her distance)* Something like that *happened,* a few years ago.

PORTER: *(Feeling this distance and resenting it)* Yes. In "real life," I know. Except *they* finally got *out.* *(He crosses abruptly into the kitchenette)*

MRS. MANNING: It's probably why you dream it though.

PORTER: *(With his back to her, takes a liquor bottle out of a cabinet and pours a fairly large shot into a glass)* Yes. No doubt. Not very original, my unconscious. *(Swigs down the shot and pours another)* But all the more reason not to go near a subway. It could happen again, *in* real life.

MRS. MANNING: *(Seeing this, rises)* Uh . . . I wish you wouldn't do that.

PORTER: What? Oh, this. You're a teetotaler, too?

MRS. MANNING: No. I just . . .

PORTER: Oh, nothing to worry about. Just a little, as the Irish say, lubrication. Not for *me.* For the Muse. *(Holds the bottle out toward her)* Can I offer you some?

MRS. MANNING: No.

PORTER: *(Puts down the bottle, starts to drink from the glass, stops, looks at her; then pours the drink back into the bottle)* There. *(Plunks the bottle back in the cabinet and turns back to her)* Tell me about your husband, Mrs. Manning.

MRS. MANNING: *(Sits again)* Oh, we're not here to talk about *him*.

PORTER: Are you intending to marry again?

MRS. MANNING: Or about *me*. Now . . . *(She picks up the pencil and pad)*

PORTER: But he was obviously a lemon. And you're still an attractive woman. Are there . . . men in your life, apart from "Him"?

MRS. MANNING: Please, can we get back to work?

PORTER: But really, Mrs. Manning, one does have one's erotic needs! . . . Or does one?

MRS. MANNING: *(Rises and picks up her coat)* I guess I'd better go.

PORTER: Why? What's the matter?

MRS. MANNING: If you're not going to dictate any more . . . *(She starts to put on the coat)*

PORTER: Of course I am—right now! The Muse is lubricated. Now take that thing off . . . *(He tries to get the coat off her)*

MRS. MANNING: *(Turning on him)* Don't!

PORTER: What?

MRS. MANNING: Touch me! Please don't do that.

PORTER: I was only . . . . Look, will you get that thing off and sit down so we can get to work? I'm paying you twice what that agency pays, and time is short!

MRS. MANNING: You . . . promise you *will* dictate?

PORTER: Yes! Right now! Now hurry, before I lose it! I feel a good one coming! *(Pulls back the small table and gestures at her place on the daybed. She, after a moment's hesitation, takes off her coat)* Good. Now come, sit. Ready your pencil. No more conversation. No more personal interruptions. The Muse is ready. Sit! *(She looks at him a moment, then drops the coat on the daybed and sits)* There, that's better. Now! *(Indicates the pad and pencil. She picks them up. He walks away, stops short, and lifts his index finger)* "And so." Yes, write that. "And so."

MRS. MANNING: *(Pointing to what he has already dictated)* What about all this?

PORTER: Cross all that out. I'm starting fresh.

(She tears the top sheet off the pad, crumples it up, lays it beside her, and writes on the fresh sheet)

MRS. MANNING: "And so."

PORTER: "And so." I know, it's kind of starting midway, but we'll get an opening later. "And so . . ." *(Hand to his head, thinking)* I had something . . . just a minute . . . something honest . . . truthful. "And so." What was it now? . . . . Yes! Yes, ready! Go! "And so on the sixth day He called us all together again . . ." That's a capital "h" on "He."

MRS. MANNING: Yes . . . but "us"?

PORTER: No, no capital on "us." "So on the sixth day He called us all together again, to reveal this truly . . . culminating idea He had. For He was so taken with how all the rest had turned out: the firmament, the stars, the fish and reptiles and mammals, especially that astonishing Leviathan . . . . Oh, looking around us at all that, we, too, were mightily awed, and from every pore exuded loud hosannahs!"

MRS. MANNING: *(Taken with the last phrase)* Mmm!

PORTER: That's h-o-s-a . . .

MRS. MANNING: I know!

PORTER: "But He was still unsatisfied. So right then and there He springs it on us: the last and greatest act, a human race, a race of *conscious* creatures, with, of all things—of *all things—freedom,* to choose, choose, *choose,* between . . . living and dying!" *(She stops writing and looks questioningly at him)* "Well, of course I warned Him against it." "Well, of course I warned Him against it!" That's the next sentence! Get it down!

MRS. MANNING: Good and evil.

PORTER: What?

MRS. MANNING: Freedom to choose between good and evil. That's what . . .

PORTER: What are you babbling about?

MRS. MANNING: The . . . assignment. It said freedom to choose between good and evil, not living and dying . . .

PORTER: Never mind! Who's writing this, you or I? Just get it down!

MRS. MANNING: *(Sighs)* All right. *(Writes)* ". . . choose between living and dying."

PORTER: "Well, of course I warned Him against it. I said to

Him: Lord, look at your—at *thy*—handiwork already complete! *(Envisioning what he describes, his voice gradually gaining eloquence and passion)* The heavenly bodies in their ordered courses on the firmament, shedding light and loveliness on the dry land and the waters between, where all those magnificently varied creatures, from the lowly jellyfish up to Leviathan himself, move in the ordered bliss of instinct—seek food, shun foes, and failing, perish; but perish *into nature,* reveling in life and knowing not of death except in the moment of transfiguration from animate to inanimate parts of the whole! Lord, I said, what more is needed? How perfect and wondrous this work of creation!" *(Stops, almost embarrassed, and turns to her)* How's that?

MRS. MANNING: Rather good—those last few sentences. But who is "I"?

PORTER: I! Me! Never mind! Just write! "Lord, I said, what more is needed? How perfect and wondrous this work of creation! Lord, don't spoil it! Know when to stop! Know when enough is enough! But He wouldn't listen! He just waved me away and held the others off and stood there vibrating, with this far off, glassy, *stoned* look in his eyes, and said: Let us make Man in our image . . ."

MRS. MANNING: *(Dropping the pencil)* Now that's blasphemy!

PORTER: Never mind! Write, damn it, write! *(Strikes a pose and intones, thunderingly)* "Let us make Man in our image, after our likeness, and let them have dominion over the fish of the sea, and over the fowl of the air . . . *(She rises)* . . . and over the cattle, and over all the earth, and over every creeping thing that creepeth upon the earth! And God saw everything that He had made, and behold, it was very good!"

(Whirling around to face her) But it wasn't good! Anyone with eyes to see could see that! You're not getting this down, damn you! *(She starts backing slowly away from him. He advances on her)* And I begged him, *begged* him to destroy this aberration, this monster He called man, *and* woman! Destroy them or we'll revolt and cast you down and do the job ourselves . . . !

MRS. MANNING: Mr. Porter . . . please . . . you're frightening me!

PORTER: *(Eye to eye with her, backing her to the wall)* But He just stared me down, with that serene, superior, patronizing look on His face, that holier-than-thou, I-believe-and-am-se-cure-and-you're-just-a-cynical-mixed-up-blaspheming-angel look, that made me want to . . . want to just . . . just . . . !

(He suddenly reaches out and starts to choke her. She screams loudly and tears his hands from her throat. He pulls back, and both stand staring aghast at the other for a long moment. Then she breaks for the door. He breaks too, beating her there, and stands with his back against the door and his arms outstretched)

MRS. MANNING: Let me out!

PORTER: *(Dazedly)* Why? I was only . . .

MRS. MANNING: Please let me out!!

PORTER: I was only . . . illustrating. I got a little . . . carried away . . .

MRS. MANNING: I've got to get out of here! Now please!

PORTER: But it's not eleven-forty. You agreed to . . .

MRS. MANNING: I know I did! *(Grabs her coat and purse)* Now let me get by, Mr. Porter, or I'll . . . I'll . . .

PORTER: Yes? You'll . . . ?

MRS. MANNING: *(Feebly)* I'll scream.

PORTER: You just did. Didn't get much response though, did you? Except from *me. (Gesturing out the door at the rest of the building)* All junkies, lushes, or simple everyday zombies who wouldn't stir if you screamed till midnight. There's *Man* for you—that wondrous miracle of the sixth day. *(He takes a key from his bathrobe pocket and locks the safety lock)*

MRS. MANNING: Please!! I must get home to my children!

PORTER: They're not there yet, Eleanor. Now . . . *(Drops the key into his bathrobe pocket and gestures at the daybed)* won't you be seated again.

MRS. MANNING: What are you going to . . . ?

PORTER: *(Gestures at the armchair)* Perhaps you'd prefer to sit *there.*

MRS. MANNING: I can't take any more of your . . . dictation . . .

PORTER: Oh, dictation's done. You've won, Eleanor. I *couldn't* fake it, not in your . . . presence.

MRS. MANNING: Then what are you going to do?

PORTER: Please be seated, Eleanor!

MRS. MANNING: *(Backing away toward the armchair, covering her body with her hands)* What are you going to do?!

PORTER: Oh now, now, Eleanor. You didn't think that I—I, who told you so movingly last night how every act of true self-sacrifice partakes of and enhances the divine—would . . . take a woman against her will? Did you?

MRS. MANNING: No, I . . . I didn't.

PORTER: Didn't. But now you do.

MRS. MANNING: I don't know!

PORTER: But I thought you knew all about me—what comes easy, what comes hard, what I mean and don't mean, feel and don't feel . . .

MRS. MANNING: *(An outcry)* I don't know anything any more!!

PORTER: A-ah.

MRS. MANNING: I don't know where I . . . am any more.

PORTER: Ah. Like me, eh, Eleanor? *(Short pause. Gently)* Come. Sit.

MRS. MANNING: Why? What do you want from me?

PORTER: Well, shall we say, at least a little further communion. With a very small "c". Just till eleven-forty. Sit, Eleanor. *(She stares at him a moment, then looks quickly at her watch, and sits on the edge of the armchair)*

PORTER: Good. *(Crosses to the small table, picks up her partly eaten donut, and breaks it in half)* I've broken bread again. *(Crosses to her, holding out one of the pieces)* Let us eat together. *(Tries to place the piece between her lips, but she keeps them closed)* Take it, Eleanor. *(Continues to try pressing the piece into her mouth)* Take it.

MRS. MANNING: *(Takes the piece out of his hand)* Mr. Porter, how can there be any kind of . . . communion with that door locked and that key in your pocket?

PORTER: *(Short pause)* You have a point, Eleanor.

MRS. MANNING: You *want* me to believe you won't . . . touch me against my will?

PORTER: Yes.

MRS. MANNING: Then trust *me*. Till eleven-forty.

PORTER: Trust you?

MRS. MANNING: Not to try and . . . escape.

PORTER: Ah. And to . . . commune, honestly?

MRS. MANNING: *(Short pause)* As honestly as I'm . . . able.

PORTER: All right then. Fair enough, Eleanor. *(Crosses quickly to the door and unlocks the safety lock; then tosses the key on the dresser)*

There! *(Crosses back to her and holds out his half donut as in a toast. She slowly holds up her half. Both put their pieces in their mouths as the telephone rings. Porter looks at the telephone, then at her, swallows his piece, crosses the telephone and, purposefully turning his back on her, picks up the receiver)* Yes? . . . Oh, Father Doyle! . . . Yes, yes, can you—uh—call back later, Father? I'm in the middle of something. . . . Eleven-forty. . . . No, I *can't* take an order now. Not till eleven-forty. All right? Good. Thank you for calling. *(Hangs up and turns back to her, with a small smile of gratification that she has not moved; then, gesturing at the telephone, almost apologetically)* One of my steadiest clients.

MRS. MANNING: *(Abashed but trying to cover it)* Well, you *said* you were . . . ecumenical.

PORTER: *(Smiling)* Yes. *(Short pause; then with a clap of the hands)* Well! Where shall we begin? Where were we before I got so carried away? Ah, yes: erotic needs, wasn't it? *(Crosses to the small table, clears everything off it, and sits)* Now then: tell me, Eleanor, in the almost two years of your husbandlessness, how often have you had . . . physical relations with members of my sex? . . . Well, *about* how often? A rough calculation will do.

MRS. MANNING: *(Short pause; matter-of-factly)* I have had *no* physical relations with members of your sex.

PORTER: None? In almost two years? You're certain of that?

MRS. MANNING: There are some things it's easy to be certain of.

PORTER: Yes. *Some* things. Well, I believe you. How often, then, with members of *your* sex?

MRS. MANNING: Come now, Mr. Porter.

PORTER: Come now, Mrs. *Manning.* An honest communion.

MRS. MANNING: I have not had physical relations with members of your sex, or mine, Mr. Porter, since . . . *(She hesitates)*

PORTER: Yes? Since?

MRS. MANNING: Since . . . well before my husband left.

PORTER: Ah! *Well* before! Approximately how *long* before, Eleanor?

MRS. MANNING: About a year.

PORTER: Ah! So that was the problem, was it? Poor hubby. Perhaps he wasn't such a lemon after all. Only driven, as it were, by your indifference to, perhaps your downright revulsion *at,* the duties of the bedchamber, to his . . . harlots and concubines? Eh, Eleanor? Poor, *maligned* hubby: I apologize for having wronged you. For I myself was often so driven. And of course, *now* these harlots—I could hardly call any of *mine* concubines—*now* these hard-eyed street harlots are my *only* resort. I confess, it does shame me, and I can really ill afford even them. But the flesh of a *man* is, alas, weak.

MRS. MANNING: *(Short pause; simply)* I think you have bit too much self-pity, Mr. Porter.

PORTER: Ye-es! You've seen that, have you, Eleanor, at last? That the "person behind the voice" is a mere morass of self-pity. *That's* where those "tears in his voice" came from, wasn't it?

MRS. MANNING: I didn't say that . . .

PORTER: After all, think of you, struggling alone, by the sweat of your brow. . . . And yet *you* don't feel sorry for yourself, do you?

MRS. MANNING: I at least . . . try not to . . .

PORTER: Yes, and successfully, too. For after all, you *now* have your belief. Your construct. Your consolation.

MRS. MANNING: *(Almost a shout, but more of protest than conviction)* Yes!

PORTER: Of course. Lucky you. And of course, your *fleshly* wants are so . . . feeble. Eh, Eleanor?

MRS. MANNING: Not really.

PORTER: No? Not feeble? Non-existent then.

MRS. MANNING: Oh, hardly that.

PORTER: Oh?

MRS. MANNING: You see, you have it all wrong, Mr. Porter. What . . . drove my husband and me apart was not problems of the flesh, but of the spirit.

PORTER: Of the . . . ?

MRS. MANNING: I am not, Mr. Porter, and never *have* been, a . . . frigid woman.

PORTER: You're not? Then . . . you mean . . . you mean you're telling me, all this self-denial, this self-deprivation, is *real? (Reaches out to touch her hands)* How I have wronged *you*, Eleanor.

MRS. MANNING: *(Pulling her hands back)* Don't! Please.

PORTER: But—in that case—how have you had the strength? Two years—no, *three*—without the solace of another's flesh, male *or* female?

MRS. MANNING: It *is* possible. Many . . . manage it, male *and* female.

PORTER: Yes—many without fleshly wants! But . . .

MRS. MANNING: And many with. There *are* . . . consolations. For *some*.

PORTER: Consolations. Ah. You mean . . . those of . . . one's *own* flesh. *(She flushes and stiffens slightly)* Ah! Have I . . . touched on something, Eleanor? I have, haven't I? *(Moves in closer to her; putting on pressure, but gently)* How often, Eleanor? How many times per month? Or week? Or day? A rough calculation will do. How often, Eleanor?

MRS. MANNING: *(Looks quickly at her watch, fighting back tears)* It's eleven-forty . . .

PORTER: *(Looks quickly at his own watch)* No. Not yet. Your watch must be fast, Eleanor. I *have* touched on something, haven't I? The secret guilt, the secret shame, of the woman behind the ears that listened and the fingers that . . . typed? Eh, Eleanor? For I'll bet—oh, I'll *bet*—you don't yet . . . report this to your confessors, do you? Do you, Eleanor?

MRS. MANNING: *(Short pause)* No. Not . . . yet . . . . *(She begins to weep)*

PORTER: *(Short pause; very gently)* Ah, I understand. Some secrets are hard to share, aren't they? Even with Him. *Especially* with Him. But now you *have* shared it, haven't you? With *me*.

And it does feel better now, doesn't it? For *I* do not judge you, Eleanor. I absolve you, completely, without even admonitions to desist from this . . . self-abuse. For *I* understand—*I* do, anyway, even if He doesn't!—what it means to be a . . . person enduring without benefit of any *true*. . . . *intra*-personal love life.

MRS. MANNING: *(Has stopped weeping; in control of herself again)* Oh, but I do have that. I have my children.

PORTER: Ah. Of course. And they you. Lucky you. *(Short pause; with ardor)* Lucky *them*. *(Short pause)* But why, Eleanor? Why no *other* love life? Surely you're not one of those who *prefer* their own flesh over . . . . There *are* those, I know. But surely not *you*. Why then? Why?

MRS. MANNING: Well, if you must know . . .

PORTER: Yes, I must! I must!

MRS. MANNING: *(Short pause)* Well, you see, I *have* thought that—once the children are grown up and on ther own—I *have* thought that I might . . . *(She hesitates)*

PORTER: Yes? That you might . . . ?

MRS. MANNING: *(Weakly)* Try and become . . . a nun.

PORTER: *(With a soft gasp)* A what?

MRS. MANNING: You heard me.

PORTER: *(Raptly)* Oh, how beautiful! You had a . . . a sign, is that it? "Get thee to a nunnery, Eleanor." And it all—everything—just fell into place. First, work, suffer, deny yourself, deprive yourself, give all for love of your children. Then, when the children depart, work, suffer, deny yourself, deprive yourself, give all for . . . for what, Eleanor? For what?

MRS. MANNING: *(Shouting at him)* You know very well for what! You spoke of it on that tape! And you did mean it! I know you meant it!

PORTER: But let me hear *you* say it. *Your* voice, Eleanor. For what?

MRS. MANNING: *(Still shouting)* For the greater glory of . . . *(Hesitates slightly; then softly)* God.

PORTER: *(Short pause; pleadingly)* Again, please. Say it again. But this time, from the person behind the voice. Please. For what, Eleanor?

MRS. MANNING: *(Longer pause; straight to him, as simply and earnestly as possible)* For the greater glory of God, Mr. Porter.

PORTER: *(Drops to his knees before her)* Will you marry me! *(She half sighs, half whimpers, and turns away from him)* Please! *(Hands in the proposing gesture)* I'll do anything. I'll be a model husband and father. I'll renounce all forms of sin, including self-abuse and self-pity. And I promise to die before your children are grown up, so you can enter that nunnery on schedule. Which you must do! Only, you must promise *me*, every morning, on waking, to say that just as you said it now. And every time before we make love, and right after it, too! And before every meal, before all breakings of bread . . .

MRS. MANNING: Please, Mr. Porter . . .

PORTER: Wilfrid! Wilfrid!

MRS. MANNING: Please . . . Wilfrid.

PORTER: You will then? You'll marry and reform and redeem me? You'll cleave to *my* flesh for a time, instead of your own? You will?

MRS. MANNING: *(Near tears again)* Get up! Please get up!

PORTER: *(Pause)* You won't, will you? I can tell. You won't. Ever. *(Pause. He whimpers slightly, then rises slowly and turns from her)* Well . . . who can blame you? *(Pause; then looking at his watch)* It's just about eleven-forty. You'd better get to that . . . subway.

MRS. MANNING: *(Turning to him)* Are you . . . are you all right?

PORTER: You can go now. Your time is up. Go on. The door is open.

MRS. MANNING: But are you . . . ? Is there anything I can . . . ?

PORTER: Oh, of course, I forgot to pay you. *(Crosses quickly to the dresser)* What do you get per hour at that agency? *(He opens the top drawer)*

MRS. MANNING: Don't be silly. That's not why I . . .

PORTER: *(Taking a pile of checks and a pen out of the drawer)* Oh, no, no, you must be paid. *(He lays the checks on the dresser and begins endorsing them one by one)*

MRS. MANNING: What are you doing?

PORTER: Endorsing these. Checks from clients for the last few weeks' work. Haven't gotten around to depositing them.

MRS. MANNING: I won't . . .

PORTER: Oh, it's a tidy sum. Over a thousand dollars, I think . . .

MRS. MANNING: I can't accept them!

PORTER: What? With three children facing starvation if the typing trade should fail? How dare you? *(Having endorsed the last check, turns and thrusts the checks out at her)* If you don't take these, I shall tear them up—all of them—right before your eyes. Then who'll be the richer?

MRS. MANNING: The . . . ministers will.

PORTER: Mrs. Manning! My clients come from the wealthiest clergy and the wealthiest churches! What is their need compared to yours? Or that of my two ex-bitch wives? Take them! *(She turns away and grabs her coat and purse. He rushes to the door and blocks it with his body)* Now I order you, on pain of . . .! *(Breaks off and moves away from the door)* No. I . . . *ask* you to accept these. Please. Take them. Please. Though you refuse to marry me, let these be my first alimony and child-support payment to you. Take them! Please!

MRS. MANNING: *(Short pause)* Why do you do this?

PORTER: "Why?" How can you, of all people, ask that? "Why?" Why, for the greater glory, Mrs. Manning. *You* know what I mean. *(Pause. She stares at him a moment, then slowly reaches out and takes the checks)* Thank you. Into your purse with them. *(Still staring at him, she opens her purse and drops them inside)*

Good. *(Turns back to the dresser)* Now you must swear—a solemn oath—that you will deposit those, or cash them, today. *(Takes the Bible off the dresser and holds it out to her)* Come, on the Holy Bible. It's a Protestant Bible, but holy nonetheless. Come. Swear. *(He reaches out to take her hand)*

MRS. MANNING: *(Pulling her hand back)* On . . . one condition.

PORTER: Yes?

MRS. MANNING: *(Short pause; then gesturing toward the cassette she brought)* You don't . . . need *that* any more, do you?

PORTER: What?

MRS. MANNING: *(Crosses to the dresser and picks up the cassette)* This.

PORTER: Oh! *(Looks at her a moment, then at the tape, and smiles slightly)* No. No, I don't, now that I have . . . *(Indicates her typescript)* this. It's yours, Eleanor. A little extra . . . bonus.

MRS. MANNING: Thank you. *(She drops the cassette into her purse)*

PORTER: *(Holding the Bible out to her again)* Now. Swear.

(She starts to reach her hand slowly out toward the Bible. He reaches out and takes the hand. She stiffens for a second, but then relaxes and allows him to lay her hand on the Bible and hold it there)

MRS. MANNING: *(Very softly)* I swear.

PORTER: Thank you. *(Releases her hand and lays the Bible back on the dresser)* If you break that oath, that same God will punish you, you know. He, and I, will be watching for those canceled checks. *(Looks at her a moment, then crosses to the door and opens it wide)* Your daughter will be wanting her lunch, Mrs. Manning. It's past eleven-forty. Forget the subway. Do you have enough cash for a taxi?

MRS. MANNING: Yes.

PORTER: Good. It's safer.

MRS. MANNING: *(Short pause; simply)* I'll . . . pray for you, Mr. Porter.

PORTER: Ah. Yes. In your way. Why not? And I for you, in mine.

(They stare briefly at each other, then she rushes out the door. He watches her off, then slowly shuts the door and stands with his back against it, breathing heavily. After a moment, he shakes himself, crosses to the dresser, starts to turn on the tape machine, stops, picks up her typescript, and fingers the pages almost caressingly. Then he lays the typescript down, picks up one of the loose sheets of paper on the dresser, scans it with a scowl, drops it, turns on the machine and picks up the microphone. He tests it, then speaks into it)

PORTER: Dearly beloved, our text today is from . . . *(The telephone rings. He stops, looks at it, then away, then back again, then bangs down the microphone, crosses to the telephone, and picks up the receiver)* Yes? . . . Oh. Oh, yes, Father Doyle. Yes, I'm . . . free now. What can I . . . ? Mm, yes, I suppose so. Any particular text? *(Picks up the pencil and starts to write on the pad)* First Corinthians, Chapter Thirteen. *(Stops writing and tosses the pencil away)* Ah, yes: "Though I speak with the tongues of men and of angels, and have not charity, I am . . ." What? Oh. Yes. "Have not *love.*" Yes, that *is* the better translation of *caritas,* isn't it? "And have not *love,* I am become as sounding brass or a tinkling cymbal. *(Continues quoting into the telephone, compulsively; picking up speed and volume as he proceeds)* And though I have the gift of prophecy, and understand all mysteries, and all knowledge; and though I have all faith, so that I could remove mountains, and have not love, I am nothing. And though I bestow all my goods to feed the poor, and though I give my body to be burned, and have not love, it profiteth me nothing!" . . . What? Oh. Oh, yes, al*most* total recall. *(Shouting, very rapidly)* "Love suffereth long and is kind! Love envieth not! Love vaunteth not itself, is not puffed up, doth not behave itself unseemly, seeketh not her own, is not easily provoked, thinketh no evil, rejoiceth not in iniquity but rejoiceth in the truth!" . . . What? Oh. Sorry. I got a bit . . . carried away. Yes, I'll get right to it. It'll be off to the typist by this afternoon. . . . Oh, not at all . . . oh. Well, bless *you,* Father." *(He hangs up and stands staring down at the telephone; more slowly and quietly)* ". . . beareth all things . . . believeth all things . . . hopeth all things . . . endureth . . . all . . . things."

Curtain

ALICE: You have to give them a chance. They do things differently here than in America. They move more slowly. Remember, we're the strangers here, not them. *(Looks about)* This is a sweet little place, don't you think?

NORMAN: What's so sweet about it?

ALICE: The way they've . . . done things. The way they've decorated it and everything. Don't you think?

NORMAN: I think it's dingy and plain. And depressing. And I say let's get out of here and go someplace less native.

ALICE: Oh, Norman, you're so ethnocentric. You have to be *open*. Open to new sights, new sounds, new smells, new tastes, new experiences. Maybe they're in the kitchen. *(Calls)* Hello? Are you in the kitchen?

NORMAN: Come on, Alice, Let's get out of here. This place gives me the creeps.

ALICE: Are you in the kitchen? Hello?

(As if in reply, the kitchen door slowly opens, revealing the Waiter. He is large, stocky, swarthy, and of indeterminate age and nationality. He wears an approximation of a waiter's jacket and carries a towel over his arm. He stands near the kitchen door, looks unsmilingly at them)

ALICE: *(To Norman)* See, I told you somebody was there. *(To Waiter)* May we please have a table? *(Pause. Waiter remains impassive. Enunciating very clearly)* May we sit down? *(Gestures)* Sit down? *(Pause. The Waiter motions them to sit down)* Oh, thank you. *(She leads Norman over to the table and they sit down. The Waiter doesn't move. Looking at him with an exaggerated smile)* May we have a menu, please? *(Pantomimes reading a menu)* A menu?

NORMAN: Look, honey, it's obvious he doesn't speak a word of English. What do you say we get out of here and go someplace else.

ALICE: Of *course* he speaks English. They all speak it. They have to. *(To Waiter, enunciating clearly)* Do you speak English? *(Inaccurately)* Habla Inglese? Sprechen-zie Deutsch? Comprendez-vous Anglais?

WAITER: *(Pause. Heavy, unidentifiable accent)* I am spik fourteen lengwiches, Misses—Hinglish de best.

ALICE: Oh, good, good. Wunderbar. *(To Norman)* See? I

told you he spoke English. *(To Waiter)* May we have a menu, please?

WAITER: *(Walking over to table)* Ees no menu. Ees een my head, de menu. *(Points to head)*

ALICE: Oh, isn't that sweet? *(To Norman)* He says the menu is in his head.

NORMAN: I heard him.

ALICE: *(To Waiter)* What do you suggest to start?

WAITER: *(Pause)* Please?

ALICE: To start. To begin. What do you suggest?

WAITER: *(Pause)* What I suggest?

ALICE: Yes. What do you suggest?

WAITER: *(Pause)* What ees "suggest"?

ALICE: Suggest? *(To Norman)* What's another word for suggest? *(To Waiter)* Recommend. What do you recommend?

WAITER: *(Pause)* Recommend?

NORMAN: Advise.

ALICE: Advise. What do you advise?

WAITER: Advise?

ALICE: Yes, what do you advise?

NORMAN: I thought you said you spoke English the best.

WAITER: Eef I spik Hinglish?

ALICE: Yes.

WAITER: So. *(Proudly)* One day a person comes to me. He ees from away. He ees America, I theenk. He say to me "Een my entire travels een dees place, I not see ever a man to spik so good de lengwich Hinglish as you." Later I find out. Thees man ees not only a native from hees cawntry, America, but also graduated of Brukeleens Cawletch.

ALICE: Of . . . ?

WAITER: Brukeleens Cawletch.

NORMAN: Brooklyn College. Well, that's certainly a very high recommendation.

WAITER: Recommen . . . ?

ALICE: . . . dation.

WAITER: *(Pause)* Ees like suggest?

ALICE: *(Enthusiastically)* Like suggest! Yes! Good! *(Gives*

Waiter's arm a quick squeeze. To Norman) You see how beautifully he related the two concepts? Recommendation and suggest?

NORMAN: Incredible. Just incredible.

ALICE: *(To Waiter)* You're very smart. Very intelligent.

WAITER: *(Humbly)* Oh, no, please . . .

ALICE: No, really. You're extremely bright.

WAITER: Sank you, Misses.

NORMAN: Look, let's order some food, what do you say? *(To Waiter)* What's the specialty of the house?

WAITER: *(Pause)* Please?

NORMAN: The specialty of the house. La specialite de la maison.

WAITER: *(Pause)* Please?

NORMAN: *(Takes guidebook from Alice and looks)* Do you have the . . . Neck of the Weak Horse?

WAITER: *(Suddenly furious)* What! *(He picks up a dish and smashes it on the floor. Norman cowers)*

ALICE: *(To Waiter)* What's the matter? Why did you do that?

WAITER: He ask eef I have the neck of a weak horse!

ALICE: No, no. What my husband meant was whether you had a dish here—a food—called the Neck of the Weak Horse. *(Takes guidebook and shows Waiter)* See? It says you have a dish here called the Neck of the Weak Horse.

NORMAN: *(Recovering)* Come on, honey. Let's get out of here. This guy's a maniac.

WAITER: *(Peering at book suspiciously)* A deesh?

ALICE: Yes. So you see, when my husband asked you if you had the Neck of the Weak Horse, he wasn't trying to insult you, he was just asking for this dish.

WAITER: *(Understands)* Ah. He asks for thees deesh.

ALICE: That's right.

WAITER: Not eef my neck ees like weak horse.

ALICE: Right.

WAITER: Ah. *(Bows to Norman. Very sincere)* Sor. I am most deeply apologize for thees outrageous and unhappy deesplay of tempers. *(Takes Norman's hand and kisses it)* Eef thees happen again, may my hand on my right side shrivel up, die, and drop off from my arm. *(Pause. To Alice)* He accepts my apologize?

ALICE: *(To Norman)* Do you accept his apologies?

NORMAN: Yes, yes, I suppose so. Look, let's just have a fast bite to eat and get out of here, O.K.? We still have to see the monument to the water commissioner, the old salad bowls museum and the broom factory. We're never going to keep on schedule at this rate, for God's—

ALICE: Fine. Don't worry, Norman. Now then. *(To Waiter)* Do you have this dish we were talking about called the Neck of the Weak Horse?

WAITER: Eef I have thees deesh?

ALICE: Yes.

WAITER: No.

ALICE: I see. Well, what *do* you have—that's good, I mean?

WAITER: We have . . . *(Pauses to think)* . . . sometheeng dot you will like berry moch. Eet ees berry . . . berry tasty and delicious.

NORMAN: What is it?

WAITER: Hees name ees Napaj Gruleek.

NORMAN: Napash Grulik.

WAITER: Gruleek. Napaj Gruleek.

NORMAN: What is it?

WAITER: Ees . . . hard to describe.

NORMAN: Try.

WAITER: Ees . . . *(Thinks hard. Then holds up three fingers)*

ALICE: *(Uncertainly)* Three words? *(Waiter nods, holds up one finger)* First word? *(Waiter nods, holds thumb and forefinger about an inch apart)* Small word. *(To Norman)* The first word is a small word. *(To Waiter)* A? The? An? *(Waiter shakes his head to all three, holds up two fingers)* Second word.

NORMAN: Come on, for God's sake. Let's just order it and get it over with.

ALICE: O.K. *(To Waiter)* Is this dish a native dish?

WAITER: How?

ALICE: Is it a native dish—a dish that the people in your country specialize in?

Dan Greenburg

Dan Greenburg's *The Restaurant,* a delightful comedy dealing with American tourists abroad, is published for the first time in this anthology.

Mr. Greenburg is the author of a number of popular books, including *How to Be a Jewish Mother; How to Make Yourself Miserable; Scoring;* and *Something's There.* His articles and short stories have appeared in most major periodicals, among them *The New Yorker, Esquire, Playboy, New York Magazine,* and *The New York Times* Book Review.

A contributor to the long-running musical *Oh! Calcutta!,* and author of two Off-Broadway plays, Mr. Greenburg also has appeared on television as a stand-up comedian and in the movie *Doc* in a serious dramatic role.

Mr. Greenburg lives in New York City and presently is at work on a new book.

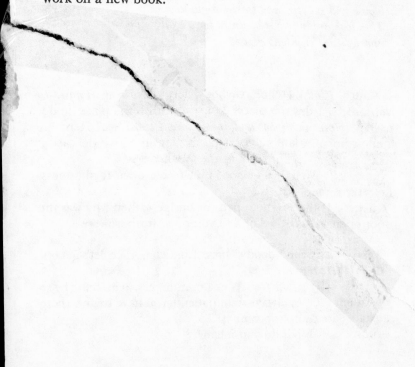

Characters:

ALICE
NORMAN
WAITER

Scene:

*A tiny restaurant in an undesignated foreign country. A small table
with a tablecloth and a lit candle on top of it, and two chairs. It is
rather gloomy and plain. A door to the kitchen at left. A door to the
outside at right.*

*After a moment, the outside door opens and two American tourists,
Norman and Alice, enter hesitantly. Norman is in his early thirties,
wears slacks, sportcoat, sportshirt, and carries a camera over his
shoulder. Alice is attractive, in her late twenties, wears a skirt,
blouse and sweater, and carries a guidebook.*

*They look around the restaurant for a waiter, shift uncomfortably
and wait. After a long pause:*

ALICE: *(Calls)* Hello? Anybody here? *(No reply. Pause. To
Norman)* Isn't this the place? I'm sure this is the place he describes. *(Opens guidebook and finds place. Points)* See? Here. "A
modest but pleasant eatery, specializing in native delicacies.
Ask for the . . . the Neck of the Weak Horse."

NORMAN: Well, it's obvious they're not open for business.
Let's try someplace else.

ALICE: If they're not open for business, then why was the
door open? *(Calls)* Hello! Are you open for business?

(No reply)

NORMAN: See? Nobody's here. Come on, Alice, let's get out
of here. *(He tugs her arm)*

ALICE: *(Wriggling free)* Wait a minute, Norman, don't be so
impatient. You're always so impatient. You have to give them
a chance in a foreign country.

NORMAN: What do you mean?

Dan Greenburg

THE RESTAURANT

WAITER: Eef we specialize een thees deesh here een my cawntry?

ALICE: Yes.

WAITER: No.

ALICE: Oh, well why don't you bring us something you *do* specialize in?

WAITER: Eef I breeng you someseeng *I* love beery moch to eat?

ALICE: Yes.

WAITER: So. One moment, only. *(Bows to Alice)* Misses . . . *(Bows to Norman)* Meester . . .

(He exits to kitchen. Pause. Waiter re-enters with two plates, puts them down on table. Alice and Norman look at plates uncertainly. Waiter waits for their approval)

ALICE: Uh, how do you call this?

WAITER: Thees?

ALICE: Yes.

WAITER: Snake.

(Norman shudders openly, but Alice attempts to be objective)

ALICE: Snake. I see. How interesting. What, uh, particular *kind* of snake?

WAITER: Dead.

ALICE: I see.

NORMAN: *(Pause)* I'm not going to eat any goddamned snake. I can tell you that—

ALICE: *(To Norman)* Sssh! *(To Waiter)* Well, we certainly never expected to get snake. At this time of the year, I mean.

NORMAN: I'm not going to eat any goddamned snake!

ALICE: *(To Norman)* Why must you always be so narrow and close-minded?

NORMAN: Are you going to eat it?

ALICE: I . . . might. I haven't decided yet.

NORMAN: Well, let me know when you decide. I'm ordering a hamburger and a Coke.

ALICE: A hamburger and a Coke? In this country? In a native restaurant that specializes in native delicacies? You're ordering a hamburger and a Coke?

NORMAN: What's wrong with that?

ALICE: You're really the original Ugly American, aren't you?

WAITER: Excuse me? You like de snake?

ALICE: *(Pause)* Uh. . . . Well, do you, uh, have something else that you could give us?

WAITER: After de snake?

ALICE: No, instead of.

WAITER: You no like de snake?

ALICE: *(Pause)* It's not so much that we don't *like* it, it's just that we . . . that we . . . *(Looks to Norman for assistance but finds none)* . . . it's just that we have this pet snake at home which we're very fond of, you see, and to eat these snakes would be like eating a friend.

WAITER: *(Pause)* You not weesh to eat de snake?

NORMAN: No. Listen, I want a hamb—

ALICE: *(Covering up his mouth)* Could you bring us something different, please?

WAITER: Yais. *(Picks up plates)*

NORMAN: What are you going to bring us?

WAITER: How?

ALICE: He wants to know what you're going to bring us.

WAITER: Ah. *(Pause)* Someseeng different.

NORMAN: Yes, but what?

WAITER: Someseeng you weel like.

NORMAN: Something *you* like?

WAITER: No.

NORMAN: Good.

ALICE: Norman!

(Waiter exits to kitchen)

ALICE: If you make any more insulting remarks to that poor man, you're going to be in big trouble.

NORMAN: What kind of trouble?

ALICE: Just don't push me too far, Norman!

(Waiter enters from kitchen with two more plates. He sets them down on the table. They stare at them stupidly. Pause)

ALICE: Isn't this, uh, the same thing you brought us before?

WAITER: How?

ALICE: Isn't this the same thing you brought us before—
the snake?

WAITER: De snake?

ALICE: Yes. That you brought us before.

WAITER: *(Pause)* Yais, I breeng you snake before . . . ?

ALICE: And isn't this the same thing? Didn't you bring us
snake again?

WAITER: You weesh me to breeng you de snake again?

NORMAN: No, isn't this—*(Points)* this here—isn't this snake
here?

WAITER: *(Understands)* Ah. Eef thees ees snake I breeng
you just now?

NORMAN: Yes. Is it?

WAITER: *(Bends down and scrutinizes the food very closely. Looks
up. Seriously)* Yais. Ees snake I breeng you now, also.

NORMAN: Why did you do that? We told you we didn't
want the snake. Why did you bring it back to us?

ALICE: Never mind. Do you have something else? Besides
the snake? Something different?

NORMAN: Do you have a hamburger and a Coke? *(Alice
glares at him)* I'm sorry, Alice, but I want a hamburger and a
Coke. *(To Waiter)* Do you know what a Coke is?

WAITER: A cowk?

NORMAN: Yes. Do you know what it is?

WAITER: *(Slightly offended)* Of *course* I know what ees cowk.

NORMAN: Good. Bring me a nice big Coke.

*(Pause. Neither Norman nor Alice look at one another. The kitchen
door opens and Waiter enters carrying large covered dish. He sets it
down on table and removes the cover with a great flourish. On the
plate is a large cow's head. Alice and Norman stare at it. Alice
turns away in disgust)*

NORMAN: Uh . . .

WAITER: Ees cowk.

NORMAN: *(Pause)* Look, do you . . . I can't believe that you
don't have Coca-Cola here. Every country in the world has
Coca-Cola. I—

WAITER: Cowka-Cola! Thees ees what you ask me for?

NORMAN: Yes.

WAITER: Of *course* we have Cowka-Cola. Before you tell me you weesh cowk, so I bring you cowk. You weesh Cowka-Cola?

NORMAN: Yes.

ALICE: Are you sure you know what he means?

WAITER: De pose dat refreshes!

ALICE: Right! *(To Norman)* Isn't he just the sweetest thing—the pause that refreshes! *(To Waiter)* Make it two, please.

WAITER: Sank you, Misses. *(He clicks his heels, turns and exits to kitchen)*

NORMAN: So Alice is having a coke!

ALICE: Oh, be quiet.

NORMAN: How ethnocentric of you.

ALICE: I said be *quiet*, Norman.

(Pause. Waiter enters from kitchen carrying two large mugs. He sets them down on table and waits for their approval. They pick up the mugs, look at them, look at each other, and put them down on table again. They look lamely at Waiter)

WAITER: Ees not Cowka-Cola?

ALICE: Yes, but . . . steaming hot?

WAITER: Ah. You weesh to have eet cold?

NORMAN: Never mind. Never mind. *(He looks at hot coke, raises mug dubiously, takes a sip, winces)*

WAITER: You weesh me to breeng you someseeng more?

ALICE: No. No, thank you. *(To Norman)* He didn't know, Norman. Apparently you have to specify if you want it cold. Just like you have to specify in our country if you want iced tea or iced coffee. Otherwise they bring it hot. *(To Waiter)* It's perfectly all right. It was our fault for not telling you.

WAITER: I am indeed sorry. Do you weesh someseeng else?

ALICE: I think not. Thank you.

NORMAN: Just get us the check, and we'll be on our way.

WAITER: Ah, the check.

(He reaches into his pocket and snaps it down on the table, then steps away discreetly and turns his back)

NORMAN: Well, they certainly have *that* down pat, don't they? *(Looks closely at check and does a double-take)* Wait a minute, this doesn't . . . Waiter?

WAITER: *(Approaches table)* Yais?

NORMAN: What is the amount here? I think there must be some mistake.

WAITER: *(Scrutinizes the check with great interest)* Ah. I see. *(Looks up)* No mistakes.

NORMAN: What is the amount?

WAITER: *(Looks briefly at check, then at Norman)* Feefty-seven and one half.

NORMAN: Fifty-seven and one half *cents?*

WAITER: Ah, no. Feefty-seven and one half *dollars.*

NORMAN: *American* dollars?

WAITER: Ah, no. Ees een *our* money.

ALICE: Oh, good. What does that come out to in American money?

WAITER: Een American monies. Excuse me. *(Calculates rapidly, sotto voce, for about ten seconds, using his hands)* Eet comes out een American money feefty-nine dollars and twenty-fife cents.

NORMAN: *Fifty-nine dollars!*

WAITER: *(Helpfully)* And twenty-fife cents.

NORMAN: That's . . . that's outrageous! That's impossible!

WAITER: Ah, no, sor. *Berry* possible.

NORMAN: Well, I'm not going to pay it, that's all.

WAITER: Excuse me, sor, but you *must* pay eet.

NORMAN: Who's in charge of this restaurant—is there a headwaiter?

WAITER: A hadwaiter?

NORMAN: Yes, is there a headwaiter here?

WAITER: Yais, but—

NORMAN: Get me the headwaiter.

WAITER: Sank you, sor. *(He clicks his heels and exits left. Pause)*

NORMAN: Can you beat that? Fifty-nine dollars for two hot cokes.

ALICE:　Don't get yourself so worked up, Norman.

NORMAN:　Worked up? You bet I'm worked up. Fifty-nine dollars, for God's sake!

(The kitchen door opens and the Waiter, now wearing a black tuxedo jacket instead of a waiter's jacket, strides smoothly up to the table)

WAITER:　Hollo, Misses, Meester . . . *(Bows)* Ees there some trauble heer?

NORMAN:　*(Pause)* I thought you were going to get the headwaiter.

WAITER:　Yais. Of course. *I* am de hadwaiter.

NORMAN:　*(Pause)* I see. *(Pause)* Is there a manager here?

WAITER:　A monoger? Yais, sor.

NORMAN:　Good. Get me the manager.

WAITER:　Sank you, sor. *(He clicks his heels and turns to go)*

NORMAN:　Just a minute there.

WAITER:　*(Stops and turns)* Sor?

NORMAN:　*You* aren't the manager, by any chance, are you?

WAITER:　No, sor, I am de hadwaiter. De *monoger* ees de monoger.

NORMAN:　O.K., fine. Get me the manager.

WAITER:　Sank you, sor. *(He turns and exits)*

NORMAN:　Can you beat that? Trying to pass himself off as the headwaiter, when—

(He stops as the Waiter, now wearing a white dinner jacket with a red carnation, saunters jauntily up to the table)

WAITER:　Hollo, Misses, Meester . . . *(Bows)* Ees there some trauble heer?

NORMAN:　*(Pause. Very quietly)* You *are* the manager, then, is that it?

WAITER:　*(Clicks his heels)* At your sorvice, sor.

NORMAN:　You're . . . the waiter, the headwaiter and the manager, all rolled into one, is that it?

WAITER:　Oh no, sor. I am de monoger only. The hadwaiter just now tells me there is some trauble weeth de check. May I be of sorvice to you een thees capacity?

NORMAN:　*(Pause. Sighs defeatedly)* Apparently not.

WAITER: Porhops you would like me to get for you de owner?

NORMAN: *(Pause)* You're the owner, too, then?

WAITER: Oh no, sor. I am de monoger only. De hadwaiter just now tell me—

NORMAN: Skip it. *(Shakes his head bemusedly. Looks up at Waiter. Pleasantly)* Look. Man to man. Very frankly. Why do you want to charge us fifty-nine dollars for two hot cokes?

WAITER: *(Pleasantly)* Mon to mon and berry fronkly, eet ees to screw you, sor. You have thees expression een your cawntry? *(Puts a comradely arm around Norman's shoulders)* Thees ees only a leetle joke and not de truth. De truth, sor, ees dat we overcharge you een the same manner as een your own cawntry, only to make you feel at home. Only because we lauv you and we weesh to make you feel at home. And because we lauv you we weesh to keep as much of you heer as we can, when you leave us. Only a memento. Only as a keepsake.

NORMAN: *(Pause)* Well, I'm not going to pay it, memento or not. It's an outrage! And if you persist in this idiocy, you leave me with but one alternative.

WAITER: What ees thees alternative, sor?

NORMAN: I'm going to have to go to the police.

WAITER: *(Sadly)* Ah, de police.

NORMAN: Yes, the police.

WAITER: *(Pause)* Dat would be most unpleasant, sor.

NORMAN: You leave me no other alternative. I'm sorry.

WAITER: *(Pause)* I see.

NORMAN: *(Pause)* Are you going to reduce the size of my check?

WAITER: *(Pause)* No, sor.

NORMAN: *(Pause)* Very well, then . . . *(Rises)* I'm afraid I'm going to have to go to the police.

(He has stood up uncomfortably close to Waiter, who blocks his passage)

WAITER: *(Gently)* You weesh me to breeng you a police-man, sor?

(Long pause as they stare at each other, eye to eye. Slowly Norman understands that Waiter is policeman as well, and slowly sinks back into his chair)

NORMAN: You're the whole town here, is that it? *(Pause)* Would you settle for thirty dollars?

(Alice, snapped out of her trance, looks at Norman's capitulation with shock)

WAITER: Please, sor. We do not make bargaining on our dinners.

NORMAN: Well, I don't *have* fifty-nine dollars. *(Takes out his wallet and empties his bills onto the table)* See? Including American dollars and your own currency, I don't have more than thirty-five, forty dollars with me.

WAITER: Thees ees extremely unfortunate, sor.

NORMAN: What do you mean?

WAITER: I mean dat I cannot to allow you to leave de premises until you pay me de amount of your check.

NORMAN: But I don't *have*—

ALICE: Let me talk to him, Norman. *(To Waiter, turning on the charm)* Please, couldn't you make an exception in this one case? You seem to be such a . . . *(Grips his arm)* . . . an understanding and a . . . an attractive person . . . *(She looks into his eyes. He returns her gaze)*

WAITER: *(Huskily)* You find me attrocteev?

ALICE: Very.

NORMAN: Alice . . .

ALICE: *(Without looking at him)* Shut up, Norman!

WAITER: *How* attrocteev?

ALICE: *(Pause) This* attractive. *(She stands and embraces Waiter)*

NORMAN: Alice, for God's sake! *(They continue to embrace, with increasing passion)* Alice, stop it this instant!

ALICE: *(Interrupts the embrace)* Stay out of this, Norman! It doesn't concern you. *(She resumes the embrace)*

NORMAN: Alice, have you taken leave of your senses? *(She continues the embrace and begins to moan in ecstasy)* Alice!

ALICE: *(Without disengaging her lips from Waiter's)* Stay out of this, Norman!

(She unbuttons the top of her blouse and the Waiter rains kisses on her throat and upper chest)

NORMAN: Alice! *(Pause. Less confidently)* Alice? *(Pause)* Alice, it's Norman, your husband. *(Pause. Alice reaches under her blouse and unhooks her bra)* Oh, my God!

(He continues to watch them helplessly. Finally they stop, gaze into each other's eyes a long moment, then they both turn to face him)

ALICE: *(A little out of breath)* Norman, I have something to tell you. *(She looks at Waiter briefly, then back at Norman)*

NORMAN: *(Dazedly)* What?

ALICE: This man and I are going away together for awhile.

NORMAN: *(Dazedly)* What?

ALICE: We're going away.

NORMAN: *(Pause)* You can't do this to me . . .

ALICE: I must do this thing, Norman, I must. It's necessary sometimes in a strange land to . . . to get off the beaten path a little . . . to get to know the people . . . to learn their customs and see how they live.

NORMAN: *(Dully)* You can't do this to me.

ALICE: I don't expect you to understand this, Norman, but perhaps, some day, after the hurt has gone away . . . you'll look back on it and see that this was for the best.

NORMAN: *(Dully)* You can't do this to me.

ALICE: *(Gently)* I was very fond of you once, Norman.

NORMAN: *(Half to himself)* She can't do this to me.

ALICE: *(To Waiter)* Are you ready?

WAITER: Only one moment, please.

(He goes to Norman, who sits dazed, staring straight ahead, and pulls him to a standing position. Then he disappears briefly into the kitchen, emerging a moment later—coatless, carrying a towel and a waiter's jacket. He briskly divests Norman of his sportcoat and camera, putting them on himself. Then he puts the waiter's jacket on Norman, raises Norman's forearm to a horizontal position and drapes a towel over it. Waiter and Alice give Norman one last look, then turn and exit right. Norman continues standing, staring into the audience as:)

The Curtain Falls

Don Evans

SUGAR-MOUTH SAM DON'T DANCE NO MORE

Don Evans

First performed in New York at the HB Studio and, subsequently, produced by the noted Negro Ensemble Company, *Sugar-Mouth Sam Don't Dance No More* drew a good deal of press attention for both play and author Don Evans. Mel Gussow of *The New York Times* was impressed by the "sharpness of the writing" while Edith Oliver declared in *The New Yorker* that "Mr. Evans' accomplishment lies in his characters, the words they speak, and the feelings that rise and ebb and change among them."

Following its New York engagement, the play was presented in many regional and university theatres, including a much lauded production at the Dashiki Playhouse in New Orleans. Writing in the *Vieux Carre Courier,* S. Joslyn Fosberg summarized the general reaction to the play: "This poignant piece about a doomed love affair is at once so specially black and so infinitely human, and the language of its expression so notably lyric, colorful, and apt that at the end my eyes were no drier than those of the rest of the house."

Author Don Evans, who holds an M.F.A. in Theatre Arts from Temple University, also is a prominent director and a leading educator and has taught courses in Black Theatre at Princeton University, Rutgers University and Cheyney State College. He has lectured extensively, contributed to dozens of periodicals and, among his many awards and citations, was named "Outstanding Educator of 1970" by the Princeton Junior Chamber of Commerce.

Mr. Evans' other works for the theatre include: *Orrin,* presented as part of a double bill at the ANTA Matinee Series, Theatre De Lys, New York; *Matters of Choice; Change of Mind; Nothin' But the Blues'* and *It's Showdown Time.* The latter, a high-spirited comedy of contemporary black life, drawn from Shakespeare's *The Taming of the Shrew,* was produced by the New Federal Theatre, New York, in 1976, and subsequently was seen on tour at the Locust Theatre, Philadelphia, and the National Theatre in Washington, D.C.

Sugar-Mouth Sam Don't Dance No More appears in an anthology for the first time in *The Best Short Plays 1978*.

The People:

VERDA MAE HOLLIS, *a black woman of approximately thirty-five years. Middle-age spread is slowly sneaking up on her, but she fights back valiantly, managing to maintain a womanly figure in spite of excess here and there. Her manner of response is often brusque, but never coarse. She looks life squarely in the eye, but with some difficulty. She would like to be less knowing and, therefore, be permitted a few small dreams*

SAMMY (SUGAR-MOUTH) WILLIAMS, *a black man in his late thirties. His manner suggests boyish optimism, but this is a cover. His struggle centers on his insistence that he at least appears to be on top of the situation. He is the barbershop orator; every groom's "best man"*

The Particulars:

Time: The present—Philadelphia, Pennsylvania

   An efficiency apartment in South Philadelphia. The large room has been screened off to form a bedroom with some privacy. Two counters meeting at a right angle separate the kitchen from the living room-dinette area of the room. Behind the counters can be seen the usual apartment-sized appliances. Fronting the downstage counter is the living room area, designated by a sofa and two chairs, centered around a low coffee table. The whole unit is in the mock-modern style of those stores which cater to "dollar-down, dollar-when-I-catch-you" urban folk. Downstage right is a small kitchen table, set for two. Up right center is a T.V.-record player console unit, topped by a series of shelf units filled with pictures, plants and other knick-knacks. The apartment is crowded, but very liveable. Stockings hanging over the screen to dry, issues of "Essence" and occasional frills identify this as a woman's home.

Scene One

It is early evening, but the drawn shades give the impression of midnight. Street sounds, mixed with bar music, filter in through the

window. A key is being unsuccessfully turned in a lock. Unper-
turbed, the guest begins to whistle as he knocks. Verda enters, wear-
ing a dressing gown, her hair tied down. She turns on a soft light,
picks up a stick and crosses warily to the door.

VERDA: *(At the door)* . . . Who's that?

SAMMY: *(Still in the hallway)* It's me, baby.

VERDA: *(Trying to recognize the voice)* Who you lookin' for?

SAMMY: How does Miss Verda Mae Hollis grab you? . . .
Come on, woman. . . . Open the door. It's me . . . Sammy.
(Excited, she places the stick on the floor and begins to unlock one of
the three locks)

VERDA: Well, I'll be damned. . . . If this ain't the surprise
of surprises. . . . *(Remembers that she is not dressed)* . . . Wait!
. . . Wait justa minute . . . I gotta put some clothes on . . .
(She starts for the bedroom. The knocking resumes, but louder)

SAMMY: Woman, you better open this door!

VERDA: *(Mumbling, but returning to the door)* . . . Wouldna'
hurt you none to call . . . *(Unfastening the remaining locks)* . . .
Poppin' up here. . . . Don't give nobody no warnin'. . . .
(Unlocks the door. Sammy starts to enter, but Verda pushes him with
her hand, holding him outside in the hall. Sammy laughs) Now close
you' eyes, y'hear me?

SAMMY: Awww, woman . . .

VERDA: Just close yo' eyes. . . . *(Moving quickly to the bed-*
room) . . . I ain't got my hair on, so just sit yo' bad self down
an' wait . . .
(She exits to bedroom. Sammy enters, one eye closed. He wears a jeff
hat and a light raincoat, his face shows the good-natured smile that
earned him his street-name, "Sugar-mouth")

SAMMY: Since when do you have to get all pretty for ol'
jive-time me? . . . *(Sets his bag down and, holding his hat, he*
moves around the room, touching things and quietly remarking that
few things have changed. Picks up a photo from the shelf above the
record player. Laughing) . . . You mean to tell me, you kept this
ugly-assed picture sittin' over there all this time? . . .

VERDA: *(From the bedroom)* . . . What? . . . I can't hear
you. . . . Can't you wait 'til I get out there? . . . *(Sammy mimics*

the pose on the picture and then laughs at himself, as Verda re-enters in "her hair," and wearing a more respectable robe. Seeing each other for the first time, both are somewhat lost for words, happy to be near each other, but fighting to avoid questions that might ruin the reunion. Verda, smiling) . . . "Must gon' rain. . . . You sneakin' up outta the woodwork. . . .

SAMMY: How ya doin', baby-cakes? You're lookin' good. . . .

VERDA: *(Crossing to the door to put on the safeties)* . . . You know me . . . I get by. Always gon' get by . . .

SAMMY: No lie . . .

VERDA: You eat yet? . . . *(Crossing to the kitchen)* I'm gettin' ready to fix myself somethin' . . .

SAMMY: *(Unbuttoning his coat)* I got me a burger down at the station. . . . Just got off the bus an' com straight here . . .

VERDA: Gimme your coat an' sit down. . . . I got some beans an' franks here. . . .

(Sammy passes her his coat and moves down to the table. Verda hangs his coat on the wall-hook near the door)

SAMMY: *(At the table)* You musta knew I was comin'. . . . *(Verda looks up)* I mean the two places . . .

VERDA: *(Reaching for the cans, getting the hot dogs, etc.)* . . . My momma always set more places than there was folks to eat. . . . Never know who's comin' in your house hungry . . .

SAMMY: *(Sitting)* . . . Y'never set but two when I was here . . .

VERDA: *(Trying to open a can of beans. Her response is "wise")* . . . but I did set *two* though, didn't I? . . . *(Crosses to him with can opener and can)* Here, see if you can open this . . . *(Gives him beans)* I never could work one of these things . . . *(Goes back and continues preparing the dinner. Just an aside)* . . . Yeah, so my wandering niggah done slipped up on me one more time . . . *(Quietly. In an offhand way)* . . . Where you been, man?

(The question bothers Sammy. His face changes to momentary concern as the now open can presents him with a way out)

SAMMY: *(Rising. Can raised like an offering)* . . . One can of Boston's best . . . *(Hands her the beans, still talking)* . . .

Y'know, baby . . . I once knew a cat who had a small yacht . . . an' whenever his funds got low, he'd wolf down a can o' Van Camp's . . . hang himself over the end of the boat and putt-putt his way wherever he'd wanna go. . . . Didn't have to buy no fuel. . . . Cat had Van Camp's gas. . . . *(Verda laughs)* . . . Yes, he did . . .

VERDA: *(Laughing. Pushes him lightly)* . . . Get on outta here, with your lyin' self . . . *(Pointing to kitchen table)* . . . an' put that picture back on that shelf where you got it, too. . . . Com 'round here messin' up.

(Sammy, still laughing, crosses to the table and gets the picture. On the way to the shelf, he holds it up appraisingly)

SAMMY: Won't such a bad lookin' niggah back then, was I?

VERDA: *(Handing him the second can of beans)* . . . I seen bettah . . .

SAMMY: *(Leaning to her)* . . . In the movies, maybe . . .

VERDA: *Had* bettah . . . an', if things go right, gon git bettah. . . . How you like that?

SAMMY: *(Returning the picture)* . . . Watch yourself . . . gon tell somethin' . . . *(Sammy sits on console and begins opening the can)*

VERDA: *(Playing worldly)* . . . Sheuuuu, I ain't got nothin' to hide . . . Not at this late date, I ain't . . . Let it hang-right-out-and-down-in-front, got it!

SAMMY: *(Mock shock)* . . . Boom! . . . Talk about bein' put in yo' place . . . *(Gives her the beans)* . . . You definitely don't play . . . *(Remembering)* . . . Hey, I almost forgot . . . *(Runs to his bag and takes out a small box of chocolates and a bottle of J. W. Harper's)* Damn things probably melted by now. *(Crosses to counter and ceremoniously places the two gifts before Verda)* Sweet chocolates for sweet chocolate . . . *(Verda takes up the chocolates and examines them like a child with a new toy. Sammy, quietly)* I'd a probably said "Good ol' times" . . . but . . . well, it was your toast. *(Verda laughs and crosses to the sofa. Sammy sits on the arm of the sofa above her)* How you been doin', girl. . . . Been takin' care o' yourself? *(Puts hands on her shoulder and begins caressing her lightly, working up to an embrace)*

VERDA: *(Moving his hand. She plays it light, but underneath her comment is real fire)* Ain't seen your black ass for damn near one whole year . . . an' here you come tap dancin' your way in here with a box o' chocolates and a bottle of I. W. Harper's . . . talkin' 'bout some "how you been doin' ". . . . Man, you somethin' else . . .

SAMMY: I been worried about you, baby . . .

VERDA: *(Gradually growing angry)* . . . Don't tell nobody you comin'. . . . Jus' knock on the damn door . . .

SAMMY: *(Not permitting the anger to grow, he jokes)* . . . It do kinda mess up a plan, don't it, Sapphire?

(The Ames-bit throws Verda. In spite of herself, she laughs)

VERDA: *(Laughing)* Man, you don't *ever* change . . .

SAMMY: *(With a wink)* . . . Ain't you glad?

VERDA: *(Rises, goes back to check the food)* . . . Yeah . . . I guess . . .

(Recognizing that the mood has grown serious, Sammy starts his "Brighten-up" campaign)

SAMMY: Hey, mamma. . . . How about one more . . . for ol' times, hunh? *(Crosses to counter. Verda, understanding his motives, but not ready to throw off her honest feelings, merely looks at him. Sammy, as if he is seeing her for the first time)* . . . You really look good, baby . . . I guess I shouldn't be surprised . . . I mean, you always . . .

VERDA: *(Cutting him, putting bowls on the counter)* . . . Go to hell, man. . . . Come back here with that same ol' B.S. . . . If I look so good, why the hell you go runnin' off like you did? . . . Sugar-mouth Sammy with the same ol' tired jive . . . *(Verda places the bowls on the table)*

SAMMY: Now, you know that ain't so . . . I've changed a lot. . . . *(Coming up behind her)* Sweeter an' sweeter . . . I keep gettin' sweeter an' sweeter . . .

(Sammy tries to pull her to him. Verda pushes him off)

VERDA: *(Lightly)* . . . Man, if you don't stop breathin' down my back, you bettah . . .

SAMMY: *(Grabbing her again)* . . . Can't stand it, hunh? *(Verda, laughing, crosses to get the silverware and other things for dinner)*

VERDA: Crazy as you can be. . . . Ain't never had good sense. . . .

(Sammy starts to play "jitterbug." Hitches up his pants. Chin jutting forward, he strikes a corner "stash" and begins a "side out of the mouth" rap)

SAMMY: *(Bopping over to and behind Verda)* Nawwwww, baby . . . Not where no broad is concerned, I ain't . . . *(Looks down her robe. Seeing him looking down her robe, Verda looks at him like "Whatchu call yourself doin'?)*

VERDA: I hope you find what you looking for . . . I ain't got no more now than I had before. . . . *(Shakes her shoulders to loosen him. Sammy, playing his silly game to the hilt, jumps back as if to fight)*

SAMMY: What you puttin' down, woman? . . . My name is Sammy Williams. . . . Don't no broad be puttin' me down, 'less I go upside her head. . . . *(Bops around the room a little, eyeing her all the while. Verda is amused)*

VERDA: If you don't sit your dried up behin' down somewhere, I mo bounce one o' these case of beans off your head, that's what I mo do . . .

(Sammy jumps in front of her, jabbing like a boxer.)

SAMMY: You bad: . . . Jump, baby . . . Come on . . . Jump . . . *(Verda quickly reaches for the stick by the door and pretends to hit him. Sammy, laughing, ducks and runs out of range)* You the best, baby . . . You are definitely theee best . . . *(Sits on sofa)* I always was weak for a woman what makes you fight for it. . . .

VERDA: *(Putting the stick up. Mock surprise)* . . . For what? . . . I ain't got nothin' you can get, so you bettah . . .

(Sammy, now standing behind her, watches her as she starts for the kitchen. Taking her arm, he gently pulls her to him. They kiss. Verda accepts the embrace coldly, giving nothing. The kiss completed, she goes back to the kitchen, leaving Sammy standing alone with his embarrassment)

SAMMY: *(After a pause)* . . . Well, I guess . . . uhhh . . . I blew that, hunh? . . . You ain't mad, are ya?

(Verda crosses to the table. The dinner is now prepared)

VERDA: Pay it no min' . . . I been kissed before. *(Verda crosses to the window and opens the curtains and then the window. The street sounds filter in)*

SAMMY: *(Going toward her)* You know me . . . I was only playin' . . .

VERDA: Yeah, like always. . . . Candy, flowers, jokes . . . Man, I been layin' up in that room for one whole year . . . wondering where the hell you was . . . worryin' about you . . .

SAMMY: *(Hands open in apology)* I'm sorry, baby . . .

VERDA: *(Quickly turning to him)* Tell me a new one, man. . . . You always been sorry.

SAMMY: *(Picking up her directness)* . . . I'm back. . . . Is that new enough for you? . . . An' I'm back for keeps.

VERDA: I pay the rent here. . . . So, I'll decide what's for keeps and what ain't . . . *(Neither of them wants the reunion to be merely a rehashing of old transgressions. Verda is sorry for her outburst)* Lookahere, Sammy . . . I'm glad to see ya . . . I really am. But we just gon sit here and eat these hare-smokes and peas . . . maybe run down some ol' laughs an' have a little fun. . . . An', then, Mr. Williams, you can just backtrack to wherever you come from . . . *(Sammy is unmoved by her last speech. He still maintains his grin as Verda begins to sit down. Rushing behind her, he gallantly holds her chair. Verda, smilingly accepting his hospitality)* . . . I meant what I said, man. . . . Don't think you gon get around me with your simple-actin' self, 'cause you ain't. . . . *(Once Verda is seated, Sammy rushes over to the console and puts on a record. Verda, as Sammy selects a record)* . . . What you jumpin' around like that for?

SAMMY: Music . . . Can't have no banquet without music, can we?

(The record plays. It is one of those old pieces featuring one of the giants backed by strings. It is lush, but not corny)

VERDA: Leave it to you to pick some o' that old-timey stuff . . .

SAMMY: *(Slightly taken back)* What you mean "ol' timey"? . . . That's Clifford . . . Clifford Brown . . .

VERDA: *Was* . . . He's dead, ain't he? . . . ol' timey.

(Sammy comes back to the table.)

SAMMY: So is Trane, Pres, Bird . . . Everybody . . . *(Sitting)* . . . Hey, you 'member that time we went down to the Earle an' he was there. . . . Him an' that yalla dude what sings . . .

VERDA: *(Starting to eat)* . . . I had on my red dress . . .

SAMMY: Um-humph . . . an' that flower up in your hair like Lady Day . . . Baby, you was lookin' fine!!! *(Laughs)*

VERDA: *(Picking up on his laugh)* . . . And don't you think I didn't know it either.

SAMMY: *(Spreading to suit the grandness of the story)* . . . I had on my blue tear-drop with the link buttons . . . Bad, baby, . . . I mean bad! . . . an' my terrible blue and white kicks . . .

VERDA: *(Pointing with her fork, laughing)* . . . An' the hat. . . . Lawd, I thought I'd die laughin' . . .

SAMMY: *(Put-down)* . . . What was wrong with my hat?

VERDA: Damn brim like to covered Broad Street . . . You looked like a black Humphrey Bogart . . . *(Quickly)* . . . But you was clean . . . I mean, everybody else gon' conservative . . . an' you still "zoot-suitin' " . . . Lawd, but you was clean!

SAMMY: I remember how my jaws got tight when that pretty-lookin' niggah up there got to talkin' 'bout some "I Apologize." . . . Lookin' straight at you . . .

VERDA: That was one fine lookin' piece o' timber . . . Still is . . .

SAMMY: All them ol' nappy-heads runnin' up there tryin' to pull his clothes off. I saw him diggin' on you . . . but I wasn't worried 'cause I knew my program was tight . . .

VERDA: *(Playfully)* . . . You know I don't like no yalla niggahs no way . . .

SAMMY: *(Seriously)* You know somethin'. . . . I think I was really jealous . . . I mean . . .

VERDA: *(Looking around on the table)* . . . I don't know why. . . . Won't nothin' he could do up on the stage. . . . Hey, whyn't you pour me some coffee?

SAMMY: *(Rising. Crossing for the coffee)* . . . Hey, woman . . . don't let my slavin' get good to you . . . *(Coming back to*

table with coffee) . . . but then, I always did like doin' for you.
. . . Kinda seemed *right,* ya know? . . . *(Pause as he pours coffee)* . . . Nawww, I'll never forget that. . . . Used up all my carfare to get them front row seats. . . Had to walk all the way to Midvale Steel Mill that whole week . . .

VERDA: *(Sipping her coffee. Trying to play it light)* . . . Man, you was in *love* . . . *(Sammy returns coffee pot)* . . . That red dress had your behin' doin' the boogaloo. . . . An' you wanna know somethin'? . . . *(Laughs)* . . . It won't even mine . . . I borrowed it from Clarice . . . *(They share a hearty laugh)*

SAMMY: No stuff? . . . Well, it ain't never looked that good on that bird-legged broad . . . *(Sammy continues to laugh. Verda quiets. She begins to toy with her food. Noticing the change, Sammy touches her hand)* Somethin' wrong?

VERDA: *(Directly. He owes her this)* . . . Where you been, man? . . . Ain't you got nothin' to say about all that?

(Cornered, Sammy moves around in his chair until he can no longer stay there. Her gaze is direct and will permit no deviation. Finally, Sammy crosses to the record player and turns it down, turning back to her with a grin)

SAMMY: You know me, baby. . . . Little time here, little time there . . . *(She doesn't buy it)* . . . D.C. . . . I was in D.C. for a while . . . *(Trying to convince her)* "The Nation's Capital" an' all that . . . *(Verda turns from him, disgusted with the game. She sips her coffee to avoid screaming at him)* Passed a few pieces of unimportant legislature . . . *(Sammy sees that he can run no further)* . . . I guess that train's passed, hunh?

VERDA: *(Not looking at him)* . . . You coulda sent a damned postcard or somethin' . . .

SAMMY: *(Crossing to her. He has an out now)* . . . Well, ya see, baby . . . I was in the slammers down there. . . .

(Verda doesn't believe him. She begins to laugh at the pains to which he'll go to avoid truth)

VERDA: *(Through the laugh)* . . . So, you was in jail, hunh?
. . . So what the hell's that supposed to mean? . . . You can't write 'cause I mo go to pieces 'cause my man's in jail. . . . Sammy, you talk like one of them Teevee shows. . . . Jail don't mean nothin' to you and me . . . an' you ain't stop

writin' 'cause you thought I was gonna crack-up. . . . You tell me somethin' better than that . . .

SAMMY: *(Disturbed that she doesn't believe him)* . . . Honest, baby . . . I did three months . . . *(Verda rises, crosses to the counter)* . . . I know it don't make no sense, but what the hell does? I'm sittin' in the bus stop . . . just me an' these three other dudes. . . . Gray cat goes into the phone booth . . . I'm waitin' to use the phone after him. . . . Finally, I go in an' there's his checkbook on the seat. . . . One of those wallet-type things. . . . So, I pick it up an' go after him, but he's gone . . . I'm broke, so I figure "what the hell." . . . Well, bam . . . you know the rest. . . . Cats get me for passin' bad checks. . . . Goddamned judge keep tellin' 'bout how lucky I am 'cause he could give five, ya know. . . . Didn't make me no nether mind. . . . Might as well be there as anywhere . . .

(Verda crosses to the sofa. Sammy stands watching her a moment)

VERDA: *(Calmly. Stating a fact)* . . . You ain't no thief, man . . . an' that ain't but three months . . .

SAMMY: *(Crossing to her)* . . . Every time I tried to write you an' tell ya . . . well, I just couldn't. . . . You'd come runnin' down there . . . stickin' by me an' holdin' me up. . . . The same ol' song in a different key. . . . Naw, baby . . . I just couldn't . . .

VERDA: *(Turns to him sharply)* . . . So you don't say nothin' . . . *(Her anger mounting)* You walk in here unannounced and you gon leave the same goddamned way, that right? . . . And good ol' faithful-ass Verda is just supposed to wait . . . one more time . . . I'm supposed to wait! . . . All right! Three months and then what, hunh? . . . *Or ain't I got the right to that either? (Verda moves from him and begins clearing the stuff on the table. Sammy sits on the sofa, locked in his own guilt feelings)*

SAMMY: *(Slowly, Creating the story as he tells it)* . . . That damned place put me through some changes. . . . Baby, jail is a trip all by itself. . . . You get to summin' up your whole damned life. . . . An' these cats they threw me in with, well, we was all bloods . . . but that's all . . . I mean, I ain't never tried to be no outlaw, ya know . . . but damn if I wasn't doin' the same goddamned time they was . . . takin' orders from

the same funky-mouthed chuck. . . . Ain't no up for us, baby
. . . It's all down . . . I looked over my whole life . . . everything . . . and you the only good thing I got . . .

(Verda now understands that his story is true. She is sorry for her outburst)

VERDA: Sammy . . .

SAMMY: An' I saw all the loose ends. . . . Made up my
mind to kinda tighten 'em up . . . tighten 'em up and
straighten 'em out, ya know . . . *(Laughs to himself)* Yeah . . .
got me an' ol' piece o' car . . . '63 Chevy . . . an' drove down
toward Virginia. . . . After I got outta the slammers, it ain't
take me but one week to shake off the man, get that car an' get
on the road . . . *(Genuinely moved)* . . . An' Verda . . . ain't
nothin' no prettier than them trees along that highway leadin'
back home . . . When I first started, it seemed like a brand
new place. . . . Like I had never been there before . . . But
soon as I turned that first corner in Manson, I knew it like I
had never left . . .

(Verda is now standing by the counter. She doesn't really hear him, but knows the routine. They speak simultaneously)

SAMMY: All the folks stoppin' me at every corner. "Hey,
ain't you Sarah Williams' boy? . . . Lawd, you ain't changed
a bit. . . . Bet you just as sassy as you ever was." . . .
Hearin' all them ol' slides and slurs. . . . Flat-talkin' we
used to call it.

VERDA: *(Crossing to the coat hanger)* Sammy-sugar don't
ever change. I ask you where you been, an' you give me a
travelogue . . . A travelin' *lie,* *(Affectionately)* Niggah got
honey in his mouth . . . Hey, man . . . I'm talking to ya.
. . . Don't ya hear me?

SAMMY: I felt good . . . an', well . . . there ain't too many
places where I feel . . .

(Verda, his jacket in hand, stands next to the door)

VERDA: Sammy . . . I'm glad to know that you're all right
an' everythin' . . . I really am . . . Ya know, I used to think
you was crazy 'cause you could talk so sweet . . . Used to
think you was simple-minded . . . I mean, you always had
good things to say . . . You could talk . . . gentle, don'tcha

know . . . The ugliest thing in the world was pretty when you got through with it . . . *(Her voice becomes harder, more determined)* . . . But, man . . . it ain't like that . . . I don't need no niggah to keep me laughin' an' tell me stories 'bout no "green trees." . . .

SAMMY: *(Sharply)* . . . What *do* you need, Verda Mae?

VERDA: The truth! . . . Just a little bit o' truth . . .

SAMMY: *(Snatching his coat from her)* . . . Well, try this, hunh, baby. . . . I left here 'cause I couldn't stand wakin' up every day and seein' the *truth* starin' me in the face . . . comin' back here empty-handed every night 'cause I couldn't find a job. . . . Cussin' and fussin' with myself just to make sure I didn't forget who I was and what I was . . . I ran because I thought it would be easier to come back here after I got things straight with my wife in Manson. . . . That I could get some bargainin' power so I could get some work when I came back. . . . An' it is ugly an' sloppy. . . . Just like you say . . . so I tell stories . . . I live as dirt so I talk about clean. . . . I drive down dark roads scared some white son-of-a-bitch is gonna pull me over an' make me kill him. . . . So, *I look at trees* . . . Do you understand that? I got a woman I don't love and a woman I can't love an' . . .

VERDA: *(Cutting him)* Sammy . . . go.

SAMMY: Can't love . . . 'cause my life is nothin' but unfulfilled promises and mistakes . . . mis-takes! . . . I got nothin' to give that ain't got strings . . .

VERDA: *(Sharply) All right!*

SAMMY: But you don't stop wantin'. . . . You stop askin', but not wantin' . . . So, I run . . . *(Pauses. The anger has gone to the wrong object. He gentles)* I ain't asked you for nothin', baby. . . . I just got in town . . . an' well, I wanted to see ya. . . . See how you was doin' . . . I know you inta some new things. . . . I mean, time don't do no waitin' . . . *(Slows down. Looks directly at her. He knows there is more than just anger in her wanting him to go. She is protecting herself)* . . . I mo move on, baby . . . but I had to see . . . if you was needin' anything . . . or . . .

VERDA: *(His naivete strikes her as wryly humorous)* . . .

Needin'. . . Man, you been in an' outta my life like a swingin' door. . . . Don't talk to me about no needin'. I can't wait on no sometime-calls no more. . . . I want somebody in that room when I come home . . .

SAMMY: I'm here to stay . . . *(Pause. Verda does not believe him. She turns away, not wanting to hear "the old story")* . . . I'm through playin' big time . . . pissin' my life away . . . That's why I come back . . .

VERDA: *(Sighs. Speaks quietly)* . . . It's too late . . . I waited on you, Sammy-man. All my life, I waited. . . . I always knew we was supposed to get together some time. . . . But you get married, move on off. . . . Now, I was happy for ya, 'cause I thought that was what you wanted . . .

SAMMY: *(Coming to her)* I was young, baby, . . . I didn't know . . .

VERDA: *(Cutting him)* . . . An' when you get finished with that an' needed some place to go . . . I was *here*. . . . And I was still waitin' . . .

SAMMY: . . . You been good to me . . . an', well . . . things just wasn't right. . . . But I'm here now . . . an' I'm ready to go all the way . . .

VERDA: *(Pulling on all her resources, she removes his arm and turns to him)* Sammy . . . I ain't the same person you left. . . . My life is all . . . changed, ya know . . . *(Sammy backs away from her. He never planned for change. Verda's voice is cold now)* . . . An' man . . . I ain't lettin' none o' you play me cheap no more. . . .

SAMMY: *("None o' you" shakes Sammy)* . . . Hey, now . . . that kinda talk ain't you, baby . . .

VERDA: The hell it ain't . . . Now you just get outta here . . . an' let me be! Go on back to Manson . . . an' let me be . . .

SAMMY: *(Sharply)* . . . Let you be what, Verda Mae? . . . By yourself? . . . Alone, so you can turn yourself into one of those man hatin', good-time-for-a-night-broads sad ol' men pick up in South Street bars? . . . Maybe you gon try gettin' yourself some religion. . . . Put it all in God's hands. . . . What you gon do when I walk out that door, baby? . . . *(Closer to her)* . . . Sammy-sugar don't never change, just like you say, baby . . . *(Verda turns to him, her face lined with tears)* . . . But neither do you. . . . You ain't never had but one man, Verda Mae . . . *(Puts jacket on the chair)* . . . And it must be somebody's joke to make him such a goddamned *fool.* . . . Not no more, baby . . . I'm tired of . . . gamin'. . . . Gamin' with you . . . with myself . . . with Charlotte . . . with everything I lay my hand to. . . . So, I went home . . . to straighten it all out. . . . *(She is in his arms now. He comforts her as he talks)* . . . For good, baby . . . I'm here for good . . . *(They kiss, slowly and warmly)* Let me stay, baby *(Pleading)* . . . let me stay . . .

(The lights dim out)

Scene Two

Several hours later.
We hear the quiet sounds of Lady Day's "One for My Baby." The room is dimly lighted by a small table lamp. After a few moments, Verda enters in a dressing gown. She walks to the coffee table and takes a cigarette from the pack, lights it and again crosses to the door to jiggle the safety chain. Satisfied that the room is secure she crosses to the window and stands looking out. Seconds later, Sammy enters. He is announced by his singing along with the record in the style of Billy Eckstine. Once in the room, he takes the broom and uses it as his mike.

VERDA: *(Laughing)* . . . You might as well quit, 'cause you don't sound nothin' like him . . . *(Sammy continues his singing. He performs like he is the "coolest" of the "cool." Verda, still laughing)* . . . You better hush up. . . . Them neighbors know I ain't got no cat . . .
(Sammy now turns the broom into a bass)
SAMMY: *(Shaking his head in the musician's cliche)* . . . Cool it, woman, . . . I'm inta my thang . . . *(Continues making bass sounds)*
VERDA: *(Sauntering teasingly in front of him)* . . . Humph . . . I thought it was *my* thang you was just inta . . .
(Sammy, surprised and amused by her comment, stops "strumming"

*and leans on the broom laughing as she moves past him, tickling his
chin as she does so)*

SAMMY: You's about one naaaaasty broad, you know that?

VERDA: *(Snaps her fingers and does a quick dance step)* . . .
Well, awwwwright!

*(Sammy sweeps the broom at her as she laughingly goes into the
bathroom)*

SAMMY: *(Crossing to replace the broom)* . . . Gon put yo'
mind out for trash next Wednesday . . .

VERDA: *(From the bathroom)* . . . You know what I wanna
do? . . .

SAMMY: *(Crossing to the sofa)* . . . We just did it . . .

VERDA: *(Lets out a whoop)* . . . Wooooooo! . . . Man, you
somethin' else . . . That ain't what I meant . . . I wanna go
for a walk . . .

SAMMY: *(Making himself comfortable on the sofa)* . . . at 2 AM?
. . . You wanna go walkin' on South Street at 2 AM? . . .

VERDA: *(Coming from the bathroom. She wears her wig and
make-up)* . . . You musta forgot everything if you don't remember South Street in the early morning. . . . *(Crossing to
the sofa)* . . . Street don't come alive 'til the bars close . . .
folks tryin' to get home. . . . Tryin' to talk somebody to make
it on back with 'em. . . . Saddest people in the world. . . .
Playin' like they "cool" so nobody won't know how very lonely
they really are. . . . Folks be laughin' 'cause two cats fightin'
over the same woman. . . . Some ol' broad what belong to a
different cat every night o' the week. . . . She standin' back
like she really count for somethin'. . . . It's loneliness. . . .
They fightin' so they won't have to face that room by they self,
that's all . . .

(Pause. Sammy walks to the window)

SAMMY: Lonely people everywhere in the world, baby . . .
*(For a moment, both Sammy and Verda run back through the past
three years of loneliness. Sammy turns, looks at Verda. His face tells
of his satisfaction. Those days are yesterday. She smiles, understanding, but unable to share her own thoughts, she turns away. Sammy
crosses toward the bedroom)*

VERDA: *(Catching his arm as he passes. Her voice is warm)* . . .
Where you goin', man . . .

SAMMY: *(Responding to her warmth)* . . . Put on my shoes. . . . So we can take a walk . . . *(Verda pulls him to her. They kiss warmly, with no reservations this time. Sammy, after the kiss)* . . . Don't do that . . . 'less you gon do it twice . . .

VERDA: *(Releasing him)* . . . Humph . . . You better take yo' black ass in there an' put them damn shoes on . . . *(Sammy laughs. Keeps walking)* Jus' like a niggah . . . ain't never satisfied! . . .

SAMMY: *(From the bedroom, laughing)* . . . So, you goin' out there in yo' bathrobe, hunh?

VERDA: Can't come in there if you in there . . . You don seen all o' me you gon' see tonight . . .

(Sammy crosses to the bathroom carrying his stuff)

SAMMY: *(As he crosses)* Gettin' prissy in your ol' age . . .

VERDA: *(Rising from the sofa)* . . . Jus' don't want you to get used to nothin', that's all . . . *(Turns off record player as she passes)* . . . Ya know, I'll betcha I coulda been a singer. . . . If she made it, I can . . . *(Goes into bedroom)*

SAMMY: An' Mohamad Ali's a punk, too . . .

VERDA: *(At the bedroom door)* . . . She just *sang* about the hard time I was *livin'*. . . . Lef' your wallet in here . . . *(Holds up wallet)*

SAMMY: *(From the bathroom)* Throw it here . . .

VERDA: Don't want nobody sayin' I'm takin' yo' money . . . *(Throws wallet. The wallet lands on the floor. Pictures and papers fall out. Verda goes to pick it up. As she gathers the stuff together, Sammy comes out. Verda has found something of interest to her)*

SAMMY: Just as crook armed as you can be . . .

(Verda is holding a picture of Charlotte, Sammy's wife. She lingers over it a minute and then, without thinking, drops everything and goes into the bedroom, leaving Sammy standing there. He slowly stoops to pick up the wallet, sees the picture, but says nothing. Dressed now, he crosses to the sofa and lights a cigarette, begins organizing the wallet, except the picture. The wallet all arranged, the picture in his hand, Sammy leans back on the sofa, smoking and running back through the last incident. Soon the sound of Verda humming quietly from the bedroom can be heard. She enters after a moment. Her manner is surprisingly bright. She refuses to be dampened)

VERDA: *(With strained brightness)* . . . Well . . . you ready? *(Sammy sits up, preparing to rise)*

SAMMY: Hey, . . . Look . . . *(Holds up the picture and starts to tear it in half)*

VERDA: *(Moves toward him)* Don't do that! . . . *(Pause. Quietly)* . . . It's bad luck . . . *(Lightly)* Anyway, that ain't no way to treat anybody you was married to for . . . how many years?

SAMMY: *(Not understanding her response)* . . . Sixteen . . . Sixteen in December . . .

(Verda crosses to table and picks up the wallet, takes the picture and begins putting the photo in place)

VERDA: That's what I mean . . . That's too much of your life . . . of *my* life to just be thrown into somebody's trash can. . . . *(Gives him the wallet)* . . . Now, come on . . . Let's go . . . I'm jus' gon put on some light . . . Ain't that crazy? . . . *(Moving around securing the apartment)* . . . Puttin' lights on so the junkies'll think somebody's home . . . *(Sammy is now standing, putting his wallet away. His mind, however, is back in Manson with Charlotte. Verda turns, sees him and crosses to him, taking his arm)* Lookahere, man . . . You took care o' all that, right? . . . I can't be jealous of the past, now, can I? . . . *(Pauses. Thinking he wants to talk about it)* . . . Okay, then, . . . sit down there . . . an' tell me about it . . . *(Verda crosses to the kitchen table, pulls out a chair and sits. Sammy moves to the window. As he moves)* . . . I mo sit right over here an' you can tell me . . . Tell me whatever's on your mind. . . . *(Pauses)* . . . What did she say?

SAMMY: Hunh?

VERDA: When you tol' her . . . well . . . When you tol' her it was . . . over . . . That you wanted out . . . *(Sammy looks away)* . . . Sammy?

SAMMY: *(After a moment)* . . . See . . . uh . . . it wasn't exactly like that . . . I mean, well *(Changes the subject)* . . . Did I tell you that she's got a little boy?

VERDA: *(Quietly)* . . . No . . . You didn't say . . .

SAMMY: He ain't mine . . . but she tol' everybody that it was . . . I was up here.

VERDA: I guess every boy needs a father, y'know . . .

SAMMY: *(Crosses to the counter)* . . . Yeah . . . He don't look nothin' like me, but he sure as hell got ways. . . . It's like, sometimes we'd be out in the yard, y'know . . . an' I'd forget . . . not just that he wasn't mine . . . but that he was hers, too . . . I'd keep thinkin' that he was *ours* . . . yours and mine . . . I mean . . . I was here with you . . . an' he does have my name . . . an' . . .

VERDA: *(Repeating her previous question)* What she say, Sammy?

SAMMY: I used to take him out to the park on Sundays. . . . He won't but five, but that dude can ride them horses an' . . . *(Remembering Verda's question)* . . . Everytime I . . . held him, my mind came back here . . . *(Looking directly at Verda)* . . . Things just don't work out right for us, baby. . . . Seems like we always gettin' to the corner after the bus is gone . . . *(Verda rises and begins turning out the lights again, starting with the bathroom. She knows the walk is for another time. She also knows that things are as they've always been. Sammy continues to talk as she moves about)* I tried to tell her . . . to keep everything in the open, y'know . . . Wanted to bring the boy . . . bring him here so we could . . . love him *together* . . . me, you . . . *(Crosses to Verda. Takes her arm)* . . . An' baby . . . he *is* mine . . . no matter whose . . . seed he is, he's mine . . . 'cause I love him . . . an' I want him. *(Verda, without speaking, moves from him. She goes to the counter and begins to mix some drinks)* I told her all that . . . an' she just turned and walked into the kitchen. *(Pauses)* I got in my car and drove downtown an' turned it in, caught the first bus outta there . . . an' . . . well, here I am . . . *(Intense)* I got to get it together, baby. . . . It's like your hol' life was up for grabs . . . *(Without speaking, Verda passes him a drink and crosses to the record pile. She begins leafing through the albums. Sammy drinks, watching her. After a moment, he speaks)* I didn't want it this way. . . . Honest to . . .

VERDA: *(Not wanting him to talk anymore, certain that further talk is useless)* . . . You know what we oughta do? . . . Set up a stand at Broad an' South . . . sell tickets. I'll betcha we could make a fortune. . . . Specially on Hallowe'en when all the

"vesties" come out. . . . Man, they be dressed to the teeth
. . . *(Putting on the record)* . . . Don't no woman dare to come
out . . . scared to be shamed by some of the funnies . . .

SAMMY: Verda . . .

VERDA: *(Overtaking him)* . . . You like Ray Bryant? . . .
(Record comes on. It is good and funky) . . . Come on . . . Let's
dance . . . *(Begins moving her body to the music)* . . . Yeah! . . .
Party time! . . . *(Grabs for Sammy)* . . . Come on ol' man . . .
Shake that thing . . . *(Sammy pulls back from her offer to dance.
She pauses momentarily, and then continues her solo "dance to ward
off ugly thoughts," talking to herself all the while. Sammy slowly
crosses to the table and sets his glass down. Verda, dancing)* . . .
Awwww, shu, now . . . I mo ball all by my lonesome. . . . Yes,
I am. . . . All by my lone . . . some . . .

*(She pauses over the word. Looks at Sammy and then quickly moves
to the counter. Sammy crosses to turn off the record player. Music
off, he pauses, turns to Verda)*

SAMMY: Baby, ain't nothin' changed . . .

VERDA: *(Sips her drink, but doesn't look at him)* . . . Not a
goddamned thing . . .

SAMMY: I'm here . . . to stay . . .

VERDA: *(Harshly)* And everything's all "straightened out"
. . .

SAMMY: Ain't nothin' back there for me . . . Y'unnerstan'
that? . . . Nothin'.

VERDA: *(Shaking her head)* . . . Not one thing . . .

SAMMY: *(Crossing to Verda)* . . . Come on . . . Let's make
that walk. . . . We can look . . .

VERDA: *(Gently)* . . . Un-unh . . . Ain't nothin' out there
that ain't in here, too. . . . So, let's just stay here . . . close an'
warm. . . . Listen to some music, drink a little . . . build up
some memories for tomorrow. . . . *(She crosses to the sofa)*

SAMMY: *(Quietly)* . . . You don't believe me . . . I'm for
real, baby . . .

VERDA: Sammy, you ain't never lied in your whole life.
. . . Not the kind that somebody can call ya down on. . . .
But stayin' ain't your style, man. . . . It just ain't your style.
. . . An' now you come around here talkin' 'bout some boy

that jus' gon give you another reason to make that split when the fun wears off.

SAMMY: . . . Well, what the hell do you want me to do. . . . Give you a written guarantee? . . . A preacher-made promise to "love, cherish, and obey?" . . .

VERDA: *(Rising. The tears starting)* . . . *That might be a reasonable start.* . . . Might let me go to bed thinkin' that you at least *intend* to be here in the mornin'. . . . Yes, dammit . . . That's exactly what I want . . . a guarantee . . .

(Verda starts for the table to get a handkerchief from her purse. Sammy moves away. He is embarrassed by her tears and the fact that he has caused them)

SAMMY: *(Quietly. After a pause)* . . . Baby, you know I'd give anything . . . everything. An' if I could marry you tomorrow . . . no, tonight . . . this minute . . .

VERDA: *(With new composure)* But . . . "that train's gone, too" . . . so our . . . *love* . . . has to be a sometime thing . . . a grunt and a groan between the 8:05 and the 9:15 . . .

SAMMY: *(Coming to her)* . . . Hey, baby . . . I didn't make this world . . .

VERDA: A quick drink and a few polite laughs about *yesterday,* or maybe somebody else's baby. *(Nasty)* Yeah, "ol' times"! . . . that's our bag . . . *(Moves quickly to the counter)* . . . Come on, man . . . You wanna raise the elbow one more time before we make that run, don't cha? Just for "ol' times"!

(Verda is trying to pour the drinks. She roughly grabs things and slams them around, dropping the bottle in the process. The whiskey spills all over the floor and splashes her dress. The combination of the dropping bottle and the tension of the room totally unsettle her, causing her to cry and swear at herself and the whole situation. Sammy rushes to her, taking her in his arms)

SAMMY: *(Comforting her)* . . . It's me, baby. . . . The whole goddamned, messed up . . . It's always been me. . . . It wasn't s'posed to get like this. . . . *(Lifting her face to him)* . . . Come on, baby . . . pull it all together. . . . Ain't nothin' worth all that . . . *(Forcing a lighter tone. Humoring her)* . . . Specially a jivetime joker like me . . . come on, now . . .

(He wipes her eyes with his hands. This kind of overt tenderness

embarrasses Verda, especially now. She moves from him on the pretense of wiping the floor. She takes the towel from behind the counter)

VERDA: *(Hiding in forced humor)* Gotta get this mess up . . . Damn roaches be high an' I'll never get rid of 'em . . .

(Verda begins wiping the floor. Sammy crosses to sofa, lights a cigarette. His face shows him to be running through the whole thing. Rather than stay with her and have things go smooth, he sees that his staying would not be like before. He moves idly about the room)

SAMMY: *(Trying to be jovial)* I wonder what folks out there on the street would think about the . . . "sights" in here . . . *(The banter sours as he plays with the answer)* . . . I guess . . . it ain't so different, is it? . . . I mean . . . up here, down there . . . *(Turns back to the window)* Y'watch that T.V. long enough you get to thinkin' that lovin' is the easiest thing in the world . . . all you got to do is want it bad enough, ya know? . . . Maybe that's why niggahs is so messed up . . . believin' all that bullshit . . . *(Verda starts to put the cloth away)* . . . Ain't a day in my life that you ain't on my mind . . . *(She continues to walk)* . . . But I just keep hop-scotchin' back an' forth between what folks call "duty," I guess . . . an' my wants . . .

(Verda looks at him a second, tries to smile, then crosses to the bedroom. Anticipating his question)

VERDA: My make-up done run all over . . . *(She continues to the door where she pauses a minute, turns back to him)* Sammy . . . maybe it ought to be some other way . . . but it ain't . . . I guess I just been actin' like I can't see, expectin' things to be different from the way they are. . . . You all tied up an' I can't have you 'til you get loose . . . an' judging from what's already gone down, it don't look like that's about to happen. . . . So, we better just take what we can . . . don't worry 'bout no long-term promises . . .

SAMMY: Un-unh . . . I'm through with "almost" this an' "almost" that. . . . For keeps . . . Baby, we got to start buildin' somethin' for us. . . . We got . . .

VERDA: *(Stopping him)* I know . . . man, I know too well . . . but let's do it one day at a time. . . . That's all we really got . . . *(Sammy, recognizing the truth of her words turns from her and back to the window. Verda, looking at her dress)* . . . I guess I better change this thing. . . Can't be walkin' out there smellin' like a bar rag . . . *(She exits into the bedroom. Sammy looks back to the bedroom, crushes his cigarette in the ashtray. He looks again at the door to the bedroom and crosses to his coat)*

SAMMY: *(Calling)* You gon be long, baby? . . . I mean, if we don't hurry up an' get out there, won't be nobody to see . . .

VERDA: *(Calling from the bedroom, a laugh in her voice)* . . . Man, give me some time. Jus' get here an' rushin' me already . . .

(Sammy picks up his coat)

SAMMY: *(Forcing a light tone)* . . . You know somethin', woman. . . . You'd be one hundred per cent better off without me. . . . I'll betcha a fat man on that . . . I mean, you need a regular cat. . . . One that can keep his own timetable . . . *(Quietly opening the locks. Pauses, his face filled with the pain of finally knowing it is over, that he has nothing to give)*

VERDA: *(Still calling)* . . . Don't think I haven't thought about it! . . . But, then who would I wait for? . . . Man, I done got so used to takin' things at half measure, I wouldn't know how to act with no regular cat. . . . *(Sammy puts key on the table—reluctantly—and quietly exits through the door as, seconds later, Verda comes into the room in a different dress)* Last time you left here, I almost . . . *(Sees him gone)* . . . Sammy? *(She stands for a moment, then crosses to the door and re-sets the locks, sees the keys, tosses them on the sofa as the lights dim)*

Curtain

Donald Kvares

THE DARNING
NEEDLE

Donald Kvares

One of Off-Off-Broadway's most prolific dramatists, Donald Kvares, was initially introduced to the area's theatregoing public in 1972 when his play, *American Gothics,* was seen at the Roundabout Theatre. Since then, thirty-five of his plays have tenanted stages of such theatrical citadels as the La Mama Experimental Theatre Club, the Judson Poets' Theatre, the New York Shakespeare Festival's Public Theatre and Playwrights Horizons.

One of the author's most popular dramas, *Mrs. Minter,* was presented at the Actors Studio both in New York and California where it was staged by Lee Strasberg, and later produced at the Queens Playhouse on Long Island.

The Darning Needle, which appears in print for the first time in this anthology, originally was given Off-Off-Broadway. The critic for the *Village Voice* admitted that "I left this play with a happy feeling of expanded possibility," while other journalists described it as "a skillfully crafted delight" and "a warmly positive examination of the duality between the earthly and the spiritual in our lives."

Mr. Kvares, who studied playwriting at New York's City College and the New School for Social Research, was the winner (for his comedy, *Smoking Pistols*) of Manhattan's first Original Short Play Festival sponsored by Samuel French at the Double Image Theatre in 1976.

Characters:

BETTY
DAVE
IDA

Scene:

The two rooms of an apartment house on 97th Street and Broadway in New York City. The apartment belongs to Betty and Max Gorner. There is a small boarder's room, and a large sitting room, near a kitchen. It is a dark, rainy night. Betty is standing by the front door looking out, her hands on her hips, furious. In Dave's room (the boarder) the record player is going full blast, and Dave is alternately typing and acting out something from several pieces of paper he holds in his hand.

BETTY: Stop belching, you'll poison the air in Central Park. *(A mumbling from the stairway)* My pot roast? It was first cut brisket, you slob! *(Raising her voice, and leaning forward so she can be heard)* And don't come back till after midnight, Max, I'm playing gin.

(She slams the front door and returns to the apartment, sets up for the card game, is attracted by the sounds from Dave's room. She walks up to the door and listens)

DAVE: "I'm sorry. I must leave now. Before it's too late. *Au revoir.*" *(He opens the door to his room and catches Betty. He is making a flamboyant gesture—and when he sees her his hand hangs in mid-air)* Oh—ex—excuse me.

BETTY: Hi!

DAVE: Hello.

BETTY: So that's what you were doing!

DAVE: What?

BETTY: This! *(She gestures the way Dave did)*

DAVE: *(Thinking)* When did I do that?

BETTY: Don't you remember?

DAVE: No.

BETTY: Oh, well. I don't know. I just thought you were—I mean—don't you go to school on Wednesdays?

DAVE: Usually. But it's kind of rainy tonight. I thought I'd stay home and work on my play.

BETTY: All right, but keep it low, will you? I didn't expect you to be home tonight. I got this gin game every Wednesday, and I told my friend you go to school, so if the jazz is blasting like that, with the acting and everything, I wouldn't want her to get the wrong impression.

DAVE: The wrong impression?

BETTY: I told her you were a nice, quiet fellow, very studious and intellectual, and you don't bother anybody, so if you just stay in your room real quiet like, and read a book or something, everything'll be fine.

(The phone rings. Betty answers. Dave closes his door with an expression of regret)

BETTY: Hello . . . So, where are you? You're not coming? What's the matter? Oh, Ida, is a little rain gonna kill you? All you gotta do is take an umbrella and cross the street. . . . But I got everything set up already. Ida, listen, it's just across the street. That's all. You won't even get wet. . . . A *phobia?* What are you talking about? . . . . You want me to come over there? Well—! Don't worry. My place is a mess, too. *(Looks out window)* I know it's raining cats and dogs. *(As she looks, the rain stops)* Ida! It stopped. *(Looks again—in shock)* Just now. You don't believe me? Take a look. Yeah, that's right. It stopped. All right, so what do you wanta do? You're comin' over? All right, I'll see you.

(Betty hangs up. Dave starts to go out. Moves towards the door)

BETTY: Dave, where are you going?

DAVE: Well, if you're playing cards, I don't want to—!

BETTY: You don't want to what?

DAVE: I don't want to be in the way.

BETTY: Don't be so sensitive. I didn't mean anything by it.

DAVE: That's all right, Mrs. Gorner. I need some cigarettes anyway.

BETTY: You want a cigarette? All you gotta do is ask.

DAVE: Oh, no. I couldn't.

BETTY: Here, take a couple. You don't have to go out. The streets are all wet. I'm sorry I spoke so short to you. It's just—I know you're an intelligent boy and I don't want people to think funny things about you—that's all!

DAVE: I understand. But I really need cigarettes.

BETTY: Don't worry about it. I got five packs. If you want one—!

DAVE: I couldn't do that.

BETTY: You'll owe me. Here. Now go inside and work on your masterpiece. You're in the mood now.

DAVE: All right. If you say so.

(He enters room. Doorbell rings)

IDA: *(As Betty answers door)* Hi!

BETTY: So, you didn't melt!

IDA: All day it poured, and then, suddenly, it stopped. I was supposed to visit my mother this afternoon.

BETTY: Your mother? She's been dead for five years.

IDA: That's what I'm saying. I was supposed to go out to the cemetery. It's her birthday today. This is the first year I missed it. I feel terrible. Oh, well, she knows how I am about the rain. She'll understand. *(Pause)* I bled all over her *Yahrtzeit* candle.

BETTY: What?

IDA: I was sewing a garment. It had to be ready by five, and I pricked my finger. Imagine me, a dressmaker for twenty-five years. Well, anyway, it drew blood, and the next thing I knew, a red stream was trickling down the side of mama's candle.

BETTY: So!

IDA: I just thought it was funny, that's all. What's that noise?

BETTY: It's my new boarder. He plays a lotta jazz records. I'd better tell him to lower it.

IDA: No, don't. Let him play. I like jazz.

BETTY: You're crazy! Come on inside. Max is gone.

(They enter the sitting room)

IDA: *(Sees the brisket)* What's this?

BETTY: It's brisket, can't you tell?

IDA: He left it again. Every Wednesday—!

BETTY: I don't know. With that man, everything has to be just so. If I cut off my right arm, he'd probably wonder.

IDA: Wonder? What would he wonder?

BETTY: Just wonder, that's all. Twenny-one years I live in this house and not once does he say, "This is a good piece of meat!"

IDA: Well, it *is* kinda tough. *(Betty shrugs)* Try it. It's stringy.

BETTY: Well, maybe it is. I don't know. I don't care really. *(Changing the subject)* So, you didn't tell me. What's with the new hat?

IDA: You like it? It cost me fifteen dollars.

BETTY: Fifteen dollars? I don't like it.

IDA: Well, I admit it is a little extravagant, but then again, Aries people are usually extravagant.

BETTY: I don't believe in all that astrology hokum.

(Dave gets sick in his room)

IDA: You should become a mystic, Betty. You'd find it so exciting.

BETTY: I'm not like you. You're always busy with a million things. Me—I just go to the track once in a while, or sit in the house! Watch TV. Maybe play some gin. I like things the way they are. The only thing I don't like is this heat lately. *(She drags out the playing cards)* You'd think the rain'd cool things off a little.

IDA: I know. It's terrible. Especially today.

BETTY: And in the middle of October, too.

IDA: I was reading somewhere that all this strange weather comes from exploding so many bombs. It mixes up the elements, pollutes the air, so to speak.

BETTY: Do me a favor, will you, Ida? Don't talk about it. I get scared enough reading the paper every day. Let's just play gin and enjoy ourselves. Okay? *(Ida nods)* Okay. *(Indicating the cards)* You wash! *(Ida washes the cards. Dave enters. Betty looks up)* What is it, Dave?

DAVE: Mrs. Gorner, do you have something for upset stomach? I feel awful.

BETTY: I got some Alka Seltzer if you want?

DAVE: Oh, thanks. That'll be all right.

BETTY: *(On her way to kitchen)* Ida, meet Dave.

(Ida and Dave look at each other. Suddenly Dave turns green)

IDA: You know, you're turning green.

DAVE: *(Laughs in shock)* Am I?

IDA: Sure. Look in the mirror.

DAVE: You're right. I am.

IDA: I told you so.

BETTY: *(Returning)* Here, Dave. Now just rest a while. You been working too hard.

(He drinks, then turns to go)

IDA: Wait. Just a minute. *(Pause) Pisces!*

DAVE: Excuse me?

IDA: You—! *(Pause)* Were born—! *(Pause)* On March 5th.

DAVE: March 3rd.

IDA: Two days off. That's not so bad, is it?

DAVE: No, not at all. Well, I guess I won't do any more writing tonight. I'll just lie down for a while.

IDA: You're a writer?

BETTY: He's a playwriter.

IDA: A playwright.

DAVE: I'm trying to be.

IDA: My cousin's sister-in-law is married to a very famous playwright. Kyle Stanford. *(Pause)* He wrote some shows for Studio One. Remember Studio One?

DAVE: Yes, quite fondly.

IDA: My, you don't look at all well. *(Pause)*

DAVE: I feel terrible. *(He finishes off his drink)*

IDA: You'd better take care of yourself. After all, geniuses have to be nurtured, don't they, Betty?

BETTY: Sure. I threw you an eight.

IDA: Don't need it.

DAVE: I guess I better get back.

IDA: Good luck.

DAVE: Thanks. I could use some. *(Exits, taking glass with him absent-mindedly)*

IDA: Nice looking boy. Intelligent, too.

BETTY: Yeah, but a hippie, like I never saw before. And the characters he brings up.

IDA: Really?

BETTY: The dregs. The absolute dregs.

IDA: My, oh, my. He must be very stimulating. I wonder what his rising sign is.

(Dave tries to sneak back into kitchen to return glass)

BETTY: Oy! You scared me.

DAVE: I'm sorry. I just wanted to return this.

BETTY: Do you have to sneak up on a person?

DAVE: I didn't want to disturb your game. I really appreciated . . .

BETTY: All right. Okay.

DAVE: Thank you.

BETTY: Anytime.

IDA: You feel better now?

DAVE: Oh, much better. In fact, a hundred percent.

IDA: Good. You're not green anymore.

DAVE: Really? *(Laughs)* That was funny.

IDA: Yes. It was.

(They chuckle a bit together)

BETTY: *(With annoyance)* Why don't you finish your play, Dave?

DAVE: Oh. Oh, sure, excuse me.

(He returns to his room. They play cards for a while. He types. A huge dragonfly, a darning needle, enters the window of his room, and buzzes about. It begins to drone. Dave notices the darning needle, and is at first terrified of it, then has a comic ballet trying to avoid it. He enters the living room quietly again)

DAVE: Mrs. Gorner . . .

BETTY: What's the matter now?

DAVE: I hate to disturb you again, but—?

BETTY: But what?

DAVE: There's a darning needle in my room.

BETTY: A darning needle? What's a darning needle?

IDA: Don't you know what a darning needle is? It's like one of those stinging bees. You know?

BETTY: I come from Canada. I don't know from stinging bees.

IDA: They're country bees, mostly. Didn't you ever see one? They got that long tail.

BETTY: What's a country bee doing in the city?

DAVE: I don't know. I was shocked by it myself. I just opened the window to get some fresh air, and it must've flown in.

BETTY: Well, what do you want me to do about it?

DAVE: If you have any Larvex, or some spray. Anything like that.

BETTY: Wait a minute? I'll look. *(She rummages through some things in the adjoining kitchen. She comes out again holding a flit-gun)* I got a flit-gun. Would that help?

DAVE: Well, gee! I don't know. I mean, it's a very big darning needle.

BETTY: Wait a minute. I want to see this thing. *(She charges over towards Dave's room. Opens door)*

DAVE: Don't go in so fast. It dives at moving objects.

(But she is already in the room, looking around. Dave and Ida enter Dave's room)

BETTY: Where is it?

DAVE: I—I don't know. It was here a minute ago.

BETTY: Maybe it flew out again. *(She turns to exit from the room, and Ida touches her on the shoulder, her eyes fastened on the wall)*

IDA: Look! Against the wall.

BETTY: *(Turns to look at the wall)* The wall—where?

IDA: *(Pointing)* Right over there.

BETTY: *(Spotting the insect on the wall. In horror)* My God— what is it?

DAVE: I told you. It's a darning needle.

BETTY: But such a size.

IDA: Isn't it fascinating? It must be a mutant.

BETTY: A what? What are you talkin' about?

IDA: You know, those things you see in science fiction pictures.

BETTY: I never go to the movies. How should I know?

IDA: Well, that's what it must be.

DAVE: What can we do?

BETTY: God! I never saw a bee so big in my life.

IDA: Maybe—if you got a chair, and stood on it.

BETTY: What good would that do?

IDA: Then you could get up close to it, to spray it.

BETTY: Who wants to get close to that thing? Are you crazy? You'd get such a bite, you'd die!

IDA: You don't have to get that close to it. Look, let me show you. *(She gets a chair and steps on it)* See. Now give me the spray, quick.

BETTY: Aim it good. There ain't much left in it.

IDA: Don't worry. I'm an expert at this. Here. Now watch. *(She leans over a little and starts to spray the darning needle)*

BETTY: Be careful, will ya? You'll fall off and break my chair.

IDA: I won't break your chair. I just want to aim it properly.

DAVE: Maybe *I* should do it. It's not right to ask anyone else.

IDA: Nonsense. It's practically dead right now.

(The darning needle springs to life, flying around the room. All three run out of the room, into the hall)

BETTY: Shut the door, quick! I thought you were such an expert. What happened?

IDA: Well, I didn't think it would start flying.

DAVE: Perhaps, if you gave me the spray, I could manage by myself. I'm sure you want to get back to your game.

BETTY: No, don't open the door! I don't want it flying through the house.

DAVE: But what am I going to do?

BETTY: Just stay with us for a while. Maybe it'll fly out again.

DAVE: But I have work. I've got a lot of typing to do.

BETTY: I don't want you to open the door, understand?

IDA: Maybe, if someone snuck in, very quietly, and turned the light off.

BETTY: How would that help?

IDA: Well, darning needles are attracted by light, aren't they, Dave?

DAVE: Yes. It's a habit of insects.

IDA: And if the light is out, maybe it would fly out again, wouldn't it?

DAVE: That's very possible.

BETTY: I don't know what this is all about! I just know I never saw a bee such a size in my whole life.

IDA: Look, Dave. Why don't you go back inside, very quietly, and turn the light off?

DAVE: Okay.

BETTY: Wait a minute! *(She pulls Ida in the living room, hides behind her)*

IDA: What are you doing?

BETTY: All right. Open it now. Well, go ahead!

DAVE: I can't. It's hovering above the door.

BETTY: Then close the door. I don't wanta' get stung.

(Dave closes the door quietly. He scratches his head)

DAVE: What should I do?

BETTY: I don't know. How should I know?

DAVE: Well, I can't stand out here all night. Maybe if you lent me one of your brooms, I could swat it to death or some such thing.

BETTY: You crazy? You'll break my broom on that thing.

IDA: So give him an old one. You got an old one, haven't you?

BETTY: Wait a minute. Lemme see. I don't know why everyone has to come bothering me about things. *(She looks in the broom closet)* I got a feather duster I don't use anymore. It's all kinky and broken through. *(Laughing a little)* You know, Ida, I remember this feather duster as far back as 1950. I never knew I still had it. It's funny the things you find hidden away.

IDA: You're telling me. I found a whole set of lace handkerchiefs in my bottom drawer that I thought I'd lost.

DAVE: Don't you have a broom?

BETTY: Just a minute, Dave. Be patient, will ya? *(Pulls out a whisk broom)* Look at this, Ida. I bought this whisk broom in 1957, in a rummage sale. I never used it.

DAVE: Perhaps I can use that then?

BETTY: Are you crazy? This is brand new. I don't want no darning needle messing it up. Here, take this one.

(He takes the broom from her and walks back to the door of his room. He opens it and the darning needle flies out into the hall)

BETTY: Dave, shut the door! That thing is in the hall now.

IDA: Let's turn out all the lights.

(They turn out all the lights)

BETTY: So now we're in the dark. So what do we do now?

IDA: Open the window!

BETTY: If I can find it. *Ouch!*

IDA: What happened?

BETTY: The settee. I bunked my leg into the settee!

IDA: You're too anxious. That's your trouble.

BETTY: *(Opens the window)* All right. What now—?

IDA: Can you see the telephone?

BETTY: I can't see a damn thing.

IDA: All right. Wait till your eyes get acclimated, and then, go over to the phone and call Min from my building across the street.

BETTY: Why should I do that? I hardly know the woman. She's your friend.

IDA: Listen, her kitchen window faces you. If she turns on her light, maybe the thing'll fly over in that direction.

BETTY: What's the sense in that? The thing would only fly into her window, wouldn't it? Why would she want that?

IDA: Her window is closed.

BETTY: Yeah. That's right. Y'know. That is a good idea.

IDA: So. Call her up.

BETTY: What's her number?

IDA: Endicott 7-7777.

BETTY: All sevens?

(Ida nods)

DAVE: Gee! I'm sorry for all this commotion.

IDA: I think it's all pretty exciting myself.

BETTY: God! I never saw such a tremendous—! *(Into the phone)* Hello. Is this Mrs. Hartman? This is Betty Gorner. I'm a friend of Ida's. Yes. That's right. Right across the way. Ida thought I could ask you a favor. I said—Ida thought I could ask you a favor! If you tell your husband to lower the television you could hear me. What?

IDA: What'd she say?

BETTY: She says she's not hard of hearing. If you ask me, she sounds like a real crab.

IDA: Not so loud, she'll hear you.

BETTY: She can't hear me, she's talking to her husband. Mrs. Hartman? Oh? I'm sorry. I thought you were talkin' to your husband. What do I want? *(Pause)* Well—it's nothing very important but —a darning needle just flew into my tenant's room a few minutes ago and he opened the door. Now the thing is flying around through the whole house and everything. Well, I'm afraid of the size of it. You should see—it's like a flying rat. . . . Well, Ida suggested if I called you, and asked you to turn on your light, maybe he'd fly out of our window . . . . No, no, he won't fly into yours. Your window is shut. I just now looked. . . . Look, Mrs. Hartman, it's not just for me. It's the principle of the thing. I know I never call up under other circumstances but it's only a simple favor. *(Pause)* Well, I think that's very unfair of you. As a matter of fact, you don't encourage friendship. If you encouraged it, I might call up under other circumstances. Well, of all the gall, what did you ever do for me?

IDA: Betty! This is so silly. Let me have the phone, will you?

(Betty gives her the phone)

BETTY: Who does she think she is anyway? Talking to me like that?

IDA: *(Into phone)* Listen, Min, what's the matter with you? Can't you be nice once in a while? Well, she's my friend and she's just asking a simple favor for me. Why didn't I call? It's her house. She should call.

BETTY: Cut it short, will you, Ida? That woman is wasting my money.

IDA: Do you know you're wasting her money like this?

BETTY: Ida, you're crazy? Don't tell her that.

IDA: *(Into phone)* All right. All right. I know you're mad. Just calm down. I know. I know. But it *is* a problem. If you saw the size of this creature you'd want to help, believe me. No, you don't have to worry about the living room light, just the kitchen light. Yes. Yes, dear. It'll be enough. I know you want to help. You're a good person. I know that. No, just the kitchen light. Yes. Yes, I'm sure that'll be enough. Min, don't go overboard. Just the kitchen light. *(Betty groans)* Yes, I know you're sorry. I'll tell her. Don't worry about it. Sure, Min. Okay, Min. Yeah . . . Okay. Yeah. I'll see you tomorrow. The usual time. So long. *(Pause)* What? NO! *I don't believe it* . . .

BETTY: All right, Ida. Hang up already! That buzzin' is drivin' me batty.

IDA: This is terrible news! When did it happen? Gut! I have to send a condolence card. Miriam's mother? Oy! And she was such a strong woman. And so young. Well, I always told you. God takes the good people early. The other kind, he lets them live longer so they can suffer.

BETTY: Ida, it's awful dark in here.

IDA: That's right. I always said that you make your own hell right here on earth.

BETTY: Ida, come on already. It's a half-hour of talking.

IDA: Stop exaggerating! It's only five minutes. No, I was just talking to Betty. Yes. Isn't Miriam a sweet thing? At least the old lady had a daughter she could be proud of. Well, I have to send a condolence card. That's all. Okay, Min. Then I'll see you tomorrow . . . No, I won't forget the dress. I have it all done . . . . Taffeta. What else? Well, I got it cheap.

BETTY: Taffeta schmafetta! Talk to her tomorrow.

IDA: Fredericks. Tenth Avenue. Finest fabrics in the world. I'm telling you, Min, it's a giveaway. Okay, I'll hold on . . .

BETTY: Ida, that bee noise is getting louder and louder. I don't know what to do.

DAVE: Maybe if I put some candles by the window?

BETTY: Oh, stop it, Dave! I have enough *tsurris* with you. You come in all the time, every hour of the night, with those ugly looking hippie girls and you play your jazz till all hours, at the very top volume. You could blow somebody's ears off! Honestly, I don't know what to do about you.

DAVE: I didn't know you felt so strongly about my jazz.

BETTY: Well, I do. And if you keep it up, I'll have to ask you to leave.

DAVE: I'll be careful in the future if it really bothers you.

BETTY: Well, it does. Just don't take so much advantage. Okay?

DAVE: Okay.

IDA: Thanks. I see it's on. What? Oh, I love sauerbraten. I can't wait.

BETTY: I got people dying to have that room for two dollars extra. I don't need all the problems I get with you. Just remember that.

DAVE: All right, Mrs. Gorner—all right.

IDA: But is it good with brisket? I like round roast myself.

BETTY: And another thing. That bathroom is always a mess when you get through with it. *(Her voice is getting angrier by the minute)* You're always traipsing over the floor in your bare feet after you take a shower. I gotta go in there with a mop and pail. I'm not a nursemaid to anyone. Understand?

IDA: How long do you cook it? You use the sour salts or the vinegar?

BETTY: Ida, will you please . . . ?

IDA: And a cup of crushed ginger snaps. Yeah, that's right? How do you like that? Our recipes tally so closely. Do you make the potato dumpling or the *latkes*. My Abe loves the *latkes*. I know it goes better, but what can you do? He's a college boy.

BETTY: Ida, will you please hang up?

IDA: Betty, control yourself. What will the woman think?

BETTY: I don't give a damn what she thinks! I just want that monster bee out of here. You just tell her to turn on the light and forget about the sauerbraten! Okay? Just tell her that.

IDA: Betty, if you weren't so excited, and just took a look out that window, you'd see the light was on.

(Betty looks out the window)

BETTY: Then what's all the buzzing about? I still hear that buzzing.

IDA: Give it time, will you? *(Pause)* Okay, I'm back. Maybe I better call you tomorrow. This is Betty's phone. I feel a little guilty talking so long . . . Around twelve. Is that okay by you? Definitely. I won't forget. Well, I've been a busy little bee. I've hardly had time to call my fabric man. Well, you know. I have my astrology and mystics' club. You've just got to come with me one day. It's enthralling. All right, Min. I have to hang up now. Okay. Yeah. No, not too much sugar in the icing. You have a tendency to sweeten everything too much. G'bye. *(She hangs up)*

BETTY: Well, finally!

IDA: Did the thing fly out yet?

BETTY: No. What do you think I'm shaking for?

DAVE: Look, this whole thing was awful of me. I mean—dragging you people into it. Maybe if I opened the door of my room again, it'll fly back in, and then it won't bother you anymore.

IDA: It'll bother *you*, won't it?

(Dave shrugs, like a martyr)

BETTY: I wonder where that thing is? It gets me aggravated just sitting here like this.

(The buzz stops)

IDA: Listen, the buzz stopped.

BETTY: It must've flew out. Quick! Let's close all the windows!

IDA: I still think it's around here. I didn't see it fly out. The buzzing stopped too quick. It could be against the wall, or the light cord, or something. *(There is a short buzz)* D'you hear that? It's still here.

BETTY: No. It's not.

IDA: I heard a buzz.

BETTY: It was just a doorbell down the hall.

IDA: No. No, it was our creature.

BETTY: Come on. Don't talk like that. Let's just play cards.

DAVE: If you want to play I could still light those candles. You could see by them, couldn't you? They're dim enough not to attract the darning needle.

IDA: Say! That's a good idea. If Betty's really frightened, that seems the most logical compromise.

DAVE: I'll get the candles.

IDA: Can you find your way?

DAVE: I'll just feel along the walls.

(He finds the door of his room and enters. Returns to the living room with candles)

BETTY: How come you have candles in your room?

DAVE: I belong to the Alchemists.

BETTY: The Alchemists? What's that?

DAVE: It's an organization, at City College. It's based on the concept of primitive metal making.

IDA: I think you've got that wrong, haven't you?

DAVE: Excuse me?

IDA: My Abe also goes to City, and he says the Alchemists are a group that practice witchcraft.

DAVE: Well, yes. In contemporary application it has taken on certain perverse characteristics. But then again, this happened only in Salem or other famous witch communities. Some Alchemists were extraordinarily intelligent men. I'm sure even Albert Einstein dabbled in Alchemy occasionally.

BETTY: God! The way he's talkin' and that buzz and all— it's almost spooky. I wish I had'na chased Max outta the house.

IDA: I love spooky things. Don't you?

DAVE: If they're effective, yes.

IDA: Talking about effectiveness, I saw that horror picture with Vincent Price the other night.

DAVE: Did you like it? I heard it was made *con amore.*

IDA: Yes. It was very *con amore.* And also terribly eerie.

BETTY: Pictures like that are stupid as far as I can see. That's why I don't go to the movies. *(She washes the cards)* I mean, if the characters were halfway real, instead of such four-eyed monsters.

DAVE: But don't you see? That's what makes them so peculiarly delectable.

BETTY: What do you mean, delectable? Pot roast is delectable, not people. And especially not monsters.

DAVE: I meant it in the cerebral sense.

BETTY: Is that the way your thoughts run? My father died of a cerebral hemorrhage. I don't like to think about such things.

DAVE: No, no, I wasn't referring to a cerebral hemorrhage. When I used the term cerebral, I meant, heady, intellectual, profound.

IDA: Give up, Dave. You're too deep for her. I'm a mystic myself, so I understand.

BETTY: I wish you would stop talking about mystics, and horrors, and things. The darkness is gettin' spookier by the minute.

IDA: Yes, it is, isn't it? How bizarre . . .

BETTY: I wish Max would get back. I can almost feel that thing buzzin' round my head. *(The table moves slightly)* What was that? The table's rattlin!

IDA: Don't move, Betty. Just sit still.

(Dave and Ida stare at each other. Their eyes become transfixed)

BETTY: But—that thing is under the table. That thing!

IDA: Don't speak! Just sit still, and be silent.

(They all sit still for a second and the table rattles again, violently. They all reach across the table and grasp each others' hands. After a moment, Dave, who has been groaning, speaks. His voice is richly feminine)

DAVE: Ida. Ida, my child.

IDA: Mama. Mama, is—is it really you?

DAVE: Yes. I missed you so.

BETTY: Hey, what's going on here? Leggo!

IDA: *Don't pull your hand away, Betty! It's my mother.*

BETTY: What are you talkin' about? Your mother's dead.

IDA: She spoke now. She really spoke, Betty.

BETTY: *(Gulping in fear)* Did she?

IDA: Mama. Mama, where are you?

DAVE: I could ask you the same question. What kinda place is this?

IDA: It's Betty's house. You know, Betty Gorner.

DAVE: You mean, that woman with the belching husband?

BETTY: Wait a minute! What is this?

IDA: She's all right, Mama. So's he. He's all right.

DAVE: He's all right? Well, I just know you came home crying once because he threw a grasshopper into your soup at the Nevele.

BETTY: How does he know?

IDA: It was just a practical joke, and so long ago. Please, Mama, don't embarrass me. Betty is my friend.

DAVE: Some friend! I should have such a friend.

IDA: She's helped me many times.

DAVE: How did she help you? She only helped you lose all

your money. That's what? I remember, that time you went to Belmont and lost everything in the fifth.

BETTY: How does she know?

DAVE: A sure thing! If she had the best bookie in the world she wouldn't be able to pick a sure thing.

BETTY: Abe Greene is not exactly a bad bookie.

DAVE: Abe Greene should have his head examined!

BETTY: *You're wrong! Abe Greene is a very good bookie.*

IDA: Betty! Mama! Don't fight. Let's not spoil it. I'm so glad you're here.

DAVE: I had to come.

IDA: I know. I couldn't come to see you today, so you came to see me.

DAVE: There's one less rock on the grave. I like the rocks to pile up.

IDA: I'll put one there tomorrow. I promise.

DAVE: How do you feel, all right?

IDA: Fine.

DAVE: Your finger's cut.

IDA: It's nothing. Just a scratch.

DAVE: If you're smart you'll wear a thimble, next time.

IDA: Oh, Mama. I wish I could see you.

DAVE: I know. But—we will see each other. Soon. Just be patient.

IDA: Is it nice where you are? Are you content? Can you tell me, Mama? Are you allowed to tell me what it's like?

DAVE: I can feel. That's the important thing. Where I am now, I'm alive. I'll tell you one thing, Ida. I'd rather be here, than where you are right now.

BETTY: Now what do you mean by that?

DAVE: Ida knows. She knows.

BETTY: What does she know? Now stop that! Just, stop that.

IDA: Betty, what are you doing?

BETTY: Give me my hand, will you? Dave, stop acting like a madman.

IDA: It's not Dave.

BETTY: It *is* Dave. It is! Leggo! Come on, leggo . . . *(She pulls away. We hear a clump, as though something heavy had hit the table)* What's the matter?

IDA: You shouldn't have pulled away like that. It could cause serious damage to any medium.

BETTY: You're crazy. He's crazy. This whole thing is crazy.

IDA: Don't worry about it, Betty. Keep calm. Nobody's crazy. Not at all. Just take his hand again.

BETTY: I will not.

IDA: We must bring him back to this plane.

BETTY: Ida, stop it!

IDA: Please, Betty. Just do it for me, okay? It's not too much to ask.

BETTY: I don't see the point to all this.

IDA: He might die.

BETTY: What—But I—Oh, my God! No . . .

IDA: Oh, yes.

BETTY: But I—I didn't mean it. Oh, God! I didn't mean it.

IDA: I know you didn't mean it, Betty, so just take his hand.

BETTY: All right! All right.

(She takes his hand again, and they sit perfectly still for a few seconds. The table rattles terribly. Then Dave struggles to life again)

IDA: You see. He's moving. He's coming back to our life. Mama. Mama, speak to me.

DAVE: Is that thing still under the table? I must've fallen asleep.

IDA: Oh, dear. We've lost her.

DAVE: Lost her? Who?

IDA: My mother's spirit came back, through you.

DAVE: Your mother? I don't understand . . .

IDA: She spoke. Through you.

DAVE: That's not possible.

IDA: But you sounded just like her. You really did.

BETTY: This all makes absolutely no sense at all. I call up a friend for a quiet game of cards and the whole evening turns into a hocus-pocus, a nightmare.

IDA: I find it very stimulating. The presence of the occult, something otherworldly. But then again, I've always had these burning visions. They come upon me so often, unawares, while I'm sewing a garment, or standing in a bus, joggling back and forth. I must be one of the blessed ones.

DAVE: It's funny. I did feel a certain heaviness settle about my body for a while.

IDA: Then it's true! You're a medium and you don't even know it.

DAVE: I can't be. That's such an extreme mystic science. It takes years to become expert at it. And so many people can prove it's a fraud after all.

IDA: But it's not a fraud. My mother's still in this room somewhere. I can feel her presence. I know she's here.

BETTY: Ida, stop it, will you?! I'm tired of this hocus-pocus, and these darning needle things. I'm gonna turn on the light. *(Turns on the light. They all see the large darning needle) Oh, my God! Look at the size of it!*

DAVE: It's grown so much bigger.

IDA: Do you believe in reincarnation?

BETTY: Ida, stop it!

IDA: That's my mother's spirit.

BETTY: Stop saying such ridiculous things. It's just a monster.

IDA: No. It's not. That's the spirit of my mother. She's come back in this form.

BETTY: Dave, listen to me. I'm gonna give you the broom. Very careful like, and I want you to sneak up on the thing, and corner it somewhere.

DAVE: But it's so big. It's almost as big as a Chihuahua!

BETTY: A what—? Oh, Dave, talk English.

DAVE: It's almost as big as a dog.

BETTY: Are you afraid of it?

DAVE: I'm not afraid of anything. Give me the broom.

IDA: No, don't do that. You'll hurt her. Don't do that!

BETTY: Ida, stop it! He's trying to kill it.

IDA: That's my mother. I know it. He's killing my mother!
(Dave smashes the darning needle about ten or twelve times)

BETTY: Your mother's been dead for five years.

IDA: My mother's spirit. Oh! Oh!

BETTY: All right, Dave. She's dead. Stop messing up my living room floor, will you?

IDA: Oh, my God! My poor mother.

BETTY: Ida, grow up, will you? All this horoscope and medium business is a lot of *nonsense*. Now stop it.

IDA: It's not nonsense. I know that was my mother.

BETTY: If you don't stop now I'll call Bellevue for you. You're acting like a madwoman. Maybe you shouldn't have hit her—I mean *it*—so much anyway, Dave.

IDA: What am I going to do? My mother returned to me, to speak with me, and now she doesn't even have her spirit left. She's not dead and she's not alive. She's nowhere, Betty. *Nowhere.*

BETTY: *You're* nowhere. Do you know that? You're living in some crazy world. I don't know what to make of you half the time.

DAVE: I wrapped it in newspaper. Is that all right?

BETTY: Yes, that's fine. Fine.

DAVE: You want me to flush it down the toilet?

BETTY: You'll stuff it up. Throw it in a garbage pail, and leave it in the hall.

DAVE: But won't it offend other people. I mean, aren't you afraid it'll offend your neighbors?

BETTY: Let it offend them, as long as it's out of this house. That's all I care about. *(Pause)* Now, go on, and please don't bother me with insects again. *(Dave goes)* Ida, let's finish our game.

IDA: Whuh?

BETTY: Finish our game, okay?

IDA: What's going to happen now? Oh, God? What's going to happen?

BETTY: Let's forget it. The thing is dead.

IDA: Is it really?

BETTY: Look. I know you're a strong believer in these cults and things, but don't you think, if your mother's spirit did come back, in that thing, she would have flew out before he smashed her? Don't you think, even a spirit wants to protect herself? Everything is self-protection in this world.

IDA: Do you really think so?

BETTY: Sure, I do. My God, I'm soundin' just as loony as you now.

IDA: No. No, it sounds logical. It sounds very logical.

BETTY: To get excited. Over a simple insect.

IDA: Betty, it wasn't a simple insect. It was very large.

BETTY: So then, it must be what you said. A mute. Or mutant—or something. Forget about it, will you? It's dead and gone. It's past history.

DAVE: *(Returning)* I put it outside.

BETTY: Okay, Dave.

DAVE: *(Notices that Ida turns slightly away from him, snubbing him)* Look. I'm sorry—this had to happen. *(He looks at Ida for some time. She is still turned away)* Really, I am.

BETTY: Okay, you're sorry. Now go to bed and forget about it, will you?

DAVE: *(After a pause)* Okay. Goodnight.

BETTY: G'night. *(He exits to his room again)* Well, you wanta play or what?

IDA: Look, Betty, let me just sit here for a few minutes. I—I'm all confused. I don't know what to think or—

BETTY: Okay, okay. Would you like some coffee and cake? *(Ida nods "no" distractedly)* It's from C & L. *(Pause. Looking for some response from Ida)* And if you don't eat it—I will. It's too good to waste. *(Still no response)* Oh, Ida, what am I gonna do with you?

(The lights dim slowly on the sitting room, and come up on the bedroom, where Dave has sat down dejectedly, in front of his typewriter, with his head in his hands. He seems as depressed as Ida.

The lights seem to focus on both of them, being dejected. After a moment, Ida relates half-heartedly to the cards again—and Dave half-heartedly to typing his play. Ida starts to wash the cards—Dave begins to pick up speed.

After a while, Dave becomes aware of another droning sound, though slightly different, more nasal sounding. He stops typing, listens for a while, and then notices a large white moth tracing a circle on the air above him. A smile of knowledge plays across his face. He rises slowly and enters the living room)

DAVE: *(Looking straight at her, with enormous warmth)* Mrs. Gorner?

BETTY: *(Slaps the cards Ida has just dealt her down)* What's the matter now?

(He moves up to her, smiling. Bafflement, and some fear, fills her face. He takes her hand, very warmly. At first she is shocked, but then slowly, seeing his eyes glaring warmly at her, she yields to him, and lets him lead her into the bedroom. She grabs hold of Ida's hand. They both enter the bedroom with Dave, inquisitively. Then they see the white moth)

DAVE: It's only a white moth, but still—!

(Betty sighs, resignedly. Ida's face lights up in a smile. Under her breath, she whispers)

IDA: Mama!!!

Blackout

Albert Innaurato

THE TRANSFIGURATION
OF BENNO BLIMPIE

Albert Innaurato

The Transfiguration of Benno Blimpie is a searing, sometimes shocking, brilliantly conceived black comedy by Albert Innaurato who, within the space of a single theatre season, rose from comparative obscurity to the upper reaches of leading young American playwrights. Opening on March 10, 1977, with James Coco giving a towering performance in the title role, the work was hailed in the press as "an incredible evening of chilling theatre" that "stuns and shatters."

Dealing with the twisted lives of people who are considered "freaks" by others, the play finds humor, as well as powerful compassion, in its harrowing recital of their plight. According to Clive Barnes' report in *The New York Times:* "As the play moves toward its surprising, tragic conclusion, Mr. Innaurato offers us scenes and monologues from this singularly bitter family life. A lot of the play is based on inner monologues, and at the end, when Blimpie pushes it to its irrevocable, inevitable climax, one does feel something of the sense of catharsis that those old Greeks gave us. This is not for the sake of blood, but blood for the sake of understanding man's inhumanity to man."

Described by critic Martin Gottfried as "a fresh and powerful new voice in the theatre," *The Transfiguration of Benno Blimpie* brought Mr. Innaurato an Off-Broadway "Obie" Award for distinguished playwriting.

The Philadelphia-reared author is a graduate of the Yale School of Drama with an M.F.A. in Playwriting. He was a 1975 recipient of a Guggenheim Fellowship and, under a Rockefeller Grant, served as playwright-in-residence at the New York Shakespeare Festival's Public Theatre.

Mr. Innaurato's other recently produced plays include *Gemini* (now in its second year on Broadway); *Earthworms;* and *Ulysses in Traction.*

Characters:

BENNO
OLD MAN
MOTHER
GIRL
FATHER

The stage throughout is divided in this way:

BENNO'S ROOM: *Benno, an enormously fat young man of twenty, sits on a stool from which he can survey the action comfortably. This should be in an area somewhat removed from the rest of the stage—upstage on a platform, for instance, or stage right. The area represents Benno's current room in which he has barricaded himself.*

A PARK: *This is still another area. There should be trash and dead leaves scattered about. This is inhabited by the young Girl and the Old Man—all their scenes take place here.*

KITCHEN: *In the home of Benno's parents, and of the young Benno. Once again, this should be in an area somewhat isolated, urban, working class.*

In the present script the following areas are indicated:

CENTER: *Benno's present room*
RIGHT: *The park*
LEFT: *Kitchen*

Benno is twenty, weighs 500 pounds, is about 5'9" or 5'10". He sits on his stool for the entire length of the play. He never leaves his area. When he is involved in a scene he acts as though he were present, and the others act the same. In the scenes he is playing a young boy and makes this plain by changing his voice slightly so that it is higher.

His clothes are very large on him, and tent-like. They look as though they haven't been washed or changed in weeks. His complexion is blotchy and pock-marked. His hair is greasy and full of tangles.

His parents are seen as they were when he was a young boy. His Father is in his early thirties or very late twenties, good looking, a former athlete. His Mother is older than the Father, less attractive.

The Old Man is Benno's grandfather, Italian immigrant, about seventy.
The Girl is from the neighborhood, thirteen, tough, Irish parents.
It should be kept in mind that Benno is remembering the scenes that transpire in the play. Thus he is controlling them and this should be made clear. He should watch these scenes with great intensity and concentration. Blackouts are indicated between scenes—but the scenes can flow into one another.

Scene One:

Lights up on Benno, center, eating.
In dim light, one by one, Mother, Father, Girl, Old Man in characteristic poses.
They freeze. Benno finishes eating and speaks to the audience.

BENNO: I am Benno. I am eating myself to death.
(Blackout)

Scene Two:

Lights up on Benno. He speaks to the audience.

BENNO: And there were weeds, feet and bugs. There were black ants and red ants and giant ants and worms. There were worms and spiders and snails. One day I crushed one hundred eighteen snails with my bare feet. I was very fat even then. It was after a rain storm. I ran in the grass and took off my shoes and socks. The snails inched out and I smashed every one I saw for an hour. I had snail blood all over my feet. My grandfather asked me what it was.

OLD MAN: *(Right, park. He speaks as though Benno were a little boy standing beside him)* Eh, Benno, what you got all over you feet, hanh? You mother gonna give me hell. Why can't you look afta youself, hanh? What is that shit on you feet?

BENNO: *(High voice, playing little boy, acting as though he were beside the Old Man)* Snail wine.

OLD MAN: You crazy, crazy!

(He hits where Benno would be standing. Benno reacts to the blow in place. The lights go down on the Old Man, but stay up on Benno. Ice cream truck jingle is heard)

BENNO: I have eaten seventeen chocolate cones today. Soft ice cream, the kind they sell in trucks. Those trucks announce themselves with tinkling, mechanical tunes played over and over. I heard the neighborhood truck making its rounds and I ran out and bought seventeen cones. Chocolate. I was out of breath from running down the stairs.

(A light up on Benno's Mother in kitchen. Benno changes his voice to a high whine. Mother reacts as though he were beside her and busies herself in the kitchen)

BENNO: *(High voice)* Momma, I wanna chocolate cone.

MOTHER: You're too fat as it is, Benno.

BENNO: I'm hungry. I wanna chocolate cone.

MOTHER: Shut up, fatsy. Why are you so fat? Tell me that. Hanh? Why are you so fat? Well, at least fat men got big ones.

BENNO: Ma, I want one.

MOTHER: I remember old Joey Fercanti around the corner in the old neighborhood. We was growin' up together. He was fatter even than you. He took my sister and me inna the alley one day and took it out and stuffed it inna his shirt pocket. He said: God provides for fat guys. An' I turned him down. I hadda go out an' marry that father of yours, the bastid. Joey was a looker even if he was fat. Better than you, God knows. Not all them blotches in the face and he didn't fall down every ten minutes. Well . . . maybe God'll give you a big one, but sure as hell, I doubt it.

BENNO: Ma, please, I want one.

MOTHER: Shut your face, fat jerk!

(Lights dim out on Mother)

BENNO: *(To Audience)* Mother. I used to think my father dropped roaches down her slit and that's why I heard her high giggle at night. There was no door between their room and mine; just a curtain with a rip in it. I heard her high giggle and I thought my father must have collected a lot of cockroaches that night in the cellar and was dropping them down her drain. A lot of them twisting in her tubes; suffocating, fornicating, giving birth; you know, whatever cockroaches do in cunts. And when she went into the bathroom and washed afterwards, you see, I thought she was flooding them out and down the toilet. Then one night I watched through the rip in the curtain. I preferred the cockroaches. Father.

(Father enters, tossing a football)

FATHER: And now, playing center quarterback and primary receiver for Bishop Neumann, Number 64, Dominick Vertucci!

(He plays wildly, pantomiming a frenzied football game. He plays as though he were the star of the team and is driving them to victory. He pantomimes hearing cheers for himself and raises his hands over his head in victory)

FATHER: Geez, geez, thanks, I couldna done it without the guys—thanks, geez . . . *(Catches himself, becomes flustered and shamefaced)* Aw, shit, was only pretendin', Benno. Even I pretend sometimes. Gotta go home anyways. You bitch mother raise hell if we're late. Come on, Benno. *(Leaves sadly. As though taking Benno's hand)* Don't trip over this curb . . . *(Benno trips)* Aw, shit, Benno!

(Father exits. Lights come up, right, park. The Girl plays. Out of the corner of her eye She watches the Old Man who watches her intently. She allows her game to take her close to him)

GIRL: *(To the Old Man)* Hey, you! Buy me a chocolate cone.

OLD MAN: You mother, what she say?

GIRL: Who's gonna tell her? *(A pause. She plays her game again)*

OLD MAN: I seen you. I seen you playing' in the street. You tough. How old?

GIRL: Buy me a cone.

OLD MAN: Can't. My Social Security check ain't come this month. Down to my last dime.

GIRL: The man'll trust you. C'mon. Buy me a chocolate cone. *(A pause)*

OLD MAN: Come on. Benno, come on.

(They walk off hand in hand)

BENNO: I was in an oven. A fat roast burning in the oven. There was a glass door to my oven and they came to it and laughed and pointed. Fat roasts are funny burning in ovens. I couldn't move. If I moved, I burned my back. If I moved I burned my side. If I turned, old burns were given to the heat. I was trapped, you see. Once I thought, wait until you're older, Benno, wait until you're older. Strength then, and force enough to burst through the oven door into the sun, into freedom. One day I did break through the glass door. But on the other side all there was was another oven with another glass door and laughing people pointing at me. And there was no sun. Has there ever been a sun? . . . I am still in the oven, I am still in the oven, I am still in the oven. And I am burning up, trapped and pierced, burning up! That's why I am eating myself to death.

(Blackout)

Scene Three:

Lights up on the park and on Benno. Benno has a flashlight with which he plays for a moment before the scene begins.

The park is lighted to suggest a very shady area. Right of center the light fades into heavy darkness.

The Girl enters barefoot. She walks slowly through the mud, humming to herself; occasionally she stops and wanders a step or two backwards.

Very slowly, the Old Man enters. He is obviously following her, and has been. The Girl realizes this but doesn't show it. As she approaches the dark area she stops and plays in place. He watches her rapt for a moment, then decides to speak.

Benno pays intense attention to the scene.

OLD MAN: What you doin' playin' inna mud?

GIRL: Walkin' barefoot.

OLD MAN: Dummy, you cut you feet.

GIRL: I want it.

OLD MAN: There are snakes and rats in here. They eat little girls, startin' down there. And swallow them, whole. Be careful.

GIRL: Ain't a little girl. An' I want to.

OLD MAN: You wanna cut you feet?

GIRL: I dunno. *(A pause. She walks a bit toward the dark area)* Maybe a man'll come by and pick the glass outta the cut. Maybe a man'll hold my foot and lick it and cry over it.

OLD MAN: You crazy! *(A pause)* Men hide around here. Under them heavy trees. They hide, you hear? And they wait. For little girls to come by, barefoot. Little girls don't fight hard. *(A pause)* Little girls, they got soft feet. Men wait with rope, to tie them, hard. Be careful!

GIRL: *(After a moment)* Take your shoes and socks off.

OLD MAN: What? Why?

GIRL: I want it. C'mon. Walk with me. Over here, in the shade, under these trees.

(She walks into the dark area and vanishes. The Old Man waits an instant, then takes his shoes and socks off. The socks are white with a pronounced yellow tinge. He walks in after the Girl.

Benno has watched and listened to this scene intently. The light brightens on him. He shines his flashlight around the area the Old Man and Girl have just left—the area which isn't dark. Then shines the flashlight into his own eyes. He squints and shudders)

BENNO: *(Quickly, passionately)* Cimabue, Giotto, Donatello, Pico Della Mirandola, Bellini, Michelangelo, Rafaello, Botticelli, Brunelleschi, I want, I want, want, want, want, Brunelleschi, Botticelli, Rafaello, Michelangelo, Bellini, Pico Della Mirandola, Donatello, Giotto, Cimabue. I want, please, please, I want—wantwantwantwantwantwant! Give me . . . give me . . . *(He is panting, his eyes are shut tightly. He has begun to cry)* No one, no one, no one . . . no . . . one . . .

(He shines the flashlight slowly into the dark area. The Old Man is caressing and kissing the Girl's feet. She moans. Hold a moment)

(Blackout)

Scene Four:

Lights up on the kitchen, and on Benno.
Benno doesn't change positions, but takes part intently in the scene.
The man and woman act as though he were present. They talk to
him as though he were sitting in the third place set at the table.
Benno uses his high voice.

MOTHER: *(To the man)* Eh, Dominick! Where's your old man?

FATHER: How the hell should I know?

MOTHER: He's your father! *(She busies herself. The man consults a racing sheet with great interest. He has a pencil in hand and figures numbers along the side of the sheet. After a while, the woman glares at him)* Look! What is your father, the star boarder? Hanh? Tell me that, what is your father? I tell him and tell him we have supper at six on the dot and does he show? Hanh? Hanh? He don't show. What am I supposed to do with the food—Benno, don't smack your lips like a pig, *pig!* Oink, oink, oink!—leave it out for the rats? I asked you, Dominick, what am I supposed to do with the food? *(The man ignores her)* That's right, Mary, slave for them and let them ignore you. Gotta cook twice, gotta clean up twice, and I work, too. What is this, a hotel? Hanh? Your no good, free-loadin' father come up to the table afta we finish, like a big rat!

FATHER: Look, fry the steak, I'm hungry. And I want it rare.

MOTHER: Awwwww! Eat it raw, you creep!

FATHER: I wanna see the blood. That's how you know it's rare, you can see the blood.

BENNO: *(High voice. Trying to make friends with his Father)* That's how you know it's rare, you can see the blood.

MOTHER: *(To Benno)* You shut up, fatty. What the hell do you know? *(To the man)* Looka him bustin' outta those pants and looka those blotches on his face. He's enough to break mirrors, God forbid! And don't get me off the topic of the star boarder. T'resa was sayin' . . .

FATHER: You got red peppers in them potatoes?

MOTHER: We run out.

FATHER: *(Suddenly angry)* God damn it to hell, you know I want red peppers in the fried potatoes! That's when they're good. They burn when they go down.

BENNO: *(As before)* They burn when they go down.

MOTHER: *(To Benno)* Shut up, you fat creep! *(To the man)* And you! Who the hell are you to start screaming at me like you own the place? Hanh? What the hell are you? Nothin', that's what! Up to your ass in debt, a lousy gambler. Who works their ass off? Who slaves? I do—Mary, that's who. I get up and work myself to the bone for you and your monster kid and your freeloading old man. I go to work at six and then have to come home to look after you and this *disgraziato* freak! How much did you give me for the house last week, hanh? Tell me that, big man, big horse player, how much did you give me for the house? A big fat fifteen dollars, that's how much! That's supposed to pay the mortgage, buy food, pay this cripple's doctor bills and keep your no good, smelly father in stogies! How far's fifteen dollars supposed to go, hanh? What's it supposed to buy—the Taj Mahal? You wanna good meal, you go to the bookie, go to the Pooch! You love him more than you love me!

FATHER: *(Retreating behind the racing form)* All right, all right.

MOTHER: You was always out bettin' them nags. This nag, this nag, Mary, you never bet on. You want red pepper! Who the hell are you to want red pepper? You can't even get it up.

FATHER: You stupid bitch! In front of the kid!

MOTHER: Kid? What kid? Where's the kid? You ever see a kid that looked like that? He's just like you—nothin'. A ton of nothin'!

FATHER: *(Angry again)* Whose fault? Hanh? Whose fault? Without red pepper he can't digest. Red peppers eat up the fat. You eat red peppers, you can eat anything, even the shit you cook and still stay thin and healthy. The shit you cook! How do you cook it, hanh? By sittin' on it? It smells of your ass! It smells of your friggin' cunt!

MOTHER: How would you know? You ain't been in it for years—all you smell is the Pooch!

FATHER: And another thing, you friggin' Napolitan bitch, you never, never put enough oregano in the gravy. And you never put enough oil. It's dry, like your tits! Not enough red pepper, not enough oregano, not enough oil, no wonder you got a freak for a son! That's why he ain't normal!

MOTHER: He ain't normal because he takes after you! He got no balls either. Your father is ball-less, you is ball-less. And your kid is ball-less. It runs in the family. I looked at him last night. There ain't nothin' down there, only flab. And your father's screwin' a thirteen-year-old girl. Everybody knows.

FATHER: You shut that big, ugly Napolitan mouth!

MOTHER: Madonna me! The whole neighborhood knows. Your father's a sex fiend and he's livin' in my house. And she's a Irish girl, the slut, the *puttana!*

FATHER: Shut up! Shut up!

MOTHER: *(Screaming)* Your father's a bum, you're a ball-less bum with no cock and your son's a good-for-nothin' ball-less bum!

FATHER: Cunt!

(He slaps her. She throws herself to the floor as though the blow had sent her reeling)

BENNO: *(High voice)* Daddy!

MOTHER: *(On the floor, hysterical)* That's right! Run off to the Pooch! You love him more than you ever loved me!

BENNO: *(High voice, crying)* Mommy!

MOTHER: Get away from me, you good-for-nothin' fatty you! You louse, you good-for-nothin'—you—fruit! *(She crawls off, weeping)*

BENNO: My steak is rare I can see the blood.

(Blackout)

Scene Five:

Lights up on Benno and the Girl.
The Girl is alone, down center. She is dancing to a very ugly, fifties rock and roll tune. She sings along for a moment. Benno stares out, abstracted.

GIRL: Last night I dreamed I was eating a boiled chicken leg. I started by licking it. I made my tongue all wet and slobbered all over it, up and down, up and down, all around. Then, with my front teeth, I tore off the leg's tip. It was a piece of skin, yellow. I rolled the skin under my teeth, sucking all the juice out of it. Then, I spit it out. Then, suddenly, I stuck all my teeth into the middle of the leg and let it dangle in my mouth. Not biting, not chewing, just letting it dangle.

(She freezes in place.

The light on her dims but does not go out. A tape of the ugly rock tune is heard. On the tape, the Girl is singing very softly into a closely held microphone. The sound is breathy and wet. Then the tape fades very slowly under the following:)

BENNO: *(He starts slowly, with little expression)* Benno loved to draw. And he loved drawings. As soon as he was old enough he stole carfare from his mother's purse and went to the big museum. He snuck in. He ran to the Renaissance paintings. And he stared at them. He stared at their designs, most particularly at their designs. And at their colors. But the designs to begin with were the most significant to him. The circle, for instance, fascinated him; and the right angle as used in a painting like "The Last Supper" thrilled him. He would trace the angles and the circles in these paintings with his fingers when the guards weren't looking. Then, on paper napkins and the dirty lined paper from the Catholic school, he would make designs like those. He drew arcs and circles, and angles and lines trying to vary them with the deception and subtlety of the masters. He wasn't interested in drawing people. He knew what they looked like. Think of the structure of the foot. The lines bend, then they curve. The arch juts up, then juts down; two angles, like a roof. Underneath there is the inverse. The sole is like a barreled vault. Then, at the front, five straight lines—but with rounded tips. Benno drew idealized feet, or distorted them in his own way. He was not interested in the imperfections of real feet. Benno's make-believe feet were curved or gracefully inclined. Real feet are crooked and crushed.

One day, out of guilt, Benno's Pop-pop bought him a paint set with a Social Security check that bounced or something and caused some discomfort. . . . Benno painted—he colored in his designs. He painted hour upon hour upon hour. He lulled himself asleep planning paintings as though they were battle campaigns. He dreamed colored designs and designs of colors and waking, tried to copy these. Once, once when he had finished painting six straight lines carefully, he stared at his painting and heard . . . heard music played up the back of his spine.

It made no difference. When he had finished a painting, Benno was still fat, ugly, and alone. Nothing makes a difference, nothing alters anything. It took Benno a very long time to learn this. And Benno wasn't sure he had learned it, really, until he started eating himself to death. Then Benno knew he had learned. For all that matters is the taste of our own flesh. It tastes horrible, particularly if we are fat and sweat a lot. But there are no disappointments there; and those feelings of horror and disgust at chewing ourselves are the only feelings we can be sure of. Benno will put his eyes out soon. Then there will be no seductive angles or circles. Benno will be left to stumble about his filthy room, the windows nailed shut, biting at himself. Thank you.

(The lights go out on Benno. They intensify on the Girl, who starts singing and dancing again)

GIRL: So anyway, then I dreamed that I tore off the bite in my mouth. Just then I was woke up by my brother screaming. He sleeps in the bed next to mine. His underpants were covered in jit. He'd had a wet dream. *(She sniggers)* He didn't know what it was. I did. I didn't tell him what it was. He started crying. He thought he was gonna die. I let him think so. I'm hungry. I hope mom serves chicken soon.

(Blackout)

Scene Six:

The lights come up on Benno and on the Park.
The Girl and Old Man are lying down. The light is heavy and shadowy.

OLD MAN: *(Looks off, nervous)* Damn kids! Make a lotta noise. Benno, why you no play wit them?

BENNO: *(High voice)* What, Pop-pop?

OLD MAN: Why you no have friends, Benno? Why you always around me?

BENNO: *(High voice)* I love you, Pop-pop. *(The Girl laughs, mocking)* I do love you, Pop-pop.

OLD MAN: *(To Benno)* Shut up, you crazy you! If you gonna stay around be quiet. Stay over there.

BENNO: *(High voice)* I'm drawing, Pop-pop. I'll be quiet.

(The Old Man draws closer to the Girl and whispers in her ear)

OLD MAN: You very pretty for an Irish girl. I like you hair, it is so long and thick. And you thighs, they very soft. When I touch them, I feel them long time after.

GIRL: You have bumps on your feet. And there's somethin' strange on your heels. It's like moss.

OLD MAN: You fingers is beautiful. You toes is beautiful. *(He sucks on her fingers)*

BENNO: *(High voice)* Pop-pop . . .

OLD MAN: *(Very annoyed)* Benno, go 'way! I'm tellin' you, go 'way. Go over to them boys in the trees over there. Go play wit them. You hear me, Benno? Go on!

(He gets up and mimes chasing Benno away. Benno reacts facially in place)

OLD MAN: *(Looking off as though following Benno with his eyes)* Maybe they be friends for him.

GIRL: Benno's so fat.

OLD MAN: He's my oldest grandchild.

GIRL: He's a monster. Ooooo! He's so ugly. Benno Blimpie, we call him.

OLD MAN: Lemme get on topa you.

GIRL: No, use your fingers like you did yesterday.

OLD MAN: I wanna do somethin' different.

GIRL: Somethin' different? *(Caresses his thigh)* What? I don't wanna do nothin' different. *(Sticks her tongue in his mouth)*

OLD MAN: I gotta do somethin' different.

GIRL: What?

OLD MAN: Somethin'. You like it.

GIRL: What'll you give me?

OLD MAN: My Social Security check comes next week. I give you if you let me.

GIRL: How much?

OLD MAN: Sixty-two twenty.

GIRL: Bring it next week. We'll see then. Use your fingers today.

OLD MAN: *(Reaches under her dress)* Like this?

GIRL: *(Spreads her legs)* Yes.

OLD MAN: Touch me.

(The girl starts to unzip him. Benno screams)

OLD MAN: Damn it to hell! That's Benno.

(They both look off and the Old Man rises)

GIRL: It's them boys. They got him.

OLD MAN: Shit! *(He starts to go off)*

GIRL: *(Holds him back)* Don't go. They're just playin'. That's how boys play nowadays. Come on. Use your fingers today. Next week bring me the check. Kiss me.

OLD MAN: Like this? *(Kisses her)*

GIRL: Use your fingers.

OLD MAN: *(Reaching under her dress)* Like this?

GIRL: *(Unzipping him)* Yes . . . yes . . .

BENNO: *(Screaming as though terrified and in pain)* Pop-pop! Pop-pop! Pop-pop!

(Blackout. Benno continues screaming for a beat in the dark. Then silence)

Scene Seven:

Lights up on the kitchen and on Benno. The Father hovers about the stove.

FATHER: Goddammit, Benno, quit followin' me. Where did she keep things, Benno? You know where that bitch, God forgive me, kept everything? Aw—how would you know? Sit down. How many eggs you want, Benno? Six enough? Benno, I make seven, that should fill us both. I hope she dies in that filthy Napolitan' shack livin' with her virgin sister. Get the black pepper, Benno—don't spill it—watch out, don't spill it. Be careful, or you'll spill it; watch out . . . shit fire, you spilled it! Why are you so clumsy, my son? *(Stoops down as though picking black pepper up off the floor)* Hey! I know what. I'll put pepperoni in the eggs. That's always good! *(Sings as he mimes adding the ingredients)* "Pepperoni hits the spot, helps you shit because it's hot." Why didn't you fight back, Benno, hanh? Why didn't you fight back? I heard, I heard, Benno what them kids did to you. Why did you lay there like some queer? Hanh? I'll turn the heat up just a tidge. And maybe we better put some milk. Is there somethin' wrong with you, my son? Are you a pansy, my son? Why ain't you out there in the street, playing ball, roughin' up like I did? Why you always in here with you mama, like a girl? Shit, the eggs is stickin' to the pan, I'll stir them. We better put a tidge of sugar in. There. Why are you so fat, my son? Why don't you exercise? I'd never of let them kids near me when I was your age. I'll put some oregano in. Never. I'll tell you, I was a holy terror, a holy terror, geez. I'd have kicked them inna balls, like this. I'd have beat them with my fists, like this. I was no fatty, no pansy. I'd have punched them, I'd have beaten them senseless. *(Dances around as though in a boxing ring)* Left, right, left, right and a kick to the balls. *(Mimes a fight)* Take that, mother-fucker, take that and that! A right to the side of the head—pow! A left to the jaw and boop!—a knee between the legs! And another left and another right!—he's down, he's bleedin'—my God!—he's out! Hey! Hey! *(Runs to the stove)* Shit! Shit fire and save the matches! The eggs is burned.

(Blackout)

Scene Eight:

Lights up on Benno and on the Girl.
The Girl is down center. Near her is a small night table with stained and sticky-looking bottles and jars on it.
When the light hits her she sprays a large amount of very smelly hair

spray on her hair; then teases her hair violently. Then she smears an enormous amount of purple lipstick on sensuously puffed out lips. During this she sings a very ugly rock tune and occasionally does a dance step to it.

GIRL:　Last night I spilled spaghetti all over me. The sauce went over my white blouse and my blue dress; and it was thick sauce with peppers and bits of meat in it. It was a big mess. And Donny, my cousin, wiped it off. He's spiffy. Twenty and in the Navy. He took his napkin, it had red stains from his mouth on it and wiped my blouse off. Wiped and wiped, not too hard but strong. Then he took another napkin, my brother's, and wiped my dress off. Wiped and wiped, makin' a small circle in my lap. Donny has big hands, a lotta hair on them around the knuckles and the veins is very thick. His fingers is thick, too, and the middle one is long and heavy. I dream about Donny's hand makin' circles in my lap.

(She freezes in place. The light on her dims)

BENNO:　Benno grew up thinking that talent and sensitivity were things people took seriously. At least, that important people took seriously—artists, for instance, and teachers. Benno grew up hoping that looks and sex didn't matter. That paintings would satisfy any longing he'd ever have. And when that longing got too strong, a quick pulling with the palm would be enough. Benno was wrong. . . . Benno has been heard to say that nothing matters save the taste of his own flesh. But since then, time has passed. For your benefit he has conjured up scenes better not remembered. And Benno realizes that he was guilty of over-simplification. There are things that matter: Looks matter, sex matters. These are all that matter. Benno feels that those who deny this are participating in a huge joke. Benno has learned his lesson. Paintings, you see, aren't enough. When loneliness and emptiness and longing congeal like a jelly nothing assuages the ache. Nothing, nothing, nothing.

It was the end of spring, the traditional season of youth, renewal and young love. Benno returned to his old neighborhood, having celebrated his twentieth birthday. He found the poorest side street in his old neighborhood. Fitzgerald Street, by name. And he rented a room on the third floor of a row house on Fitzgerald Street. Benno nailed shut all the windows in that room, even though it was summer. Something about imbibing his own smell. Benno is not as isolated as you might think. He hears the horrible street noises. He hears the monster children screaming. He even allows himself to have his shade up one-half hour a day. Today at one PM, Benno had his shade up. He stared out his nailed window, stared through the caked dirt that streaks the window's glass. He saw a wild circle flashing red across the street. He stared at that circle and was tempted to . . . never mind. He was tempted and stared and was tempted some more. And then he saw the agent of that circle. It was a little girl. A beautiful little girl. Oh, yes, Benno knows beauty. He knows if he tells you. Once, when he saw something beautiful, it would flash across his eyes like a hot knife and he would peer, eyes stuck there until they ached. Once, he tells you, no longer. For beauty has lost his power over me, it has lost its power, no more beauty, no more longing to grasp it within me and smother it with my bulk, please God, no more beauty.

(He is almost weeping. He eats passionately and slowly pulls himself together)

GIRL: *(Unfreezes and continues with her make-up)* When Donny finished wiping me off, I smiled up at him and his eyes, they're black, got very big. When Ma wasn't looking, I let my fingers take a walk along his thigh. I saw the big bump in the middle of his thigh get bigger. Then, when Ma was clearin' the table, I spilled the plate of meatballs all over me. While she was in the kitchen, Donny licked them off with his tongue. Ma caught him and gave him hell. Pop laughed. Donny ran into the bathroom and puked all over, like a sissy. I changed my mind about Donny. I think Donny is a jerk-off.

(Lights out on Girl)

BENNO: Benno has decided: He will no longer lift the shade, he will no longer look out into the street. . . . Benno stayed in this tiny room. He left every two days to buy food. Otherwise he never went out. Except in cases of emergency such as when the ice cream truck came along. He did nothing. He ate continually from when he awoke until he fell asleep. He did nothing save remember.

When I become so fat I cannot get into his clothes and can barely move, I will nail the door shut. I will put his eyes out with a long nail and I will bite at himself until he dies. In the middle of this filthy hole on the third floor of a row house in the poorest side street of my old neighborhood there will I be: A mountain of flesh. There are rats in this room. I see them slithering along the sides of the wall. They will eat me. These rats will find Benno beautiful. They will long for him. He will be a sexual object to them. They will make the devouring of Benno's body an erotic act. They will gnaw hollows into his face, into his belly. And in those hollows, they will fornicate. Then, they will perish. The instant before he is ready to die, Benno will swallow a huge draught of poison. These rats in eating Benno will be eating poisoned meat. The poison will cause a fearful splitting of stomachs, vital rat organs will swell up and burst even while the rats are making love. Even while they are eating. Posthumously, Benno will have been loved.

(Blackout)

Scene Nine:

Lights up on park and on Benno.
The Girl and the Old Man are seated together on the ground. The Old Man has a wine bottle in a paper bag with him and takes swigs from it. The Girl is in a Catholic schoolgirl's uniform—white blouse, blue, rather long skirt and white ankle socks with blue oxfords. She has a school satchel nearby.

OLD MAN: Benno, you stay over there and draw. Don' bother me. You old enough to go pee-pee by yourself.
GIRL: He's funny, retarded.
OLD MAN: You hear me, Benno?
BENNO: *(High voice)* Yes, Pop-pop.
GIRL: *(Mimicking)* Yes, Pop-pop.

OLD MAN: Just be sure you stay away! An' don' you go tellin' you bitch mother, either.

BENNO: *(High voice)* I won't, Pop-pop.

GIRL: Queerie!

OLD MAN: You hear me good, Benno. Leave me alone today.

BENNO: *(High voice)* Yes, Pop-pop. *(Quietly to himself, high voice)* I love you, Pop-pop. *(Normal voice, to the audience)* And Benno wept. He didn't realize at that time that there is nothing funnier than a fat boy, weeping. Nothing funnier. Nothing.

(A pause. He laughs dryly.
The light dims somewhat on Benno. But he stares at the scene intently)

OLD MAN: *(Takes a drink, offers the bottle to the girl)* Drink this!

GIRL: Don' wan' none.

OLD MAN: Drink.

GIRL: Don' wan' none, I said! *(Takes a long swig and grimaces)* Oooooooh! What is it?

OLD MAN: *La vita, carina, la vita.*

GIRL: Don' know Eyetalian. You bring the check?

OLD MAN: Sixty-two twenty.

GIRL: Lemme see.

OLD MAN: Later.

GIRL: Lemme see. *(He reaches into his back pocket, and presents her with the check. She scrutinizes it)* Yeah . . . yeah . . . sixty-two twenty. Sign it over to me.

OLD MAN: What do you mean?

GIRL: You know what I mean. Sign it over.

OLD MAN: Can't write.

GIRL: Make yer sign.

OLD MAN: Got no pencil.

GIRL: Got one in my schoolbag. *(Reaches into her schoolbag and removes a pencil)* New point. Come on.

OLD MAN: All right. *(He makes his mark on the check. The Girl reaches for the wine and takes a long pull)*

GIRL: *(As he notices her drinking)* Didn't have no lunch today. On a diet. Give it to me.

OLD MAN: Afta. *(He puts check in his back pocket)*

GIRL: Benno hangs around you a lot. Why? He ain't normal.

OLD MAN: Kiss me.

GIRL: My brother beat him up, broke his glasses. Said he wanted to crush his nose against his face like a pimple.

OLD MAN: Touch me.

GIRL: You love Benno?

OLD MAN: Let me do it now, I be gentle.

GIRL: Do you love him?

OLD MAN: I take you top off.

GIRL: *(Twists away)* Yesterday my brother told me he gonna beat Benno up afta school on Monday. You gonna try and stop him?

OLD MAN: Help me wit you buttons.

GIRL: Not yet. Use your fingers.

OLD MAN: Want more today. Help me wit the buttons.

GIRL: *(He tries to start undressing the Girl. She resists but in a lazy, teasing way. The Old Man sometimes stops trying to remove her top and caresses her)* Why is Benno so weird? Drawing all the time. Never playin' in the street? In school on Tuesday—c'mon, cut it out—he started talkin' about this Eyetalian painter. Just started talking; Sister didn't call on him or nothing. Cut that out! Then Benno showed us his drawings. They was weird. One was supposed to be a old man. He was long and thin with these blurry features. Looked like my brother's dickie floatin' in the bathtub. Stop it! I don't like you slobbering on me!

OLD MAN: Drink some more. *(He takes a long swig and passes her the bottle)*

GIRL: Lick my feet like you did before. *(Drinks)*

OLD MAN: I want more—I want more. *(He gets on top of her)*

BENNO: *(High voice, loudly)* Pop-pop, look what I drew. Look, see the circles . . .

OLD MAN: *(Jumping off the Girl)* God damn it to hell, Benno! Get away from here, go on! *(Acts as though chasing Benno off)* Damn kid, always around, always in the way! *(He lies down beside the Girl)*

GIRL: *(Giggles)* Benno couldn't genuflect at Mass on Wednesday. He couldn't get that far down. And when he did get down on his knees, he couldn't get up. Even Sister laughed. Then we all had to go to confession for laughing at Mass. Even Sister. I smelled the priest in the confessional. All sweaty and underarmy. But nice. Do you love Benno?

OLD MAN: *(Caressing her, kissing her hair)* You *carina,* you I love; all of you. Fine Irish hair and the little hairs down there. I wanna scoop you up with my mouth. You hear me, with my mouth! I wanna bury my teeth, bury them, in there, in and in and in. Come to me, *cara,* I ready. I wan' . . .

GIRL: *(Squirming away)* You wanna, you wanna, you wanna! You're drunk, you're a slob!

OLD MAN: I wan' more from you this time, this time more!

GIRL: Hey, hey! *(He reaches under her dress)* I'm not in the mood! *(She reaches for the bottle and takes a long swig)*

OLD MAN: *(Lies back and strokes her)* In the *paese,* over there, over the seas, I took a little girl inna wood. I was how old? Nineteen maybe, who knows? I take her inna the wood and swallow her whole. You hear, swallow her whole?! I start at her feet. *(Grabs the Girl's foot. She utters an annoyed cry)* Took her toes inna my mouth and bite them off, one by one. Then I bite inna her leg *(Grabs her leg and holds it tight while she struggles)* . . . and chew onna the bone. It was hard that bone, but then, then I have good teeth and chew hard. I ate all of her, and today, today I wan' more . . .

(The Girl finally pushes him away with all her strength)

GIRL: No! I'm sick of you and your yellow skin and your sores and your smell!

OLD MAN: *(Trying to get on top of her)* Bella mia, mia bella, ti voglio! I wanna dig inna you skin!

GIRL: *(Twisting away)* Dago shit! Smelly!

BENNO: *(High voice)* Pop-pop! Pop-pop!

(The Old Man has begun to chase the Girl, reaching out for her. This has started slowly but becomes wild. The Old Man starts gasping for breath and getting dizzy)

BENNO: *(High voice)* Why are you running like that, Pop-pop? Stop it, I'm scared!

GIRL: *(Dodging the Old Man as though it were a game)* Grandson's a queerie, grandad's a smelly!

OLD MAN: *(Still chasing her, panting)* I wan' more, more!

BENNO: *(High voice)* Please, Pop-pop!

GIRL: Smelly!

BENNO: *(High voice)* Leave her alone, Pop-pop!

OLD MAN: *(Gasping) Mia! Bella mia, ti voglio! Fermati! T'amo!*

GIRL: Wop bastard!

(The Old Man lunges and catches the Girl. She utters a cry and fights him. Neither is playful. The Old Man throws her to the ground. She screams. He tries to hurl himself on top of her but she moves at the last minute and he hits the ground with a thud and a cry. He is stunned briefly)

BENNO: *(High voice)* Oh! Oh, Pop-pop . . .

(The Girl runs to the wine bottle and breaks it)

GIRL: *(Waving the broken bottle)* Come on, dago shit, come on!

OLD MAN: *(Laughs) Tigra, tigra,* come on, *tigra!*

(They circle each other slowly. Occasionally the Girl strikes out at the Old Man. He is playful but she is very serious. From his stool Benno watches in terror)

BENNO: Pop-pop, should I run for the police?

OLD MAN: *(To the Girl, still circling)* I wann chew you up!

GIRL: Asshole! *(She lunges again and cuts him on the arm)*

OLD MAN: *(Yells but chases her more violently) Mia, vieni!*

BENNO: Leave her alone, Pop-pop, she's crazy!

(The Old Man acts as though Benno is tugging at him and turns to push him away)

OLD MAN: Go home, queerie, go home! Today I wan' more . . .

(With a scream the Girl lunges and stabs the Old Man in the back with the broken bottle. He screams and falls)

OLD MAN: *(Screaming) Aiuto, aiuto,* Benno, help me!

(He twists desperately in the mud as though trying to stop the pain in his back. Benno gasps, then stares. The Girl also stares wide-eyed. The Old Man continues to scream and throws up in the mud)

GIRL: *(In a stunned whisper)* Go 'head, puke, you wop bastard!

OLD MAN: *(Almost voiceless)* I . . . I . . . I . . .
(He dies. There is a pause. The Girl becomes suddenly hysterical)
GIRL: Bastard! Bastard! Filthy wop bastard! Oh, my God,
my God, I've . . . I've . . . he's . . . *(With a cry she throws
the bottle down. It shatters. She looks at it frightened, then bends over the
corpse, screaming)* Dago, dago, wop, filthy, dago bastard, bastard,
bitch, dago, jerk-off, bitch, mother-fucker, filthy . . . mother . . .
(She is gasping. She pulls herself together suddenly and looks around)
Geez . . . the check! *(She searches the body for the check and finds
it. She removes it from the back pocket)* Muddy. *(Wipes the check on
her skirt)* Hey . . . hey . . . you kiddin'? *(Kicks the body)* Oh
. . . oh, Caarist! Hey, Benno, your Pop-pop's dead. Don't you
tell nobody or my brother'll get you good. Oh . . . *(Looks at the
body)* Oh . . . Caarist! *(She runs off)*
BENNO: *(A pause. Then he whispers, normal voice)* Pop-pop.
(Blackout)

Scene Ten:

Lights up on Benno and the kitchen. The Father is pacing tensely.

FATHER: Where the hell is your mother, Benno? Hanh?
Mary! Mary! Where the hell are you! We should be there!
Mary!
MOTHER: *(Offstage)* All right, for Christ's sake, I'm comin'!
FATHER: Jesus Christ—let me make sure everythin' is
ready, Benno. *(Opens ice box)* Yep, got the spare ribs for the
gravy—Uncle Fonse likes them—Benno—don't eat the cake,
it's for the relatives, afta. *(Calling)* Mary, for Christ's sake,
hurry.
MOTHER: *(Off)* Jesus Christ in Heaven shove that friggin'
racin' form in that big mouth, I'm comin'!
*(A pause. She enters. She seems ashamed. The dress she is wearing is
too small for her. He looks at her)*
FATHER: Jesus—is that all you had to wear?
MOTHER: Ain't had no money to buy a dress in years—

FATHER: Well, at least they'll know you was Benno's mother and you eat well—wear a shawl or somethin'. Come on.

MOTHER: Not yet.

FATHER: Oh, Jesus!

MOTHER: I ain't ready yet! Gotta get inna the mood. I don't like wakes. You go on, I'll come later. Not ready I tell you.

FATHER: And the kid?

MOTHER: Why can't you take him, you ashamed? You think they'll think he's my fault if he comes in wit me? Hanh? Is that what you think? Oh, their little Dominick could never commit somethin' like this flabby monster. He could never cause such ugliness to come inna the world. It's Mary's fault.

FATHER: Look you, none of your shit tonight! You keep that big ugly Napolitan mouth shut. And you bring the kid. It's my father's wake and I want you to show some respect, or so help me God, I'll take the strap to you right there.

MOTHER: All right, all right, get the hell out!

FATHER: Make sure that kid keeps decent, too! *(He exits)*

MOTHER: Let's have some coffee, Benno. I need it. *(Heats coffee)* Oh, Jesus, Jesus, how'm I gonna face it? All them relatives of his: his sister Edith, that witch of a prune face, *faccia brutt', Virgine, ti conosci'*, Benno stop slobberin', and his brother, Basil—face like a rhinoceros' ass—how'm I gonna face them? They hate me. They look down on me—Mary the peasant, they call me. But it was me, the virgin knows, me, Mary the horse, put the old man up. Me! I hadda see him come and spit inna the sink every day. Me! And I hadda run the vacuum cleaner to get up the scales from his sores. Those damn scales were everywhere, like fairy dust. I even found 'em on the window sill. How did they get on the window sill? What did he do, scratch them while watchin' some broad walk down the street? And do they thank me for cleanin' up afta him week afta friggin' week? Nah! Benno, why you puttin' five teaspoons of sugar in you coffee, hanh? Why can't you put two like a human being? Three, even three I could see, God knows, but five? Who do you take afta? Hanh? *(Gets up and pours coffee for herself)* Take some coffee, Mary. Weep into them grounds. And them goddamned lousy shits look down at me. My father, my friggin' father, God rest his soul, was eight times, nah, nine times the man theirs was! Nine times, you hear me? The day before he died I went a see him. Couldn't find him. Where was he, where? Then, suddenly, I hear this clang, this loud clang. *Clang!* It come from the cellar. I run down. There he is, seventy-six, at least, chasing' rats with the shovel. He screamed: *Ecco! Ecco!* and then he smashes one with the shovel. *Clang!!* It splattered all over the cellar. That was a real man. Not a ball-less bum like you no good bastard father. Well, have a cookie Mary, you deserve it.

(To Benno) No more for you, Dinosaur, you've had seven. No more, I said. You shit, you! *(Pantomimes reaching over and slapping his hand. Benno winces in place, as though fighting back tears)* Cry baby! Looka him hold back the tears. No good sissy! Men don't cry. And looka! Just a big lump of lard. Jesus, I could store you up and cook with you. What did I do, oh Virgin, to deserve all this suffering? Hanh? Looka them pimples. Don't scratch them you no good! If only you wasn't so flabby. If only you had some muscle on them monster arms and legs. But all you is, is a huge, flabby rat. You hear me? A rat; with them big, black dartin' eyes.

I'm sick a you; and sick a that creep you no good bastard father. Who goes out and works like a dog? Me! Who comes home and cleans like a horse? Hanh? I do! And who put that no good bum, your Pop-pop, God rest his soul, up for years and years and then he has to go out and let some nigger stab him with his own wine bottle and we don't even get his last check, god damn it all to hell, *I* did and *I* do, that's who! Mary! Mary the horse! Mary the horse, they call me—don't take another cookie, you pig—Mary the horse. *(She is becoming hysterical)* They used a call me Bella, beautiful, you know that? Beautiful and I had red hair, flaming, and big boobs, almost as big as yours, you little queer, and a shape, Madone', what a shape! Old Joey Fercanti, I coulda married him, said my lips should be on the silver screen, that's how big they were and thick and red. Bella, Bella they called me. And when I danced they looked at me and when I walked home from the market even with a dozen other girls, they looked at me and when I got married all the guys in the neighborhood got drunk. Bella! And look at me now—I'm almost as ugly as you, I'm a hag, a bitch! Got no shape no more and my hair's grey and fallin' out and your father, your father that no good lousy son-of-a-bitch did this to me, worked at me and worked at me, a rat, chewin' at me, with big dartin' eyes and tearin' me to pieces!

Look at me, look at me good. Oh my God, my God, how did I wind up like this, with the peelin' wallpaper and nothin' else, no furniture, no money, not a decent dress. What am I gonna wear to that wake? They'll laugh, you hear me, they'll laugh! *(She has reached a frenzy and sobs for a moment, then slowly begins to calm down. Occasionally her chest heaves from sobbing. Benno stares wide-eyed. She has calmed down. Slowly she rises and pours herself another cup of coffee)* Have some more coffee, Mary. That's all you got, caffeine, that's all you got in the whole world. *(To Benno)* And you, monster, you with them big eyes, them big black eyes, what do you want now?

BENNO: *(High voice; soft)* A cookie.
(Mother sobs. Lights dim on mother)

Scene Eleven:

Benno speaks urgently to the audience.

BENNO: And what about love? Specifically, what about sexual love? Did or did not this fat one ever have congress with anything other than his palm?

Benno wonders: should he describe his sexual past? Benno is ravenous for himself and time it presses on. Benno must cease this night or face yet one other two-day cycle.

(Out of the shadows comes the Old Man. He is dressed in a long butcher's apron. It is abnormally white and quite long. The Old Man's hair has been whitened and so has his face. There is a golden aura about him so that even though he is recognizably a butcher,

*there is something angelic in his appearance as well. He carries a
golden meat cleaver and a black crayon.*

*During the following, as Benno speaks, the Old Man pulls over his
head an enormous white robe. When the robe is fully on Benno, the
Old Man prepares to draw on it with his crayon. He will draw on
Benno a butcher's chart identifying the various slices of meat.
Benno submits to all this without paying any attention. Benno
speaks laconically and with a certain irony. The light on him becomes brighter and brighter as he speaks)*

BENNO: Benno and sex: a story. Benno went out one night.
He was fourteen. His Pop-pop had been dead—how many
years? They blur too much for Benno to know for sure. Had
Benno been an intellectual he would have concerned himself
with the nature of time. Benno felt that the secret of time was
perhaps his secret. Maybe Benno was the product of a time
warp. Benno then would have been the bloated issue of an
inverted time womb which, due to God's joke, or cosmic
spasm, vomited him out long before or long after his true
time. But when, he asks you, when would have been Benno's
time? Some of us, it seems, exist outside of nature and no one
knows where we fit. Nature has her claws in all of you but not
in we who exist outside her. You have your claws in us. . . . I
see that you all think Benno speaks nonsense. My mouth is
dry. Perhaps what he says to you, even to the very words is
unfamiliar. Perhaps it is Hungarian he speaks or some curious combination of frothy dipthongs. Benno always had a
problem with his saliva.

(Out of the dark come the voices of the Father and Mother)

MOTHER'S VOICE: Not only a fatty, but he drools, too.
Looka that: it's like a broken water fountain!

FATHER'S VOICE: Is there something wrong with you, my
son?

BENNO: Benno ran out one night. In the best tradition of
arts and letters there beat in him the age-old desperation.
Benno felt those horrible waves of longing wash over him and
tumble back on himself and he could do nothing about it.
There was no cure for that longing in Benno. No church
socials sponsored his dreams of satiety; no youth organization

provided him with a concourse to fulfillment; and double dating was out. There was no cure out of popular sentiment nor out of clinical misassessment. Benno was singular and had to suffer alone. Sometimes I want to run to my nailed windows and vomit out them. The force, the force of my vomit would explode through the window onto the passersby and crush them. And crush them. *(He pauses for a moment. The Old Man is now ready to draw on him)* Benno Blimpie: The sensuous Fatso. Prefatory to his supper of self.

OLD MAN: Breast! *(He draws the lines around Benno's breast, as a butcher's chart would show them, and labels them)*

BENNO: The fourteen-year-old Benno ran out one night . . .

OLD MAN: Rib! *(As before, draws the lines and labels them)*

BENNO: Benno was looking for love.

OLD MAN: Chuck! *(As before, draws and labels lines)*

BENNO: Benno was looking for love!

MOTHER'S VOICE: *(Off. In the dark)* You think we should put him away?

FATHER'S VOICE: Who?

MOTHER'S VOICE: Who else? Our humpback of Notre Dame son!

BENNO: For love.

OLD MAN: Round. *(As before draws on Benno and labels him)*

BENNO: Benno took a walk. He ended up in Edgar Allen Poe schoolyard. A place of concrete, broken glass and dog shit of the peculiarly urban sort. In the schoolyard, Benno saw three boys. They lounged about in the shadows, some distance from him. They were older than Benno, from his neighborhood. He saw the schoolyard to be a place of waste; to be a locus of the city's fecal matter. Yes, he saw that broken glass, that concrete with the brown grass jutting and that hard dog shit to be part of a gigantic fecal mass; yes, and he saw those boys with their tee shirts and torn dungarees also as so many turds. Nor was Benno himself exempt; he too was waste. All was waste. Waste. Through the haze of this decay, Benno saw these boys, and chose to wait.

OLD MAN: Sirloin . . . *(As before, draws, then labels)*

BENNO: In due course, the boys noticed Benno. They performed the usual ritual of greeting Benno. They pointed and giggled.

OLD MAN: Rump. *(As before, draws, then labels)*

BENNO: Hey kid, one said, hey kid. They beckoned me closer. I went. What you name, kid, they asked. They knew already. Benno, he replied. Hey, they sang out, Benno Blimpie. Hey fellas, meet Benno Blimpie.

OLD MAN: Loin. *(Draws and labels as before)*

BENNO: The tallest said: Hey Benno, know what this is? He grabbed his crotch. My mouth was dry. Yes, Benno was heard to whisper, I know. They laughed. Hey fellas, they sang out, Benno Blimpie knows.

OLD MAN: Liver. *(Draws and labels Benno)*

BENNO: The oldest lowered his voice and said: Hey Benno, you wanna eat me?

OLD MAN: Kidney. *(Draws and labels Benno)*

BENNO: I said nothing. Sure he does, one said. Benno wants to eat us all. The oldest said: Sure, Benno wants a big meal, he wants to eat us all. They settled the order, one taking watch, one watching me, the other being served. They pushed me down, it took all three. And one after the other I ate them. I ate all three.

OLD MAN: Heart. *(Draws and labels on Benno)*

BENNO: I ate all three. One, two and three. I caught on after a bit. They were happy during it and pranced around. They enjoyed it. When Benno had finished all three, they bloodied his nose and forced one eye shut by pounding it. Then they picked up pieces of glass and dried dog shit and stuffed them into Benno's bleeding mouth. Laughing, they ran off. I was left lying like a blimp in the middle of the public schoolyard. In the middle of all that concrete, with come and shit and glass in my mouth. I couldn't cry; Benno couldn't scream. He lay there; and in that instant, time stopped. And feeling, it stopped too, and seemed to merge with time, and with space. My sense of identity seeped out of me into the cracks in the concrete. And for a few seconds I was out of myself, totally free of myself. Totally. Free. Free. And this I call: The Transfiguration of Benno Blimpie.

Scene Twelve:

Lights come up intensely on everyone. The Old Man hands Benno the meat cleaver.

OLD MAN: You ready now!
(Slowly, Benno rises from his chair with great effort. He raises the meat cleaver. Everyone turns and watches him in silence)
BENNO: I am Benno. I am eating myself to death.
(Slowly he lowers the meat cleaver as though to cut off some part of himself. The others watch intently. As he reaches that part, quick blackout)

Author's Notes for Production

In writing detailed instructions about a particular play, a playwright takes a considerable risk. About a play there must always be ambiguities and mysteries, and more harm than good may be caused by attempting to pin down truths better found by a careful reading of the text. Also, in giving instructions, the playwright risks inhibiting and cramping the imaginations of the actors and director, whose contributions are vital to the life of any play. This is not my intention. After experiencing a number of different productions of *Benno Blimpie,* under a variety of circumstances, it seems wise to me to answer those questions in advance which, in my experience, have always come up regarding the performance of this play.

It is well to remember also that the particular form of *Benno* can be confusing because it is so compressed and abbreviated. For better or worse, a three-act play has been squeezed into sixty minutes playing time; unless this is kept in mind, problems in realizing the text may result.

Therefore, I offer the following suggestions, making them as general as possible, hoping to point the way toward a fair realization of the play.

CASTING

BENNO: Benno is meant to be a young man between seventeen and twenty-two, who weighs five hundred pounds. Type-casting here is not feasible, because none of the five-hundred-pound adolescents in existence appear to be actors. Producers sometimes express confusion as to what path to follow in finding an actor for this part. I must insist that the best path is casting the actor, fat or slim, young or old, who has the necessary emotional and technical resources for a grueling part. I have seen actors of all sizes play the part successfully and, since even a fat actor will have to be padded to suggest the extreme state of obesity, there is no reason not to pad a thin actor who may be more appropriate emotionally, technically or intellectually.

Similarly, in the matter of ages: I have seen young men in their twenties play the part, and mature men past forty. Again, the youth of the character must be more a matter of acting technique than strictly of type. It is most important that the actor, regardless of his actual age, be able to suggest the vulnerability and innocence of the character, as well as his adolescent obsessiveness and self-dramatization.

OLD MAN: Much the same is true for the part of the Old Man. I have seen a young man still in his twenties play this part very successfully, for he was able to suggest the character's debility and desperation, and also his charm and peculiar sexual allure.

GIRL: The Girl is meant to be twelve or thirteen. Again, it is wiser to cast an actress who can suggest the character's paradoxical qualities—decadence and innocence, toughness and charm—than to strive to find an actual thirteen-year-old, or settle for someone who can easily look that age.

ACTING VALUES

It is well for the director of the play to understand that *Benno Blimpie* is a memory play, that we are perceiving the characters as they are remembered by Benno. Not only remembered in general, but in particular; their actions are selected so as to make a case for his suicide. This is not to suggest that Benno has fabricated the actions and attitudes of these characters; nor, under any circumstances, should the acting be "distorted" or unreal. Actors, in preparing their parts, must remember that these characters were probably perceived by other people as perfectly normal and ordinary; and that anyone, were various elements or actions of his life to be taken out of context, might appear monstrous. Every attempt must be made to ground these characters in everyday reality, even though we see them only at relatively extreme moments. Biographies might be constructed by individual actors so as to imagine the ordinariness of these characters most of the time—the Girl in school, the Mother at work, etc., so that a continuity can be achieved between the everyday aspects of their lives and the particular extremes represented by the play and Benno's memory.

BENNO: Many people are tempted to think so, but Benno does not represent the author, nor does he speak for the author. He is a character in a work of fiction, and thus his attitudes may be wrong, his interpretations of reality may be debatable.

Benno is like an attorney, making a case for his suicide, with which, finally, he hopes to elicit the love and approval he feels have been denied him because of his appearance. As a result, he takes certain actions out of context, interprets them in a certain way. In a sense, he is putting on a show for the audience, acting as an "entertainer." Like many entertainers, Benno's style is conflicting; he can be alternately cajoling and offensive, self-pitying and abrasive. In his final monologue he settles for a controlled simplicity.

An actor playing the part must keep in mind the need for variety of color in handling the speeches, as well as keeping a balance between the character's intensity and obsessiveness and his objectivity and irony. There should be something vulnerable and open about Benno, as well as something repulsive and horrible. The actor must not comment on the character's ugliness, which can speak for itself, nor must he sentimentalize a part whose sad aspects are clear enough.

OLD MAN and GIRL: Some actors are tempted to play these parts in a ghoulish and caricatured manner. This is not the author's intention. Though the writing in these scenes is somewhat abbreviated, a fairly real picture of an erotic interchange is intended. The Old Man feels himself aging, perhaps dying, and is desperate to recapture, even for an instant, his youth. He is intense, but not a monster. He is grandfatherly, teasing and affectionate with the Girl. He seeks pleasure from her, and seeks to give her pleasure, but does not perceive what he is doing as ugly, abnormal or shameful.

Similarly, the Girl is a tough street kid who acts towards the Old Man as she thinks a tough girl should. But, at first, she likes him, and their interaction should have the aspect of a faintly naughty game.

Under no circumstances should the end of their relationship be played from the beginning. Instead, in their first scenes and, in fact, up to the last minute, they are having a wonderful time. When the Girl kills the Old Man, she does so mostly accidentally. Her outburst of curses afterwards is her way of expressing a hysterical horror at what she has done.

My point is that, while neither of these characters is meant to be totally sympathetic, they are not meant to be horrendous monstrosities either. A playful seductiveness is an important part of their scenes.

MOTHER: Some actresses do not understand the source of this character's venom. It is that she is in a trap as inexorable and horrible as Benno's, and the only way she can continue her life is to turn its incessant sadness and disappointment into an ugly and sadistic humorousness. This is very clear in the writing of her long speech and is, in fact, a tactic adopted by many working-class women in similar straits; one can think of a number of comediennes who have adapted this style as their professional persona. The Mother's marriage is a total failure, her husband is a cruel disappointment to her and has lost interest in her as a woman; the child Benno becomes a shameful, living, inescapable reminder of the failure of her life. One must remember that, like most working-class women, there is little opportunity for self-actualization or escape in her life. And this vicious circle is the cause of her own continued viciousness, as well as her self-loathing.

In her early scenes, the Mother behaves very much as one of those comediennes mentioned above; she probably acts and says the same things every day, and nothing her husband or son might do would find her at a loss for a funny, probably insulting line. Pricking her husband into hitting her is the only way she can have any contact with him, and her insulting manner with her son, perhaps, becomes a twisted way of attempting to make contact with him.

In her final scene this style gradually gives way to the grief and horror underneath, and even then she remains somewhat trapped in the surface of her behavior.

THE SET

The play has been given both in the round and the proscenium. In the round it is somewhat easier to unify the set, and to suggest that Benno is remembering the locales represented.

The different areas can be very simply suggested: a park bench, large wire ashcan, and leaves can do for the park; a kitchen table, perhaps on linoleum, can do for the kitchen. If more elaborate kitchen fixtures are used, as for instance a stove, sink, refrigerator, they should be believable in a working-class, poor kitchen from about 1952 or so. The kitchen fixtures need not be functional, nor need real food be used.

Benno's area should suggest a small room in which he has imprisoned himself. Old food containers may be in evidence, paper cups, plates, trash bags, etc. may be near him.

PERIOD

The play takes place in two time periods: The present—Benno as he is now, remembering, committing suicide; and the past—the scenes remembered by Benno when he was a young boy. The actual period of the past may depend on the age of the actor playing Benno—if he is, as suggested in the script, actually young, or able to play young (for instance, in his early twenties) then the time in the past is the early nineteen fifties (about 1952–56), and the rock music that accompanies the soliloquies of the Girl should be chosen accordingly, as well as the costumes and hair styles of everyone but Benno. If Benno is older, then the time period, of course, will be pushed back to the forties, thirties, etc. The author prefers the fifties as the chosen time period for the scenes in the past.

ACCENTS

The Mother and Father are working-class, Italian Americans. That is, their parents were immigrants. They have been raised in predominantly Italian neighborhoods, generally poor, in American cities.

The Old Man is the father's father. He is an Italian immigrant who speaks broken English.

The Girl is a working-class youngster from a poor neighborhood. Her parents are Irish Americans, but she speaks with a street accent.

Benno clearly has read and educated himself, thus he speaks standard middle-class English.

Rochelle Owens

MOUNTAIN RITES

Rochelle Owens

With *Mountain Rites,* which appears in print for the first time in this anthology, Rochelle Owens takes on a new guise as author of "a modern Gothic fantasy with satirical overtones." Written straightforwardly (the satire is beneath the surface), there are all the elements of "pop-Goth"—the gentlemanly camaraderie, the beauteous but ambiguous heroine, an exotic locale and mysteriously monstrous doings accompanied by ominous sound effects.

Rochelle Owens is the award-winning author of many controversial and innovative plays. Honors include several "Obies" (the *Village Voice* Drama Awards), the Drama Desk Award, and honors from the New York Drama Critics' Circle. Her plays have been produced throughout the world and presented at festivals in Edinburgh, Berlin, Paris and Rome. In addition to writing for the theatre, she has published five books of poetry, three collections of plays, and has given many readings throughout the country and in Europe. A recipient of Guggenheim, Yale School of Drama, Creative Artists Program Service, Rockefeller, and The National Endowment for the Arts Fellowships, she is a founding member of The New York Theatre Strategy and a sponsor of The Women's InterArt Center, Inc.

Miss Owens stepped into the international theatrical limelight with her first play, *Futz,* which excited considerable critical and audience interest. Described by Edith Oliver of *The New Yorker* as "a witty, harsh, farcical, and touching dramatic poem," it was presented at Café La Mama in 1967, subsequently toured England and Europe, and was performed at the Edinburgh Festival. In 1968, the drama returned to Off-Broadway, this time at the Theatre De Lys where it ran for 233 performances and garnered an "Obie" award for distinguished playwriting. *Futz* and his companions, however, would not stay ballasted to Greenwich Village, and soon they were to be seen in theatres of Sweden, Germany, Canada and other countries, as well as on the screen in a movie version released in 1969.

Miss Owens' plays have engendered much journalistic space, both approbatory and disparaging, but whether one is pro or con, it must be conceded that she has an exceptionally gifted hand for stirring the cauldron of theatrical excitement. Harold Clurman, one of her many distinguished votaries, has written, "Her work is not realism; it is real. It is the product of a complex imagination in which deep layers of the author's subconscious emerge in wild gusts of stage imagery. . . . I know of no contemporary playwright like Rochelle Owens."

At the time of her initial publication in *The Best Short Plays* series, Miss Owens supplied the following biographical information: "I was born in Brooklyn, New York, on April 2, 1936. Having completed my public school education, I moved to Manhattan where I studied at the New School for Social Research and with Herbert Berghof at the HB Studio. At that time, neither an academic degree nor a career as an actress appealed to me, so I worked at numerous jobs, read a great deal, and wrote poetry. In 1959, my poetry began to appear in several of the most prominent little magazines and, since then, I have published three books of poems and have contributed to many literary journals and anthologies.

"In 1962, I married George Economou, poet and college professor, then editor of *Trobar* poetry magazine. Shortly before meeting my husband, I wrote my first play, *Futz*. Since then I have written many full-length and short plays, among them: *The Queen of Greece; Istanboul; He Wants Shih!; Beclch; Homo;* and *Kontraption*.

"Although I wrote *The String Game* after *Futz*, it was the first of my plays to be staged, in 1965, at the Judson Poets' Theatre. Subsequently, my plays have been performed Off-Broadway, Off-Off-Broadway, in regional and college theatres, on television, and abroad."

The author's published works include: *Not Be Essence That Cannot Be; Salt and Core; Futz and What Came After; I Am the Babe of Joseph Stalin's Daughter; Poems from Joe's Garage; The Karl Marx Play and Others; The Joe 82 Creation Poems;* and *Spontaneous Combustion*.

Miss Owens previously was represented in these annuals with *The Karl Marx Play (The Best Short Plays 1971)* and *The Widow and the Colonel (The Best Short Plays 1977)*.

Characters:

PROF. RAYMOND LONGTIN: NARRATOR
CONSTANTINE DOWLING, *intense and idealistic*
PROF. GARRISON BOGG, *ambitious and autocratic*
EMERSON SPEARS, *worldly but suspicious*
HERA, *spirited and intelligent*
HERMES, *a typical boy*
CHARIS, *the friend of Hera*
WAITER
TELEPHONE CALLER
PROF. PAUL SPECTOR, *a rational individual*

Time:

The present.

Place:

England and Greece.
Using little more than lighting effects to ease transitions and enhance the swirling sense of life which engulfs these locales, we are taken on an excursion into a modern Gothic fantasy with satirical overtones.

(The dining room at the faculty club, England)

NARRATOR-LONGTIN: Dr. Constantine Dowling! How wonderful to see you again at the club. The whole university has had you in mind since news of the disaster that befell Dr. Garrison Bogg in that remote mountain village in Greece. Welcome back!

DOWLING: Dr. Longtin, I am very glad to be back in London and I can assure you that to be able to relax in the university's faculty club will never be a mundane experience for me again.

NARRATOR-LONGTIN: Everyone was horrified at the reports from Greece about the gruesome death of Dr. Bogg. It will be added to the list of the most fantastic crimes of the century! Don't you agree, Constantine?

DOWLING: The manner in which Dr. Bogg died will always fascinate those who are hungry for a good mystery.

NARRATOR-LONGTIN: Hungry for a good mystery! You are forever ironic! And after what you have suffered.

DOWLING: It is a way to keep sane; irony. That and pity— pity for the man who tried to ruin me. The man who tried to besmirch my reputation as a scholar!

NARRATOR-LONGTIN: For a second Constantine Dowling's eyes showed disturbance as he leaned forward in his chair and began to tell the story of his relationship with the late Dr. Garrison Bogg, a renowned Greek scholar.

(Musical interlude)

DOWLING: When I first came up to London I had rooms in Harrison street near the university. All of my time was spent studying those branches of Greek literature which would make me more efficient in writing my dissertation. I had insights of incredible scholastic importance, principally through my new discovery which I was hesitant to reveal. However, my professor, Dr. Garrison Bogg, and I became friends and I was able to confide to him the nature of my theory. One afternoon we were together in his office—

BOGG: Constantine, your methods of research are unorthodox indeed and your hypothesis is fascinating but it is hardly realistic scholarship. Scholarship is grueling, systematic work.

DOWLING: Professor Bogg, I realize how strange my idea sounds—my idea that certain hymns of a small group of hill people living in central Greece could be traced almost in a straight line directly back to pagan times.

BOGG: Yes, you explained your theory—that these hymns are the prayers to the old gods and goddesses and in particular to Aphrodite the goddess of love! Absolutely absurd! Constantine, your theory is far-flung and imaginative but not scientific! Human culture is dynamic—there were numerous foreign invasions that changed the racial and linguistic character of the present day population. Invasions of Franks, Saracens, Slavs, Turks and including 2000 years of Christianity! It is impossible to believe that these Byzantine hymns are in reality authentic prayers to ancient pagan deities!

DOWLING: Dr. Bogg, I respect you immensely—but you must listen to my story. I've mentioned to you before that my mother was Greek and that three years ago I visited the village where she was born. One day I went to a fair in the village; a friend was with me, an American sculptor by the name of Emerson Spears. We were returning by mule to the house that we had rented.

(Distant sounds of Greek music)

(The Greek countryside; on a narrow road)

SPEARS: Constantine, have you ever been to a Greek village fair before where the men dance so incredibly—holding a cafe table between their teeth?

DOWLING: I have never seen that stunt done except in films.

SPEARS: Ahh, now, Constantine, you have seen it in the flesh! Do you know that a man can paralyze his jaw for a month after performing that difficult feat?

DOWLING: How ghastly! But I suppose there's not much else to do in the local villages any more. So many of the young Greeks leave to find work in Western Europe.

SPEARS: Or else they marry and live with the wife's parents.

DOWLING: I believe it is the other way around. The wife goes to live with her in-laws.

(Distant thunder)

SPEARS: Another rain storm! Zeus is preparing to hurl a bolt of lightning. Well, we don't have much further to go.

DOWLING: The thunder sounded rather odd—like a tape recording with too much bass!

SPEARS: Look, Constantine! There—there is your Zeus! A couple of children!

DOWLING: Very amusing! Two children! A very pretty girl

of about fifteen I'd say, and a boy who appears to be about eight—and they're carrying a tape cassette! So that's where the thunder came from—a tape cassette!

SPEARS: Here we are in a primitive village in the Balkans where one would expect to hear real thunder and we meet two children playing sound effects on tape recording equipment of a fairly late design!

DOWLING: Little girl, do you and your young friend make it a habit to frighten tourists away with the power of Zeus's lightning bolts! *(To Spears)* What a lovely girl! She resembles those archaic sculptures of the Mycenaean age. Emerson, I can see why you enjoy using the local young people as models.

SPEARS: Constantine, the boy looks like a Ganymede! With eyes of sapphire!

DOWLING: Where are you going, children?

HERMES: To the celebration! Hera and I are going together!

HERA: Hermes, you must not tell the foreigner where we are going!

HERMES: I have told the gentlemen nothing! All I said was that we are going to the celebration.

SPEARS: Another Christian saint's feast day. Not unusual at all when you consider the many hundreds of saints and martyrs that are revered in the Greek orthodox tradition.

HERMES: Today's celebration is not for any Christian saint!

HERA: Hermes, you are terrible to say that! You promised the priest and our own parents that you would never tell lies!—Gentlemen, he's making up a story! That's all. My little brother enjoys telling fairy tales!

HERMES: It's not a fairy tale! It's true! We are going to a celebration for the goddess Aphrodite!

HERA: *(Slapping Hermes' face)* You little imp! You liar! Goddess Aphrodite! There is no such person as that!—Only the blessed Virgin Mary! Say it, Hermes, say it! There is only the blessed Virgin Mary! And never never say the name of Aphrodite again!

(Hermes cries and runs off)

DOWLING: Young lady, Hera, where did you get that name?

HERA: Sir, I should think even a foreigner would know that a child is named by her parents! They named me Hera.

SPEARS: But that's the name of an ancient Greek goddess. The wife of Zeus. It's not a Christian name.

DOWLING: Emerson, many Greeks have classical names instead of Christian. After all, you surely have heard of Aristotle and Diogenes—this beauty is called Hera. It's an appropriate name—look how large and mysterious her eyes are.

SPEARS: Hera, I'll give you a hundred *drachmas* if you will take us to where this celebration of Aphrodite is.

HERA: I have money! I don't need any from a curious stranger! I cannot be bribed to tell anything I don't want to. . . . Celebration of the goddess Aphrodite—how ridiculous!

DOWLING: Emerson, she is right. Your request to be taken to a pagan celebration is something only a tourist who has imbibed too much *ouzo* might dream up.

HERA: Your friend thinks he can buy whatever he wants— if it was so—he would have bought some common sense!

SPEARS: Hera, you are an intelligent and blunt girl. I admit it was rude of me to bribe you. But if there is some celebration, an unusual event that will take place or perhaps is in the process of taking place right at this moment, I would like very much to be there.

HERA: I have been to schools in England and Germany! I even took a course in video technology. I'm going to make experimental films one day. I'm not a peasant girl. I detest being patronized!

SPEARS: Hera, I'm sorry we've made you so angry. I am a sculptor whose only interest is art and I wonder if you would do me the favor of modeling for me.

HERA: Naked I suppose. Well, I'm not too shy to model naked for someone I like. But I don't like you. I like your friend Constantine. I like his eyes.

DOWLING: Well, Emerson, she has picked the right man. How old are you, little Hera?

HERA: I am *eighteen!* Listen, I can't stay with you here any longer. I must leave. But meet me tomorrow afternoon at this exact place without your friend! Do you have anything made of copper?

DOWLING: Copper? Why, no—only some pennies.

HERA: Here, take this bracelet and wear it when I meet you tomorrow afternoon. At three oclock. Don't forget exactly at three oclock!

(Hera runs off)

SPEARS: Constantine, I certainly hope you're not going to meet that little wench. If you do, her boyfriend will come after you with a knife.

DOWLING: Emerson, don't be so melodramatic. She's not an ordinary village girl. Can't you tell by her attitude? And she's even taken a course in video technology. Emerson, the whole wide world is modernizing more or less, you know. And when it comes to science and art why shouldn't this delightful and beautiful girl also be interested? I must say that I am a bit curious as to why she wants me to wear this cheap copper bracelet that she just gave me.

SPEARS: I've seen those bracelets in novelty stores. They are supposed to ward off the evil eye and prevent certain maladies. Constantine, you ought to take care concerning that girl—these village people are obsessed with guarding the virtue of their wives and daughters.

DOWLING: I'm not interested in anyone's wife or daughter! Besides, you sound like you're quoting lines from a cheap novel about love, terror and intrigue in the Greek mountains!

SPEARS: Constantine, are you going to meet that girl?

DOWLING: Indeed I am.

SPEARS: She really might have a jealous lover, you know.

DOWLING: Emerson, you've already suggested that idea. I'm eager to learn about the social relationships that exist between these village people. Frankly, I'm tired of being with artists and scholars even if they are Greek, English, German or American. I want to have a sense of the life of the unsophisticated villager.

SPEARS: You are contradicting yourself! You said before that Hera's not an ordinary village girl. She owns a tape cassette with intricate sound effects that she carries around surprising gullible tourists—now who is painting cliché images about village people in Greece. Unsophisticated villager! Don't be absurd!

(Musical interlude)

(Hera and her friend Charis are in a field. We hear distant sounds of sheep, birds, the wind)

HERA: I met a young Englishman today. He's very handsome and educated. He's also a Grecophile!

CHARIS: You mean one of those sentimental Western Europeans who believe that we Greeks are more passionate and alive than they. Like my brother Stavros who is as nervous as a hen when he has to talk to a woman.

HERA: It is ironical—the maudlin attitudes some foreigners have about Greece. They like to idealize us as simple earthy people without any neurosis. They ought to see my mother when she feels she has been snubbed by the priest's wife. She retires to her bed for days and sulks. Then she invites my Aunt Katherine to the house for coffee and they tell each other stories about how their families take them for granted and how hard they work and how lazy everyone else is and what terrible gossips people are—if I don't leave this village soon I will go crazy with boredom!

CHARIS: Where do you want to go?

HERA: Athens or a large city in Western Europe. I really want to make an important film and I must be somewhere where I can take an advanced film-making course.

CHARIS: How exciting! I envy you. Hera, I have a strong suspicion that you will dazzle this Englishman that you are meeting tomorrow. But I think that you ought to appear less intellectual.

HERA: Why?

CHARIS: Because you might scare him away with your brilliant mind. You ought to play another role.

HERA: Charis, you are right! I've decided that I will play the role of a laconic sex-object.

CHARIS: That should be fun.

HERA: Yes, it should be fun.

CHARIS: Do you want to go with him to the celebration?

HERA: I don't know. I want to find out more about him. Constantine told me that he loves to wander along the dusty roads of his mother's village.

CHARIS: How romantic! To wander along remote places and the dusty roads that wind up and down among the foot-hills of mountains, through the pine forests and above the bays of the Aegean—so beautiful—and the woods smell of dust and incense! And the god Pan blows his pipes—

HERA: *(Ironic)* I'm sure that Greece has a strong effect on him.

CHARIS: Perhaps you and he ought to take a ride on a donkey together.

HERA: I'm sure that would bring out his romantic nature. He might have the desire to take off his clothes and dance through the wild gardens and fig trees.

CHARIS: Two years ago there was an American student at the festival who became convinced that he was the incarnation of the god of wine, Dionysus. He said that he felt his whole body was saturated by the brilliant blue of the Greek sky. And in the middle of a rainstorm the American began to insist that the sun was burning the alpha and omega into the center of his forehead! Yes, I remember that event!

HERA: He was so exhilarated by the rites of the celebration that he died of a stroke.

CHARIS: But he had the thrill of witnessing the secret rites. He died believing that he was the god, Dionysus!

CHARIS AND HERA: Two by two and one by one the call of the owl starts the fun. Five by five both fat and thin Greeks and Turks both love gin. Seven by seven bowl of butter an Englishman is made of rubber.

CHARIS: *(Calling after Hera as she runs off)* Good-bye, Hera, Good-bye!

(Musical interlude)

(In the woods)

HERA: Constantine, I'm so happy to see you again. And you kept your word. It's exactly three o'clock.

DOWLING: When a beautiful girl asks me to do something and if I want to please her, I always do what she asks.

HERA: How thoughtful and generous you are. *(Pause)* How do you feel today, Constantine?

DOWLING: You're looking at the copper band on my wrist. Hera, I feel wonderful and I'm sure that this band of copper that you gave me is causing just the right vibrations between us.

HERA: *(Serious)* You must wear it always, otherwise you will die.

DOWLING: Of course. I believe in the folk customs of rural people everywhere in the world. And when I'm in Africa I always wear a string of monkey's teeth around my neck if it's the custom.

HERA: I'm very serious. Last year in this village, a young French artist contracted cholera and died. The peculiar thing was that he was the only person to get the disease. No one else in the village had been infected.

DOWLING: Hera, you're smiling! I think you enjoy telling me these stories of horror!

HERA: No, Constantine. I don't enjoy telling you such things.

DOWLING: Then why are you smiling?

HERA: I am smiling because you are a fool.

DOWLING: Then why did you agree to meet me here?

HERA: I don't know why. Perhaps because I think your eyes are exciting.

DOWLING: Be with me tonight, Hera. We could take a boat ride through the islands and swim in the moonlight—

HERA: I would rather swim during the day and enjoy the sun and then have dinner in a wonderful little restaurant by the edge of the sea. Would you like that also, Constantine?

DOWLING: Yes, Hera, I would like that very much.

(Musical Interlude)

(The dining room at the faculty club)

NARRATOR-LONGTIN: A month later Constantine Dowling and his friend Emerson Spears were having lunch together.

(Greece)

SPEARS: And so, Constantine, you are having a love affair with that little village girl, Hera. How lucky you are! Lucky in love. At least I hope that you are.

DOWLING: Well, Hera takes up all of my days and nights—if that's what you can call being lucky—then I'm a lucky fellow. Unfortunately, I'm not doing enough research work on my scholarly project. My time just seems to slip away.

SPEARS: Constantine, a love affair is always time-consuming.

DOWLING: *(Ironically)* Hera has opened up incredible vistas in my being.

SPEARS: I'm sure you are not mistaken. She's a beautiful young woman, Constantine.

DOWLING: I wonder if—if—no. No. It's not a realistic thought.

SPEARS: Say what is on your mind, Constantine.

DOWLING: Emerson, if I were to marry Hera—marriage would stabilize our relationship. Surely after a year or so she would want to settle down a bit and concentrate on film-making. She really is very talented.

SPEARS: Are you mad? Marry that village girl! How ridiculous! What would everyone in London say?!

DOWLING: They will say that they envy me! Remember Heinrich Schleimann? He was the famous German archeologist who discovered the ancient city of Troy—he married a seventeen-year-old Greek girl.

SPEARS: But that was a century ago! Young girls were different then—now they are ambitious and desirous of having careers of their own. Hera doesn't want to sit in your shadow! Hera doesn't want that!

DOWLING: I don't believe that is the real reason why you think I should not marry her.

SPEARS: What do you mean?

DOWLING: I mean that you do not want me to marry Hera because she is very much a woman. You are jealous.

SPEARS: Maybe. Maybe I am jealous of your success with women. But Constantine, I do have your best interests at heart. I really do. Your scholarly career should be the most important objective in your life.

DOWLING: I know. You're right. That's why if I marry the girl—if I marry Hera—we will finally—we will finally—

SPEARS: Constantine, what is wrong? You are so pale.

DOWLING: I don't feel well—

SPEARS: Are you ill? *(Dowling falls to the floor with a loud thud)* Oh, my God! He's fainted! Someone! Quick! Quick! Bring a glass of water—bring smelling salts!

THE WAITER: Here—we must loosen his belt! Quick—rub his wrists while I try to call the doctor—How terrible—I just realized that the doctor left town this morning.

SPEARS: Constantine! Constantine!

(Musical Interlude)

NARRATOR-LONGTIN: The next day our little friends, Hera, Charis and Hermes were together.

HERA: *(In the woods)* Hermes, why didn't you tell me that Emerson Spears asked you to model for him?

HERMES: Because if I had told you you would have told mother and she would not have let me model for him.

CHARIS: There's a good reason why you ought not to model for that odd sculptor.

HERMES: I know what you're thinking. But it's not true. He's a kind man and he gives me money. He's like a priest! He even asked me to call him papa!

CHARIS: Are you serious? He asked you to call him papa?

HERMES: Do you think that he's a vampire? A vampire who wants to drink the blood of young children! But I tell you—he's a very kind man! He's given me a lot of money just for sitting for him while he sculpts me in clay. . . . At least I don't cause people to have fainting spells!

HERA: Hermes, why did you say that?

HERMES: You know exactly why I said that. And Charis does, too.

HERA: Hermes, when people faint it is a sign that they are sick or that they are suffering from the terrible heat of summer.

HERMES: Or that someone is doing something to them to make them sick!

HERA: What a vivid imagination you have, Hermes. And who is doing what to whom?

HERMES: Three by three and carrying gifts rolling and swirling the wine-sea drifts.

(Hermes runs off)

NARRATOR-LONGTIN: That same evening Constantine Dowling was visited by his friend, Emerson Spears.

(At Constantine's house)

SPEARS: Constantine, I'm glad to see that you are feeling better—but are you aware of what has happened—your, your condition?

DOWLING: What do you mean—my condition! I simply had a brief fainting spell last night. It was too hot in the taverna.

SPEARS: When will you be seeing a doctor?

DOWLING: What? Because of a fainting spell!

SPEARS: I think it is much more serious than that.

DOWLING: I'm not going to see a doctor about a fainting spell! Can't you understand it was just too damned hot in that lousy taverna! Just too damned hot!

SPEARS: Get hold of yourself, man! I'm worried about your—about your emotional stability and some other things. You ought to go to Geneva for a complete medical examination.

DOWLING: Will you get out!

SPEARS: Will you be seeing Hera again?

DOWLING: Of course, you damned fool! Now get out!

SPEARS: If you could only convince yourself that you need professional help—

DOWLING: Why are you speaking to me like this?! Why! Why are you preaching at me! As if I were some cretin imbecile!

SPEARS: I'm worried about your health—you're in terrible danger! I don't trust Hera! Constantine, have you seen yourself in a mirror lately? Have you noticed what's happening to your bones—the bones in your face—and your wrists, Constantine, what's happening to your wrists? And let me ask you another question—Why is your face so white and-and powdery? You're becoming less and less human-looking. You must see a medical specialist about your condition.

DOWLING: Leave me alone! Leave me alone! *(He begins to sob loudly)*

NARRATOR-LONGTIN: Constantine Dowling had become afflicted with a disease of unknown origin. He visited a hospital in Geneva to find out the nature of the illness. The entire medical staff could offer him no explanation as to the cause or the cure of the malady. He returned to Greece exhilarated and told everyone that he felt strong and healthy! Indeed that was the mysterious factor about the peculiar nature of the disease; it caused a biological change that was by any stretch of the imagination impossible to believe. Constantine Dowling was growing taller and larger! Perfectly normal development for an adolescent boy but not for a man of twenty-eight! Two weeks later Constantine Dowling and Emerson Spears met in the village taverna.

(In the taverna)

DOWLING: It's the sulphurous springs that I've been bathing in. The waters have stimulated my endocrine glands and that must be the reason for my height development and the increase of muscle tissue. Hera says that this condition—will—will gradually normalize!

SPEARS: When will this condition normalize, Constantine?

DOWLING: Hera says in about a month! I won't grow beyond seven feet!

SPEARS: Seven feet! My God! How does Hera know that?

DOWLING: Frankly, I don't know. But that's what Hera says! I'm not worried though. I feel healthy and all my body functions are normal. I've even begun work on the research that I must do. . . . Who gives a damn if I look like a basketball star and not a university professor!

SPEARS: You are so very optimistic. What if you don't stop growing?

DOWLING: If I'm an optimist—then you are a pessimist. I'll tell you what will happen if I don't stop growing—something that will satisfy you, Emerson. I'll join a freak show! Does that idea satisfy you?

SPEARS: I'm sorry.

DOWLING: You get on my nerves, Emerson! Always judging!

SPEARS: Let's change the subject. Have you heard anymore about the celebration that is going to take place?

DOWLING: I've heard a few things from Hera—I promised not to tell anyone. There's an incredible secrecy attached to this forthcoming celebration.

SPEARS: Where and when will it take place?

DOWLING: I don't know—I promised not to tell anyone—

SPEARS: I am not just anyone! I'm your old friend! A very close friend!

DOWLING: Then stop prying into my life! What's wrong with you! You ought to broaden your interests—expand your horizons. You are always cooped up in your studio sculpting sentimental neo-Hellenistic statues of young boys! Hera says that you're not up to date about current art forms—that you're fixated on derivative forms.

SPEARS: So now you're listening to the opinions of a little village girl!

DOWLING: I don't like the tone of your voice when you say "little village girl"! There's contempt in your voice. Emerson, I don't think that you're going to like what I want to say—

SPEARS: I'll be the judge of that. Say what you want.

DOWLING: Our relationship—our friendship is over. We had better not see each other anymore.

SPEARS: (Pushing the table away and knocking over glasses) I knew it! I knew it! Oh, I just knew it! She's driven us apart. That cheap vicious village girl has completely changed you! She's changed you! And all your feelings toward me have changed! She's taken you away from me! Constantine, I won't let you leave me!

DOWLING: Calm down, Emerson! The men in the taverna are staring at you!

SPEARS: I don't care what they think! Constantine, I won't let you leave me!

DOWLING: That's what I'm doing, Emerson. I'm leaving you! *(He gets up noisily from his chair and leaves)*

SPEARS: Come back to me! Constantine, come back to me! *(The laughter of the village men merges with the sound of bouzouki music)*

NARRATOR-LONGTIN: Three days later Hera and Constantine were together in the hills.

HERA: Constantine, do you see those hills? Follow your gaze directly along the line of my finger. That one—that pretty hill with the cloud above it. In the valley of that hill the celebration of Dionysus will take place.

DOWLING: Dionysus? I thought it was a celebration for the goddess Aphrodite?

HERA: You are mistaken, Constantine. It is for Dionysus.

DOWLING: Oh. *(Pause)* When will the celebration take place?

HERA: Tomorrow evening. It begins at seven o'clock. Will you be prepared?

DOWLING: Yes. I know exactly what I must do. I must pretend that I just wandered into the festivities—that I'm lost—

HERA: That is what you must do. You will tell the people that you simply wandered off from your friends and that you are lost. Remember, the people must not suspect you of being a curiosity seeker. As I've told you, these village people actually believe that they are practicing the ancient Greek religion of worshipping pagan deities.

DOWLING: They do share certain customs that no other village in Greece practices.

HERA: Constantine, do you believe that these village people are practicing the ancient worship of the old gods? Zeus, Hera? The goddess, the goddess that I am named after! *(Laughs)* Constantine, are they really followers of Dionysus?

DOWLING: Yes. It is entirely possible. Even their marriage customs are not like those of the people in the same region. And of course their hymns—I am fascinated with the language that the hymns are written in. They are written in ancient Greek and not in Byzantine Greek, which is the language of the church. And you know that my scholastic field of interest focuses on the language and culture influences on Byzantine hymnology. I've even written to my advisor in London, Professor Garrison Bogg. I've explained to him my convictions and theory about the hymns.

HERA: Constantine, I believe that when you finish your thesis it will be a major contribution to the study of ancient Greek civilization.

DOWLING: However, I am not doing nearly as much work on my project as I must.

HERA: *(Coyly)* And whose fault is that?

DOWLING: It is your fault, my darling Hera—they should have named you after the goddess of love! Aphrodite!

(Musical Interlude)

NARRATOR-LONGTIN: Meanwhile, Charis, Hermes and Emerson Spears are together in the same vicinity as Constantine and Hera.

SPEARS: Constantine and Hera are like two bugs in a rug. Hermes, would you like to look at them through my field-glasses? You can borrow them if you like.

CHARIS: Emerson, it's a nasty trick to spy on lovers!

HERMES: Are they lovers? Are they really lovers? . . . With these field-glasses I can see the bumblebees on the flowers! Do you think that Hera and Constantine will get married?

SPEARS: I think that Constantine wants to marry Hera. He mentioned it to me a while ago.

CHARIS: How can he marry anyone? A dead man cannot marry.

SPEARS: What did you say?

HERMES: With these field-glasses—I can even see their noses!

SPEARS: Charis, what did you say? What did you just say? Something about a dead man?

CHARIS: It's just a line from a poem. A poem about a sailor who has died and his mother weeps about the terrible fact that her young son will never marry—

HERMES: Because he's dead! Because he's dead! With

these field-glasses I can see Constantine and Hera as clearly as flies in a glass of water! How tall Constantine has become! He looks like a huge statue!

SPEARS: Charis, what is causing the abnormal growth of Constantine's body? You must know the secret.

CHARIS: Of course I know. It is part of the plan leading up to the sacred rites of the festival. But his huge height and muscularity is not permanent and he will gradually shrink back to his normal size.

SPEARS: Are you sure?

CHARIS: Of course. Have you ever seen any other individual in this region who is seven feet tall? Of course not.

SPEARS: Yes, I have! The caretaker of the church is at least seven feet tall. He looks and walks like a robot.

CHARIS: Oh, yes, you are right. I forgot about Nikos Deligiorgios.

SPEARS: Strange to think that once Constantine was as tall as I am—five-feet-eleven-inches—and now he is seven feet!

HERMES: Constantine looks like a statue of an ancient Greek god!

(Low thunder)

DOWLING: Hera, at times I feel such—I feel strong impulses to do terrible things! I have hideous urges!

HERA: I know, Constantine.

DOWLING: How can you say you know? I've never revealed anything about my feelings. I've never told you about these urges! These grotesque urges! I'm so frightened of what I might do!

HERA: You are feeling a profound new strength. A power!

(Lightning strikes)

DOWLING: Hera, why are my hands so chalky-looking? *(With a nervous laugh)* Do you know that sometimes I am tempted to stand for long periods of time as if I was rooted to the earth like a tree!

HERA: Gradually you will become used to the variety of changes that are happening to your body and spirit. The waters of the sulphurous springs are miraculous!

DOWLING: But why do the waters only have an effect on

me? Except for the caretaker, Nikos, I am the only person who is a giant! Is it—is it—!

HERA: Is it what, Constantine?

(Low thunder)

DOWLING: Is it an evil thing that is happening?

HERA: You are a scholar. A very rational man. It is unlike you to describe these extraordinary changes as evil. My darling Constantine, do not be melodramatic.

DOWLING: Then why did I do that—that—horrible thing to the nest of birds?! What I did was evil!

HERA: You must no longer judge your actions as good or evil. You are beyond good and evil.

(Lightning strikes)

DOWLING: For awhile I thought I was beginning again to be involved with the research work I must do to prove my theory about the hymns and their relation to the ancient prayers of the pre-Hellenistic Greeks. But I can't concentrate! My mind is racing away from me. I have these hideous compulsive thoughts!

HERA: Constantine, you will be able to do your work with immense concentration later—after the celebration.

DOWLING: But when is the celebration? I can't stand the suspense any longer! When is the damned celebration?!

HERA: Constantine! Look! A raven has just settled on that rock! How marvelous! Look how it's watching us!

DOWLING: It's staring at us. It looks as if it's able to see right through to our livers and hearts! *(Pause)* I feel dizzy. My head is spinning with crazy ideas. These urges in me—that make me want to—*(Screams)*

HERA: Constantine, you know what you must do now! You know exactly what you have to do right now! You must help yourself!

DOWLING: I can't do that! No! No! I will not do that! That terrible thing!

HERA: Your will-power cannot restrain your terrible need! Submit, Constantine, submit to your great need!

DOWLING: *(Desperately)* It's too grotesque. Please help me! Help me!

HERA: The act will be a sublime experience! Do the necessary sublime act!

DOWLING: That evil bird sees through me! It sees through
to my soul! Make it stop staring at us, Hera! Make it stop
looking through me!

*(Blackout. Wild bird screams and beating of wings merges with
music; flutes)*

NARRATOR-LONGTIN: After Garrison Bogg received a letter
from Emerson Spears he left London for Greece immediately.
The two men met each other and Spears told Bogg all the
circumstances of terror and the unknown surrounding Constantine. Bogg was shocked to learn of a new development to
the strange story: the disappearance of Constantine Dowling.

(Greece)

BOGG: And so, Emerson, you have not heard from Constantine for three weeks!

SPEARS: I have heard absolutely nothing!

BOGG: It's hard to believe that a man could drop out of
sight without some sign of his whereabouts. And you say that
there was an argument between the two of you.

SPEARS: We argued all the time. I think that he was having
a nervous breakdown. He wouldn't take any advice from me.
If Constantine took a trip somewhere—or if he has left
Greece—why should he have let me know? He no longer
wanted my friendship. That girl made him become more
and more irrational!

BOGG: What did he do?

SPEARS: He did several things that one might describe as
being mad! And he completely lost interest in his scholarship.

BOGG: His so-called scholarship had become mere flights
of fantasy! I never approved of his methods of research. They
were absurd!

SPEARS: Somehow I feel that when he became involved
with the girl Hera—I feel—

BOGG: You feel what, Emerson?

SPEARS: She was leading him on, toying with him. She
wanted to make a fool out of him.

BOGG: In your letter you said that Hera was interested in making experimental films. That's unusual for a village girl, don't you agree?

SPEARS: She's not a typical village girl. She comes from an educated background and she is one of the most charismatic females that I've ever known! She has a relentless power over Constantine. Her ideas about experimental film-making are very unique.

BOGG: Her film project that you told me about is most unusual. And you say that she doesn't know where Constantine is?

SPEARS: I am sure she doesn't know.

BOGG: This whole affair sounds like a mystery drama!

SPEARS: I must say that I don't understand a great many things, especially the excessive calcification and muscle tissue development of Constantine.

BOGG: And now the poor wretch has disappeared. (Pause) I must admit that I'm a bit curious about the so-called Dionysian rites that are supposed to take place during the forthcoming festival. I told Constantine that I didn't believe it had anything to do with the religious rites of the ancient Greeks. It's probably just an isolated circumstance. When does the festival begin?

SPEARS: It happens each month, when the moon is in its quarter.

BOGG: I must see it with my own eyes! I want to be there!

SPEARS: Professor Bogg, what if these people are really practicing ancient pagan rites?

BOGG: Then the scholar who could prove it, prove the theory—would become the most heralded scientific mind of the twentieth century! A giant of our age!

SPEARS: How ironical! A giant of our age! Like Constantine who is over seven feet tall!

NARRATOR-LONGTIN: The next evening Emerson Spears received a telephone call from Garrison Bogg.

(In Bogg's room)

BOGG: Hello, Emerson? Emerson, something incredible has happened!

SPEARS: Speak louder, Professor Bogg. We have a bad connection. I can't hear you very well.

BOGG: I say something incredible has happened!

SPEARS: Well, speak up! What's happened?

BOGG: This morning when I returned to my room after breakfast I found a note on my bed written in Greek. It says that I must go to the other side of Spanos mountain tonight at 5:45 in order to be a witness to the sacred rites of the festival!

SPEARS: Professor Bogg, somebody is playing a joke on you. I suggest that you remain in your room and drink a hot toddy and forget about going to the other side of Spanos mountain!

BOGG: Emerson, I came to Greece to find out what the devil is happening—and to discover the whereabouts of Constantine. I intend to be at the ceremony tonight!

SPEARS: Professor Bogg, you must stay in your room tonight. Stay in your room! Do not go outside! I'm warning you for your own good. Professor Bogg, drink *two* hot toddies.

(Spears hangs up)

BOGG: What a ridiculous fellow! Stay inside my room and drink hot toddies! How dare he mock me! How dare he! However, I will take precautions—I'm no fool! I will carry my revolver with me just in case there are some wild dogs around the other side of Spanos mountain. *(The telephone rings)* It's probably Spears calling back. *(He picks up the receiver)* Hello, hello. *(The sound of heavy breathing is heard over the telephone)* Some crackpot is doing the heavy breathing stunt. Well, go ahead you damned idiot! Breathe your brains out! *(He slams the receiver down)*

NARRATOR-LONGTIN: And that same evening, Charis, Hera and Hermes were together admiring Hera's film equipment.

HERMES: Hera, you will be able to make a wonderful film with this expensive equipment. Now you must buy a fake mustache to wear—so that you can look like a famous film director.

HERA: You are very wrong, Hermes. There are already several important women directors and after I have finished making my film about the extraordinary event that we will witness tonight—I will join the ranks of the most influential film directors of all time!

CHARIS: Hera, I hope that no one breaks your camera. You know how the people feel about intruders!

HERA: Constantine will take care of that problem.

HERMES: Charis, don't you know that our English friend Constantine has become the incarnation of the god, Dionysus!

CHARIS: Of course I know that.

HERA: Tonight Constantine will perform a sacred rite of healing. It will be glorious to film!

CHARIS: Tonight the god Dionysus will attend the ceremony! The giant Constantine is now the god Dionysus!

HERA: Constantine's huge size will prove to the people the magical and healing powers of the ancient pagan religion! The people will be so mesmerized by him that they will ignore the film equipment. Everything will run smoothly tonight! Do not forget to wear white robes for the celebration! Tradition demands the wearing of white robes.

HERMES: I'm going to wear garlands on my head. The people will think that I'm Cupid!

HERA: How does that little poem go—the one from an old European fairy tale? Do you remember it, Hermes?

HERMES: Fee fie fo fum I smell the blood of an Englishman! Fee fie fo fum I smell the blood of an Englishman!

(Interlude: wind instruments)

(Garrison Bogg is in his room)

BOGG: Hell! I can't find my other shoe! I must have accidentally kicked it under the armoire—no, that's not possible! The armoire rests solidly on the floor. I've got to leave soon! Oh, there's my other shoe! My left shoe! I've got the right shoe on already. So that must be my left shoe. What in hell is it doing on the window sill! I don't remember putting my shoe on the window sill! *(Pause)* I can't seem to be able to find my keys! Oh, the desk clerk has it, of course.

(The telephone rings)

TELEPHONE CALLER: Fee fie fo fum I smell the blood of

Garrison Bogg. If the Englishman doesn't die by and by he will fly.

(Caller hangs up)

BOGG: Emerson Spears again! What a lunatic! I wonder why he's resorting to all these stupid attempts to keep me from tonight's celebration? Perhaps the disappearance of Constantine has driven him mad. I'm going to find out what's really happening. The truth. Because if Constantine's theory proves to be correct and there is a definite connection between the hymns sung by this group of hill people and the prayers to the ancient pagan gods—if it's true—and if it can be proven! Then I know exactly what must be done!

(He leaves, slamming the door)

(At the celebration. Distant chanting, music of flutes, etc.)

HERA: The sun will set in a few minutes. And the rites will commence. The rites of mystery!

HERMES: The sacred rites of Dionysus and his blessed followers.

CHARIS: As Aristotle said: "Those undergoing an initiatory rite are not to learn anything, but to experience something and get into another frame of mind."

HERA: Where is Constantine?

SPEARS: He has not yet come.

HERA: I'm happy to see that no one has forgotten to wear the only piece of jewelry allowed—the copper bracelet. And that no one is wearing purple, black or any embroidered fabric.

SPEARS: We are wearing our beautiful white robes! *(Chanting)* As those who dispose of their dead, we walk in a grim file looking, looking for the plants and flowers—

HERMES: *(Chanting)* Looking for the plants and flowers—

CHARIS: *(Chanting)* Our hearts beating to the killing sounds—

HERA: The people joyous as the wedding guests—

SPEARS: *(Chanting)* Dionysus is among us—

HERA: *(Chanting)* Soft as a dream his blood darkens—

SPEARS: *(Chanting)* Tooth and udder, heart and spirit—

HERA: He who is Dionysus must dance in the healing springs!

HERMES: *(Chanting)* Look look there is the god Dionysus!

SPEARS: Oh, oh, oh! Constantine looks divine! He is as tall as a pine tree; and more magnificent! He seems to be hypnotized or drugged—instead of a knife—he carries a bayonet!

HERA: He is possessed!

HERMES: His eyes look like a blindman's eyes! The whole crowd is weaving towards Constantine. They want to touch the god, Dionysus! Closer and closer they come!

HERA: The people are totally absorbed in watching Constantine. Now we are ready to begin shooting the film.

HERMES: Constantine looks like an English rock-star. A super-star! He waves the shining bayonet over his head!

HERA: I'm going to create the effect of a thousand shooting stars circling his head! This will be the most exciting film at the international film festival this year! It will dazzle everyone!

SPEARS: A hundred years from now the film will be a document proving the fact of this incredible event that we're witnessing! This film will tell others who were not present— what we saw! A man over eleven feet tall whirling in a mad dance and ready to perform a sacrificial rite. He holds the bayonet high like an ancient priest! He looks drunk! Drunk on the spirit of the god! Where is the sacrificial goat? I see only three skinny chickens in a wire basket!

HERA: Homer talks about animal sacrifice! The human spirit demands vital confrontation with the life force! Obedience to the power of the gods is manifested by animal sacrifice!

HERA: I want to take some footage of the surging crowd around Constantine! See the incredible white smoke behind the people! The eyes of the people have the look of frenzied madness—madness or spiritual devotion! The crowd is hypnotized by what they see! Now words are useless to describe what we are about to see! *(Long pause)* He has bit the head off the first chicken and now he's ready to bite off the other two heads!

SPEARS: And God said let us make a man in our own image.

(The noise of the crowd increases; rising anger)

HERA: These are difficult shots to film! I can't see very clearly but the crowd seems to have taken hold of something—a donkey—no, it appears to be a woman! . . . No, it's a *man!*

SPEARS: And God said, let us take a man and test his faith!

BOGG: *(Screaming)* Let me go! You're crushing me! Let me go! I can't stand up any longer! Please, I can't breathe! I can't breathe! Please, stop tearing at me! Stop tearing at me! Stop tearing at my body!

(The dining room at the faculty club)

NARRATOR-LONGTIN: Scarcely had Constantine Dowling uttered the last words of his bizarre story when one of the listeners was seized with hysterical laughter; then he flew into an indignant tirade of condemnation, his eyes filled with scorn!

SPECTOR: Constantine Dowling, we have been at the mercy of your solipsism for a rather long period of time. You have detained us with a grotesque and preposterious tale of Gothic fiction. I have been impressed with the tone of conviction in your voice during the telling of these ghastly events, but you cannot expect any of us who are grounded in rational principles to believe these absurdities of supernatural horror. I hesitate to point out the numerous erroneous aspects of your story because I do not care to admonish a man of your reputation who has indeed contributed an important piece of scholarship to the world. But I wish to ask you a direct question concerning your height in relation to the story you have told us. You are standing before us, and anyone can see that you are about five-feet-eleven-inches tall and not the eleven-foot giant as you claim you had become because of the power of the sulphurous springs you had bathed in. What caused the change back to your normal height?

DOWLING: Professor Spector, gentlemen. The story that I told you is completely true, and, as for the reversion back to my normal height, you can accept or reject what I will tell you—but my height gradually diminished as I began to eat what I had been instructed by Hera, a radish and greens salad—I had been advised by her to eat this specially prepared salad every day for one month—and the prescription was a success, the patient was finally cured. By the way, gentlemen, Hera and I were married and although I'm sure she would have liked to invite you herself, I will do the honor of asking you all to be my guests at the auditorium this evening at eight o'clock for the private screening of a new experimental film directed and produced by my wife, Hera. Tonight, we will witness the extraordinary circumstances of my journey to Greece and the gruesome details of the death of a human being, Dr. Garrison Bogg, by acts of cannibalism. I ask all of you to be there at least ten minutes before the film begins so that proper seating can be arranged.

NARRATOR-LONGTIN: The film succeeded in convincing us all that the incredible story was indeed true. As I left the auditorium that night I shuddered at the thought of human desire convulsed and distorted, heightened to unbearable madness and depravity. I remembered also that the film had caught some moments of fascinating beauty.

Curtain

Jan Hartman

SAMUEL HOOPES READING FROM HIS OWN WORKS

Jan Hartman

The solo drama or one-character play long has been a staple of the theatre but was never quite so popular as it has been in recent years. Witness the success of Julie Harris in *The Belle of Amherst,* Hal Holbrook's interpretation of Mark Twain, Emlyn Williams as Dylan Thomas, James Earl Jones' portrait of Paul Robeson, and James Whitmore as President Truman in *Give 'em Hell, Harry.* Now there may be added Jan Hartman's ingenious *Samuel Hoopes Reading from His Own Works,* a revealing drama in which the sole character, an aging author, reads from the singular works which are his life—and his epitaph.

One of our most prolific and imaginative writers, Jan Hartman was educated at Phillips Academy and Harvard College. His produced plays include: *The American War Crimes Trial; Fragment of a Last Judgement; Final Solutions; Freeman! Freeman!; Antique Masks; The Shadow of the Valley;* and *Legend of Daniel Boone,* a large-scale outdoor drama presented annually in Harrodsburg, Kentucky.

Mr. Hartman also has written over seventy dramatic and documentary scripts for network television, the most recent being the highly acclaimed *The Great Wallendas,* a drama dealing with the famed circus high wire troupe, which starred Lloyd Bridges and Britt Ekland.

Among his many screenplays are: *The Cursed Medallion; The Kastner Affair; The Dwarf; Hail to the Chief;* and *The Longest Love Affair.*

Jan Hartman, who was awarded a Guggenheim Fellowship for playwriting, makes his first appearance in these annuals with *Samuel Hoopes Reading from His Own Works.*

Characters:

SAMUEL HOOPES

Scene:

A lecture hall. The speaker waits for a moment before beginning.

HOOPES: My name is Samuel Hoopes. But you know that or you wouldn't be here. I will tell you immediately that I detest public readings. I do not like reading to audiences, whether of one person or a thousand! But tonight I am making an exception, for a very particular purpose. As I was saying, tonight's reading has a very particular purpose which will make itself evident later in the evening.

(He pauses. Takes a sip of water. Pulls a silver pill box from his vest pocket and takes a pill)

Pardon me.

I shall begin with a piece reflecting my childhood. Tonight's reading will, in fact, encompass my entire lifetime. Parts of the reading you will find are very personal. I will not subject you to maudlin personal confessions, which I deplore. I despise sentiment. What I have to say I shall try to say impersonally.

My first piece is entitled *The Monument*. It is a short story and one of the first I wrote. I dislike it. It is badly written and fills me with rancor. But for what I intend to say tonight . . . for what I intend to do before the evening is over . . . it is important!

Please. Excuse me. I have . . . no . . . it's just that I am sometimes upset by my work . . . it is not always easy to expose oneself . . . bear with me.

Bear with me.

The Monument:

Vertically, the letters on the small square blocks read Y, M, Z, Q, and W . . . no vowels. But then, the monument was not conceived to be read. As a model for something larger it was perfect, and it covered almost half the nursery floor. But soon Mother's leg would be in front of his eyes and he would have to put the blocks away. But now it was no concern to Little Icarus that he had to put them away. The model was finished. Now, in the woods, he could begin to build it full-size. And then, there it would stand, tall and high, challenging the very height of the pines. It would be his, his monument alone, no one but he would know. That was enough. It would stand there by itself, untouched, defiant. And then he thought of a horn on a rhinoceros and a picture he once saw of a white horse with a twisted horn on its nose . . .

But there was Mother's heavy walking shoe. Time to stop thinking!

The rustling throughout the forest was, to Little Icarus, a kind of silence he could hear. The browned leaves and dry pine needles came up over his sandals. He wriggled his toes in order to watch the leaves and needles dance off his foot. He would need them. They would make a good final layer, and he might even stuff the cracks with them. But, more importantly, they would serve to hide the work while it was in progress.

When he arrived at the small clearing ringed with low rocks, the silence and the sun-rays streaming down reminded him of a cathedral he had once visited.

Nothing had changed since last time. The lights, the leaves, the shadows, and the silence were all as he had left them. And under a natural grotto formed by two round rocks roofed by a flat piece of slate were carefully cut sticks, the knife, the basket for mixing mud, some small smooth stones, and an old rusted trowel found handle-deep in mud at the other side of the forest.

Carefully, Little Icarus selected eighteen perfectly smooth rocks for the foundation. Eighteen was his own number; one he had selected with the same care as the rocks.

Now the eighteen rocks formed the design he would build on: neither a circle nor an ellipse, but a raindrop like a tear!

As he looked at the shape, contemplating the next step, the spreading of the mortar-like mud, he thought—impossible in the lonely wood—that he felt eyes watching him from high up. They made him uncomfortable. But he banished the sensation from his mind. It could only be imagination, for no one knew but he . . . no one!

When finally the mud had been packed between the rocks and the base finished, his cathedral began to darken, and he knew he must go back to the playroom. He put the mud-basket away, carefully removed the improvised cover-alls from his body, folded them, and put everything into the grotto. Having washed his hands in a nearby stream, he headed for home, with the vision of his monument that would last forever, sharp in his mind. But as he left, he was disturbed by the snapping of a twig. Could someone know? No! He had been too careful in selecting the place. And didn't the fact that it was his own, his very own, protect it from intruders?

As the weeks passed, the monument grew until Little Icarus had to work at it from the over-hanging limb of a nearby tree.

Once the frame was finished, the time was at hand to begin covering it with the red clay he had found very near his clearing. If the sun shone long enough in the next few days, his monument, hard as brick, would be finished, dominating the empty clearing.

As he slid down the trunk of the tree, anticipating the feel of the soft clay against his palms, he felt the eyes upon him again. He shuddered slightly; but Little Icarus could hardly be called frightened. He wanted to know the challenge, to face it openly.

As he walked toward the clay pit, he worried about guarding the monument. Nothing must come near it. For it was his own, his claim to a place in time, a thing that must stand not only until he had left childhood, but well past the moment he was laid into the clay or scattered as ash to the wind.

If someone should place another name upon it, all would be futile! The feeling of being observed had stirred a doubt tentatively in the back of Little Icarus' mind; a doubt that it was useless, that he would no longer feel pride at its standing there for him. But he found such thoughts congenial only for the shortest instant before he shut them forever away!

The monument was completed. On a bright day in the cathedral of the wood it stood towering over its little creator, tiny crystals of light playing off its surface. But the last work, the application of clay and the final washing and shaping, had been accompanied by that dread which the unseen eyes stirred in Little Icarus. Now, he felt them all around him, always, even in the room with Mother.

He could not dismiss it. For now, the extremely delicate but painful malaise was lost in the first flood of joy at seeing the monument whole in front of his eyes.

He sat on a stump looking at it. Done! And I did it! There it stands, telling the world beyond the treetops and beyond the forest: I am the product of a creator, Little Icarus, and hearing this, Little Icarus would only respond with a quiet whisper, you are mine! I am a creator! God!

The sun disappeared from the wood, but even then he did not stir, but sat, waiting for the moonlight to fall across his creation. As a dark shape in the night, the monument was more impressive than before. Little Icarus shuddered at the hulk of it looming over him. For the first time it seemed a thing apart from its creator. But that could not be. Yet it must be. The monument stood; an extension of Little Icarus, yet a thing alone! He sat in darkness, hypnotized by the terrifying size of the thing he had created, waiting to leave. And then, the crack of a twig broke sharply into his reverie. He jumped from his stump, and knowing he was watched, frightened of encounter, he ran through the woods, ran and ran until he could run no more; twigs slapping into his face, his muscles twitching beyond control. He fled—screaming—from the very core of his Being.

But even as the panic fired his mind, he knew that he should remain and defend his creation. Yet he could not turn. Not in the night when the moon threw shadows on the creation and the creator would crouch and tremble at its foot.

Icarus was a fool! Too much caring about being destroyed by his own actions! A damned fool!

Months passed before Little Icarus could return. The blocks on the nursery floor lay gathering dust. He huddled in corners and dared not think of the Cathedral in the Wood.

A day dawned, full of sun, and Little Icarus felt the gloom lift like a shroud from his hunched little shoulders, and set out that day to see what had been so perfect about his monument.

The stillness of a tomb hung over the wood.

He pushed through the walls of trees toward the clearing. At first he could not be sure he had remembered the path. Although the rocks were ringing the clearing and the trees were as he remembered, the monument was gone! No hint of clay, no crust of leaves was left.

Little Icarus could no longer know whether he had built it, or whether the textures of the memories were textures of dreams.

Or was this the dream? He could not know.

He ventured carefully to where the center of the monument had stood under the well-remembered over-hanging branch. And directly there, someone had carefully placed a small, gray tombstone. And as he knelt, he saw in the slanting rays of evening that the letters, horizontally, read, I,C,A,R,U,S, Icarus.

He wanted to last, you see. Little Icarus wanted something that would last beyond himself.

Poor Little Icarus! He learned, he and I learned, that those monuments are only tombstones. Pieces of slab they drive into your dead corpse to mark the space in which you are rotting! Rot! Everybody rots!

You are rotting right now!

I said this was a story of childhood, my childhood which was lived amidst visions of monuments proclaiming the everlasting being of Samuel Hoopes!

Of course that is all nonsense. Nonsense which I was dedicated to exposing. Nonsense I shall make clear to you this evening.

Little Icarus was the beginning of this theme in my writing and was written after I'd determined . . . or rather, been led into becoming a writer. This next piece is from my diary.

Being concerned with immortality I shall leave a diary behind me.

April 24-25, 1938. Back from walking. Now rain starts to beat against the window. Rain makes no music to accompany the churning of thought. I met an old man, whose beard gave him the appearance of a prophet. He even talked like one in some half-biblical, half-modern style with a lisp, that lisp being the touch of the absurd with which Nature joys in cursing Man. He knew my name and spoke it like cold water running down my back. "Thamuel Hoopth." He had horrible eyes: little green pupils floating in thick gray clouds of mucus. "I am old," he said, "and have almost reached the dust time." That's how he talked. "I have almost reached the dust time! Nothing on earth will remain after me once I am gone." Eyes! I hate men's eyes . . . they accuse or forgive without language! The old man talked on about fables and tales, about the mystical stories of the past. About books. "A book, a printed page," he said, "reaches every heart that wants it." And then he told me tales of the Java seas and other far places, and tales of the heroical dead. I feel a life stirring in my brain. All the misty figures I have felt so long whispering in my ears have come to life! "Thoughts can never turn to ash": his last line. He disappeared then into the fog. His face branded on my mind forever; the beard, the deep wrinkles around the floating green eyes. Where did he come from! God damn him!

That was the beginning of a career. It is strange how I have always hated that old man, but then again, hate is part of us, easier than love. The entry from that night continues:

Why has God cursed me with a will to live beyond myself into everlasting time? I am haunted not with the Now but Then; not with death but the after-death. Looking at myself in the mirror I see only an absurdly round-faced man with hollow glass eyes. I laugh that one so physically cursed should want to join the immortals. They will build a fat statue to me one day; bald, pudgy, holding a quill in fleshy hands with bitten nails! But I shall strike it down with lightning from Hell . . . my only statue will be carved in language, in the rich rock of words, and Samuel Hoopes shall live forever!

Stupid, isn't it? That kind of wild ambition? If you don't think so you're as disgusting as that young man who wrote that diary entry! He is as remote to me as to you.

Bitter with life, he still wanted something that would live beyond himself. Stupid, ignoble drive toward immortality. We see it around us every day. Everyone . . . you, too . . . wants his niche in immortality! Oblivion! I know. I tried to defy it and I know how uncompromising it is! This next selection will show you that I *knew* the truth before I *learned* it—creativity sneaks truth into lying hearts. This next will not bore you because it is not so personal. It is from my novel, *The Hall of Statues,* born on that night so many years ago. Samuel Parapet arrives at an obscure village in the European mountains. The chapter is called *Waxworks*.

Arriving at Dofsplatz, Samuel, as usual, inquired about the local wonders. A rheumy concierge, snuffling and wiping his eyes, handed him a brightly-colored pamphlet and directed him to the left, down a steeply declining cobblestone street.

Samuel would never know why he hated cobblestones and quaintness; but he fully understood, and eagerly anticipated, the chaos he could excite in such surroundings, and nothing seemed more to his purpose than an announcement in the little colored brochure that the pride of Dofsplatz lay at the bottom of the cobblestone decline, lay unsuspecting in a small wax museum enshrining the ancestors and burghers of this little town.

With full heart and keen anticipation Samuel skipped down the hill hungry for the confusion he would excite in his clean mountain air.

The huge door of the museum surpassed his expectations. It was an immense piece, probably paid by village subscriptions, ornately decorated with mythical creatures: satyrs, chimerae, winged horses, man-headed birds, and a crowd of lesser characters from the world's pantheons. Instinctively, Samuel reached into his pocket for a knife to draw across the reliefs, but a voice within him told him to forego the lesser pleasure for greater ones inside.

At the entry he was stopped by a guard in a green uniform, thin as a fence-rail and sporting a walrus mustache.

"Nobody pay," he said. "The town make pay. Visitors free." And he motioned Samuel past with a courtly bow.

Parapet found himself in a long, marble room into which light flooded through a skylight in the roof. The ceiling was the highest Samuel had thus far encountered in Europe. He gaped.

On either side of the room the burghers, their wives, their children, and even an occasional dog were propped or sat or leaned looking with waxen composure toward the entry way. They were fat, thin, tall, bald, hairy, ruddy, pale, and all, without exception, smug, self-satisfied, and repulsive.

Samuel moved toward his left, toward one Herr von Myerhaffenkitzenkatz, who stood with hands folded benignly over an immense paunch girdled by a heavily laden watch chain. The Herr was dressed for the day in a maroon tail-coat.

Not a detail of the Burgher missed Samuel's gaze: broad nose, tiny eyes sunk in folds of flesh, a wart fastidiously fastened to the left of the nose.

Samuel's anger rose as he read a card attached to the base of the statute. Here stood Herr Myerhaffenkitzenkatz, three-hundredth burgomeister of Dofsplatz, inspirer of a wax museum, statuary fund, a village-subsidized pub, and above all, he had personally supervised—being a contractor by trade—the erection of a commemorative obelisk upon which all the burgomeisters' names, past, present, and future, were or would be inscribed. A monstrous vanity was described here, and it worked upon Samuel's fury to such an extent that all the well-known signs of his strange weakness manifested themselves.

Samuel jutted his sharp chin at the bearded burgomeister: "Why did they put you here, eh? What did you ever do?"

No answer.

"You just ran your stupid quaint little village and ate and ate and ate, you fat-bellied bastard! Didn't you! Didn't you!"

Nothing is more infuriating, particularly to one of Samuel's nature, than to abuse someone in vain.

"Bastard! Big-bellied, flat-footed bastard!"

But still the three-hundredth burgomeister remained deaf and mute.

Samuel turned violently against all the figures then, screaming, "What did you ever do? Any of you, to stand here! Huh? Smug! Smug! All of you! Well, you're not so safe when Samuel Parapet's around. I'll show you!" he screamed.

Just then the guard entered.

"Vat you doing?"

"Why the hell should you care!"

Bewildered, the guard said, "Maybe you leave, no?"

"NO!" roared Samuel, picking up a waxen dachshund and throwing it at the guard.

"Help! Help me!" He screamed in German, whereupon Samuel hit him over the head with a brass post used to rope off the waxen figures. Without a sound the guard slid to the marble floor.

Delightful! I still enjoy this book . . . in a somewhat childish way! Strange, the dimension one's own work takes for one after years have passed. Strange. *(He looks at his watch)* We must proceed.

As the guard's mustache hit the floor, the demonic spirit that had driven Samuel to Europe possessed him fully. As he spun away from the guard, his eyes took in the prides of Dofsplatz's history. Nothing could stop Samuel as with one jerk of a golden rope he pulled the barriers and brass posts crashing to the ground!

One by one, he grabbed the burghers and their families, their dogs and their medals, and flung them into a huge mound in the center of the marble floor. Arms broke off, ears rolled tentatively across the floor only to spin themselves flat and lifeless in one spot. Clothes ripped: but there were no screams except those Samuel heard reverberating through his skull as he threw Herr Doofenspatzerkitzenstuber into the heap and heard him groan.

When the pile had mounted well beyond Samuel's head and the hall lay covered with tatters and random human limbs, the guard awoke, staggered to his feet, and ran from the room screaming incoherently. There was not much time left. Quickly, Samuel dumped the contents of his carpet bag on the floor beside the pile of bodies. Then, stuffing his own clothing and loose bits of paper into the base of the pile, he took a match from his pocket, struck it, and watched as the blaze sizzled to the fringe of some *fräulein's* dress, to the wig of one of the children, until it roared into a pyre.

Now Samuel could laugh.

Nothing he had accomplished so far: the toppling of Nelson's statue in London, the burning of the grass at Versailles, the painting of the obelisk in the Place de la Bastille, or any of the other accomplishments of his trip fed his purpose more heartily than this. He watched, in utter delight, as noses ran across faces, as fingers elongated, as mouths twisted and twitched, as those waxen burghers slowly dissolved into themselves, becoming the waxen blobs they were at heart.

Samuel was thoroughly and undeniably happy. The past was melting in front of his eyes. He was proving to all of them everywhere—whoever they might be—that the past did melt. The truth belonged to him alone and he wanted to teach the world.

Wasn't this a great humanitarian act? Or was it just a comedy played out in an obscure alpine village? Whatever it was, it gave Samuel a pleasure that he felt was rightfully his.

He had travelled far and wide with his message and he had suffered much. But what he did not hear (perhaps because outside a crowd was screaming and he knew that he must make his escape, or perhaps because his mind was closed to all such possibilities) was the little subconscious voice whispering that if the world listened and learned, perhaps they would erect a monument to Samuel Parapet; one that could not be toppled, painted, or melted.

But as he ran from Dofsplatz with the crowd screaming behind in the distance, he never thought that even he would disappear from the spinning ball along which he trotted; that even the spinning ball would disappear; and even, in time, the empty heaven that held it.

There you have Parapet, crusher of idols, destroyer of statues, dedicated executioner of men's memorabilia.

Parapet, you see, hated the past as I used to. Neither of us knew then, as I do now, that the future destroys itself as well.

The book was awarded a high literary prize. This next reading is from my diary, dated April 24, 1940.

A telegram arrived a few hours ago awarding me the Pulitzer Prize for *The Hall of Statues.* "A brilliant satiric novel in an age when satire threatens to die; a novel reflecting the bitter mood of the times, and inspiring thought-provoking laughter!" Bitter are the turnings of one's own success. I am no closer to my own fulfillment than I was after the Old Man's first visit. Nothing works. Each word on paper leaves me feeling as though a piece of me has dropped off into oblivion, leaving me as hungry for satisfaction as before.

One keeps hoping that each new creation, each new volume will demonstrate that I am not finite, but as the shelf of my works expands, my life . . . my life seems to ebb away as though each volume sucked a bit of me into itself. The only truth seems to be that *no* monuments are lasting! In an eon, epoch, or millennium this prize, those beautifully bound books that won it will whirl with the cosmic dust which will replace this tortured globe.

The old man standing in the rain that night was wrong! From the first, man has been fooling himself, trying to leave bits of himself behind for others to remember. Even our memory of the first civilization is no more than myth. Yet those cavemen existed only a few moments ago in the time of the Universe! Always and ever this torture! This horrible knowledge that Hoopes will disappear! Why? We begin nowhere and end nowhere, and meanwhile we fill ourselves with hope! One day I might hope to leave a memory in a single mind through an act of complete violence and absurdity! But the books will do me no good and even the man carrying the memory of my acts will disappear in time.

The day I received the telegram, my drive for the absurd end began.

If the futility of Man is my theme, then my own life must be the perfect dramatization of that theme!

But there is the tortuous paradox! If tonight I become a symbol of futility, then I become what I repudiate: for a moment, immortal!

It's all nonsense of course!

This next piece was started almost twenty years after that day and finished soon after I began writing it. If ever I threw myself into a work, this was the one. In it I hoped to record all the futility I have found in life. The story itself is inspired by one of the Javanese tales the Old Man told me on the river bank that night. Here is the legend:

A witch doctor took for a pet a baby octopus that he watched grow to its full size and weight. When the octopus had reached maturity, and its tentacles were fine and strong, its head round and smooth and all its parts perfectly formed, the witch doctor realized that, in fact, the octopus is an ugly monster not pleasant to look upon. He loved his pet but wanted it to shine out among others. So, in order to make it beautiful, he employed magic and turned it into crystal that shone and sparkled in the sunlight and moonlight. The witch doctor now doted on his pet which outshone all the other animals and fishes of the island.

But the time came when the crystal octopus became hungry. He reached for food and the tentacle which was beginning to uncoil snapped off. Then, in his agony, the octopus stretched all his other tentacles and they fell to the ground with such a shattering ring of glass that the witch doctor was forever deafened. The beautiful octopus died with the broken fragments of its tentacles glittering around it in the moonlight. Its master was never heard to speak again. Not ever.

You may think of this next piece as being entitled: *Tentacles of Glass*.

Twisted ravings of tortured thought! A prologue statement for the death of a man! Death! I only die because all my beginnings are exhausted! Days alone as a child playing with imaginary friends. Mother didn't like them, because she couldn't see them.

She used to kick my blocks off the playroom floor, clattering and scattering into an empty sky. She was the first to go. Broken by the nib of a pen. Only a sketch scrawled and scratched on a yellow-ruled pad—a goldenrod tablet (That was the trade name)—

Adolescent hands wrote: *Mother was a Gargoyle.* Ha! Comic relief!

Her hair smelled of straw and usually looked it, though my eyes never wandered so far. My memories stopped at the knees. And, of course, those heavy shoes for kicking blocks.

Cry! Cry tears like the spattering of rain on pavement. Seven novels, twelve plays, and a galaxy of poems later, I try to write an epitaph. To think! So much destruction in the tools of thought; pens and typewriters. Mother's body, then, lay on Goldenrod.

And what do Mother's heavy shoes have to do with it? Answer: I hate life and all meaninglessness. I am a failure. Every little thing I have touched has failed.

The whole of the pain, really, did not start when I buried Mother. Then only, I learned that creation is the destruction of inspiration. I created Mother on paper and destroyed her in my heart. The whole pain started long before that in the middle of the sun-drenched nursery floor.

I grew, somehow. Or at least aged. Until the day of my mother's death. A simple, rain-spattered day. Alone, in front of the yellow-lined pad, a pen, and a shaky adolescent hand sketching the portrait of a brutal madonna.

Now I write about myself. But I anticipate.

She was gone from my heart. I forgot her and went on. Youth, the human flowering, unfolded me and the world grew sensual. Blocks of time became blocks of loneliness. The recall, the memory of me wandering tear-spattered streets, not hearing the city-sounds through my thoughts, not seeing faces rushing past, but only wrapped tightly in the vision of puppets, not yet recorded.

A room somewhere. Thick with hangings. I was never poor. Systematic, careful reachings. Now that the first arm had dropped, I dared not lose another. Book followed book; page followed fluttering page: the process of slow decay.

Even you, sitting there, quizzical, are fragments of my mind. You see, it is a power, this mind behind my eyes.

I learned one lesson. All men live and die, beginning and ending nowhere. Exhaustion, not even despair. Only numbness. I gave up my battle in my tiny hung room. The fight ended, decay began. Even the wind whipping my dust will die. There you are, then, a whole story from beginning to end . . . only, there are no beginnings. Birth, the end of nonexistence. Death, the end of birth. The end of end.

My spirit is dead.

And now I rest in the dark shell of my self, feeling and wanting nothing. I have no more arms left with which to reach. Even the ultimate metaphor of my life is dying.

It is now only a matter of minutes. Had I but the pleasure of Faust, I might be anguished at this moment. But I have chosen it as it is. I leave a life behind me as meaningless as the lifelessness ahead. Perhaps the face was that of oblivion. I shall never know. There can be no more. My life is my epitaph.

Of all I have read and spoken tonight, this moment is the last chapter.

At the start of the reading I took a poison that has just about finished its work, but before it takes me, I want you to know why I have deliberately chosen this moment to die.

I pity what you are seeing: a man alone with his soul. When I look out at your faces, soft and white in the dark hall, I seem to see all the faces of Hoopes staring back at me.

But you see, all life is absurd and particularly the life that seeks immortality, because there is no room for us to live forever. I wanted immortality and used to sit in the nursery, building little monuments which would live beyond myself. And as I entered adolescence I thought of being an architect so that I could build towering glass and brick monuments to Samuel Hoopes, but that dream dissolved when I saw the dust that used to be ancient civilizations.

My hunger had grown. That old man in the rain showed me that ideas could live and I began activating my ideas on paper in stories, verses, essays, dramas.

But the world will end, even the people carrying the idea of Hoopes.

I want a monument, something, anything, that will scream to the world, "Hoopes lived!"

That's why I've chosen to die here, in front of you. You'll carry the memory of this with you . . . till you die. How many of you have ever watched a man die?

But I'll never know the image in your minds. I'll never see my only true monument. I'll never know if I've failed again in trying to snatch even a moment after life in which people will say, *Hoopes lived!*

I can't talk any longer . . . tell your children . . . so that . . . they will tell theirs. The reading is over. Remember . . . please . . . all of you . . . remember . . . Hoopes!

Curtain

Stanley Richards

Since the publication of his first collection in 1968, Stanley Richards has become one of our leading editors and play anthologists, earning rare encomiums from the nation's press (the *Writers Guild of America News* described him as "easily the best anthologist of plays in America"), and the admiration of a multitude of devoted readers.

Mr. Richards has edited the following anthologies and series: *The Best Short Plays 1978; The Best Short Plays 1977; The Best Short Plays 1976; The Best Short Plays 1975; The Best Short Plays 1974; The Best Short Plays 1973; The Best Short Plays 1972; The Best Short Plays 1971; The Best Short Plays 1970; The Best Short Plays 1969; The Best Short Plays 1968; Great Musicals of the American Theatre: Volume One; Great Musicals of the American Theatre: Volume Two; America on Stage: Ten Great Plays of American History; Best Plays of the Sixties; Best Mystery and Suspense Plays of the Modern Theatre; 10 Classic Mystery and Suspense Plays of the Modern Theatre* (the latter six, The Fireside Theatre–Literary Guild selections); *The Tony Winners; Twenty One-Act Plays; Best Short Plays of the World Theatre: 1968–1973; Best Short Plays of the World Theatre: 1958–1967; Great Rock Musicals; Modern Short Comedies from Broadway and London;* and *Canada on Stage*.

An established playwright as well, he has written twenty-five plays, twelve of which (including *Through a Glass, Darkly; Tunnel of Love; August Heat; Sun Deck; O Distant Land;* and *District of Columbia*) were originally published in earlier volumes of *The Best One-Act Plays* and *The Best Short Plays*.

Journey to Bahia, which he adapted from a prize-winning Brazilian play and film, *O Pagador de Promessas,* premiered at the Berkshire Playhouse, Massachusetts, and later was produced in Washington, D.C., under the auspices of the Brazilian Ambassador and the Brazilian American Cultural Institute. The play also had a successful Off-Broadway engagement and subsequently was performed in a Spanish translation at Lincoln Center. During the summer of 1975, the play was presented at the Edinburgh International Festival in Scotland, after a tour of several British cities.

Mr. Richards' plays have been translated for production

and publication abroad into Portuguese, Afrikaans, Dutch, Tagalog, French, German, Korean, Italian and Spanish.

He also has been the New York theatre critic for *Players Magazine* and a frequent contributor to *Pl iybill, Theatre Arts, The Theatre* and *Actors' Equity Magazine,* among many other periodicals.

As an American Theatre Specialist, Mr. Richards was awarded three successive grants by the U. S. Department of State's International Cultural Exchange Program to teach playwriting and directing in Chile and Brazil. He taught playwriting in Canada for over ten years and was Visiting Professor of Drama at the University of Guelph, Ontario. He has produced and directed plays and has lectured extensively on theatre at universities in the United States, Canada and South America.

Mr. Richards, a New York City resident, is now at work on *The Best Short Plays 1979.*